From Bureaucracy
to Public Management

From Bureaucracy to Public Management

::

THE ADMINISTRATIVE CULTURE
OF THE GOVERNMENT OF CANADA

::

O.P. Dwivedi
& James Iain Gow

broadview press

CANADIAN CATALOGUING IN PUBLICATION DATA

Main entry under title:

Dwivedi, O. P., 1937–
    From bureaucracy to public management

ISBN 1-55111-271-X

1. Civil service — Canada.   2. Political culture — Canada
I. Gow, Iain.   II. Institute of Public Administration of Canada
III. Title

JL108.D88 1999   352.6'3'0971   C99-930990-0

BROADVIEW PRESS, LTD.
is an independent, international publishing house, incorporated in 1985.

North America
Post Office Box 1243, Peterborough, Ontario, Canada K9J 7H5
3576 California Road, Orchard Park, New York, USA 14127
TEL (705) 743-8990; FAX (705) 743-8353; E-MAIL 75322.44@compuserve.com

United Kingdom and Europe
Turpin Distribution Services, Ltd., Blackhorse Rd.,
Letchworth, Hertfordshire, SG6 1HN
TEL (1462) 672555; FAX (1462) 480947; E-MAIL turpin@rsc.org

Australia
St. Clair Press, Post Office Box 287, Rozelle, NSW 2039
TEL (612) 818-1942; FAX (612) 418-1923

www.broadviewpress.com

Canadä

Broadview Press gratefully acknowledges the support of the Ministry of Canadian Heritage through the Book Publishing Industry Development Program.

This book is a joint publication of the Institute of Public Administration and Broadview Press.

IPAC
1075 Bay Street, Suite 401, Toronto, Ontario M5S 2B1

Cover design by Zack Taylor and Liz Broes, Black Eye Design.
Typeset by Zack Taylor, Black Eye Design.

Printed in Canada

Contents

5

7

SIX CANADIAN ADMINISTRATIVE CULTURE BETWEEN PAST AND PRESENT

List of Tables

DEDICATED TO

John Edwin Hodgetts

Remarkable student and teacher of Public Administration,

Influential contributor to public affairs in Canada,

Person of great integrity and humanity.

Preface

We came to write this book because we wanted to explore the relationship between the official values put forward by the Canadian administration and the values and meanings experienced by Canadian public servants. We are both former students of J.E. Hodgetts and so have been made sensitive to the importance of history in the life of a nation's administration and to the intricate relationship between the latter and its environment.

Our own backgrounds also dispose us to take an interest in these questions. One of us comes from India, where another transplanted version of the British system operates, and combines a career teaching and researching public administration in Canada with extensive travel, study, and consultative work in the Third World. The other was made sensitive to cultural differences during time spent as a Canadian diplomat and later as an Ontarian transplanted in Quebec, making his career in a French language university. In addition, we both bring different approaches to the study of public administration. While Dwivedi prefers the deontological perspective, Gow emphasises a teleological approach. Combining these two perspectives into the study of administrative culture was also a challenge.

We have been witnesses to many cycles of administrative reform, have read many analyses as to why they almost always disappoint their sponsors. Then, with others in our field, we became aware of an increased interest in organization culture in the 1980s. At the same time, the New Public Management movement has had a strong impact on Canadian politicians and officials. While there are now several good studies of public management in Canada, we wanted to examine the relationship between this new doctrine and the observable values and sensibilities of the Canadian public service.

The book is intended for advanced students who may be in need of a general overview of Canadian administration as well as the detailed knowledge of its various aspects they have acquired in specialized courses. It is also directed at our colleagues as part of the ongoing dialogue and debate about where we come from, what is happening to our administrative system, what it means, and what possibilities and problems these tendencies offer.

We wish to acknowledge the research assistance of Magali Marc and François Simard and the helpful comments on earlier versions of this book by colleagues Gerald E. Caiden, Keith Henderson, and Ivo Krupka; the two anonymous reviewers, and the IPAC's Canadian Public Administration series editor Paul Pross and Research Officer Geoff McIlroy.

Finally, Michael Harrison of Broadview Press deserves a special vote of thanks for his helpful suggestions and initiative for this publication.

O.P. Dwivedi
James Iain Gow

ONE

Introduction: Administrative Culture and Values

Public administration is going through a period of turmoil, both in practice and in theory. After a period of unprecedented growth from the end of World War II until the mid-1970s, the developed world experienced increasing financial difficulties and a sense of disappointment with the bureaucracies that had been created. This led to strong challenges by politicians, people in business, and academics. The result was a dramatic increase in the tendency to turn to management practices used in the business sector, even as business itself continued to change. The resulting public management movement presents a strong challenge to the bureaucratic methods developed by modern welfare states.

There are good reasons to believe that challenges are good for individuals and organizations, in the sense that those challenged often tend to be more innovative and adaptable than those who are not.[1] However, challenges and new solutions may call administrative methods into question. In the context in which we write, the main challenge facing public administration may be what Robert Denhardt has called "the pursuit of significance."[2]

Focussing on this concern directs our attention to the culture of public administration. Underlying an administration's actions and ideas, people and the products of their labours, there is something which we call culture, which gives meaning to what administrators do and to what influences them from without. It describes the limits of the possible, determines the nature of the desirable and the undesirable, and permits the interpretation of outcomes.

In this book, we are interested in the administrative culture of the Government of Canada. Administrative culture has received a lot of attention in recent years. Like most other concepts used in the social sciences, it does not always mean the same thing, nor do students and actors in the field draw similar conclusions from what they think they see. It is our purpose in this chapter to define our terms with regard to the following questions: What is culture and where does it come from? What are organizational culture, corporate culture, and administrative culture? Where do values fit in? How may administrative culture, and particularly its values, be studied in a reasonably objective way? We give our answers to these four sets of questions in the pages that follow.

1 · Culture as Manifest in Organizations

The concept of culture, as it is used in anthropology, goes back to the nineteenth century. In the study of government and organizations, it has been used since the early 1960s, but the theme of organization culture has been most actively studied since 1980.[3] The reasons for this probably come from the world outside organizations: Joseph Smucker has identified such factors as the fascination in the West with the apparently successful Japanese model of management, the tensions among personnel created by mergers and acquisitions in the business world since the beginning of the 1970s, the need for business organizations to adapt more rapidly than in the past to accelerating change in the world economy, and the questioning of masculine values in many business standards and practices that resulted from the increase of more women in management.[4]

We start here with a discussion of culture as anthropologists have defined it, and proceed afterwards to examine its applications in the world of organizations and public administration.

CULTURE IN THE ANTHROPOLOGICAL SENSE

Anthropologists tend to define culture in broad terms. According to Singer, the anthropological concept of culture covers all facets of humans in society: knowledge, behaviour, beliefs, art, morals, law, custom, etc. However, according to Goodenough, culture is "not a material phenomenon; it does not consist of things, people, behaviour or emotions. It is rather an organization of these things that people have in mind, their models for perceiving, relating and otherwise interpreting them."[5] Thus for Singer, culture is composed of norms or standards, ideologies, and broad general principles of selectivity and ordering. Boudon and Bourricaud see it rather as "the system of fundamental values of a society."[6]

Despite some differences of emphasis, there seems to be agreement among anthropologists that a culture is the way of life of a given society. This approach has several implications. First, it is holistic, involving entire societies. Second, a certain coherence among the elements of a culture is implied; there is a pattern that contributes to its distinctive nature.[7] This pattern reveals the fundamental values of a society, but also the meanings it attributes to actions, events, and things. As Boudon and Bourricaud state, humans "live in a symbolic universe" of their own creation.[8] For A.L. Froeber and C. Kluckholn, "Culture consists of patterns, explicit and implicit, of and for behaviour acquired and transmitted by symbols."[9] This transmission takes place through socialization, particularly within social networks such as marriage, business, and administration.

Even so basic a definition as the one given above requires some clarification. To recognize a certain level of coherence is only to admit that there is a pattern that we may call a distinct culture. All cultures are composed of subcultures, which pull them in different directions, and may be based on sex, age, work or territory. A good deal of change occurs through the relationships among these subcultures. Nevertheless, they must have some common referent, or else we must consider that they have ceased to belong to the same larger culture.

While culture provides the interpretative code to the world, all is not culture. There is an outside world, even if we must view it through the joint prisms of our culture and our personality. This outside world is made up of what Geert Hofstede calls "the forces of nature and the forces of man."[10] Natural forces, such as the topography and the climate, affect all cultures. Other societies also influence cultures — as trading partners, enemies, and sources of religions and philosophies. Scientific discoveries and technological innovation are other external influences. While they are products of humans in society, once they exist, they become objective influences that cannot be ignored.

Much of the impetus for change in a culture comes from these outside influences. Other pressures come from competing subcultures. Still further changes come from some combination of cultural and physical factors, as in the case given by Boudon and Bourricaud: when mortality rates fall and birthrates remain the same, the result is a structural change in the population.

The study of culture in anthropology attracts our attention to the world of symbols and meanings — values and patterns which constitute particular ways of seeing, interpreting, and judging the world. Transmission of culture seems to occur through social institutions, consciously or unconsciously.

ORGANIZATIONAL CULTURE AND CORPORATE CULTURE

Gareth Morgan writes, "organizations are mini-societies that have their own distinctive patterns of culture and subculture" and "every aspect of organization is rich in symbolic meaning."[11] It is thus not an abusive extension to postulate an organizational culture that follows closely the anthropological definition. As Nadine Lemaître puts it, "Culture is a system of representations and values shared by all the members of an enterprise."[12] In everyday language, it is "the way we do things around here."[13]

Controversy quickly arises when we consider the relative importance given to the general membership of the organization or to its management. Gladys Symons has shown that many view organization culture as "corporate culture" that is created and manipulated by management.[14] This, however, seems to involve displacement of concepts: as she points out, it views management as an ideology rather than as a variable affecting and reflecting all the members of the organization. An analysis of 192 articles published in the United States on the subject of organization culture over almost ten years from June 1975 to December 1984 showed that those who wrote for practitioners were successful in influencing their academic colleagues towards the view that organization culture may be manipulated to increase both productivity and social integration.[15]

Thus there is a difference of opinion, if not a controversy, over what the culture of an organization is and how best to apprehend it. On the one hand, there are those who believe that culture pervades every aspect of an organization, and should be studied from an anthropological or sociological perspective. On the other, a whole managerial literature is given over to creating a corporate culture, at least among senior managers.[16] We think that the broader definition should be kept. Values and meanings are not the exclusive property of senior management.[17] To adopt a "corporate culture" view — to study how political and administrative leadership tries to develop and convey a coherent set of values and symbols for an organization — relegates other values and symbols to the status of obstacles or causes of resistance. While this is an understandable point of view for senior management, for the outside student, it seems to downplay the attitudes, opinions, and mythologies of middle level and lower level employees as well of those of partners, suppliers, and customers. As Latouche states, the search for symbols in an organization may lead one to consider the following realms: the ideal (ideas, values, myths, beliefs), the behaviourial (procedures, gestures, rituals, customs), the narrative (slogans, stories, legends, parables, glossaries, songs), and the material (architecture, flags, insignia).[18] Many of these are the result of deliberate choice, but not all. In the study that follows, we will emphasize the anthropological tradition.

ADMINISTRATIVE CULTURE

Is there any reason for making a distinction between organizational culture and administrative culture when dealing with the administration of the

Canadian government? There are two. The first is that the administration is larger and more complex than any single organization, being composed of many departments, agencies, corporations, and so on. It is certainly possible to speak of a corporate management and of a corporate culture in the Canadian government,[19] but we think it at least prudent to keep in mind the great complexity of such a vast conglomeration of administrative units. In the words of Gérard Bergeron, the state is "an organization of organizations."[20] Indeed, Carolyn Ban has argued that in the American case

> It is questionable whether the basic values shared by federal managers constitute a "federal culture." Most managers identify with their individual agencies rather than with the federal government as a whole.[21]

While the latter statement is probably true in Canada also, it is an exaggeration to argue that there is no larger federal administrative culture. Just as Ban argues that all American federal managers share a belief in rational problem-solving and in technical solutions, Gow found that the majority — two-thirds — of respondents to a survey of members of the Institute of Public Administration of Canada, held a common outlook that included pragmatism, suspicion of theory, moderate reform tendencies, and a view of public servants as the agents of administrative change in the political system.[22]

More than this, however, is the fact that the Canadian political system has much greater uniformity than the American. The classification system has long provided a common vocabulary for federal managers. Over time, the emergence of the Treasury Board and the Civil Service Commission provided uniform regulation of most departments and agencies. More recently still, the introduction of collective bargaining obligated the Treasury Board to adopt common wage and benefit policies that, in turn, caused unions representing broad professional categories to develop their positions. Reading the newspapers in any capital, including Ottawa, reveals a range of items on public service issues (pay, working conditions, parking, etc.) that indicate common interests and values.

The second reason to retain the idea of administrative culture is that it is part of the political culture. Kuruvilla traces this notion back to the works of Gabriel Almond, Sidney Verba, and Bingham Powell. Following their definitions, Kuruvilla defines administrative culture as "the administrative system as internalized in the cognitions and perceptions of the nation's population" concerning the administration.[23]

Reference to political culture reminds us of the large part played by notions of culture in comparative public administration. The weight of ambient culture has been considerably disputed by the experts. The cultural explanation of French bureaucratic behaviour proposed by Michel Crozier was not universally accepted.[24] It was nevertheless generally recognized that even among countries of similar levels of development and type of government, the range of bureaucratic behaviour is considerable.[25]

The debate about the influence of ambient culture was most active in the area of development administration. Fred Riggs was one of the first to formulate the idea that the degree of institutional specialization in a society, and the consequent attitudes towards equality, status, and markets could determine the success or failure of modern administrative institutions and practices in developing countries.[26] While this notion was adopted by many academics, it led to a kind of defeatism that both practitioners and funding agencies did not like: if you can't change the culture of an entire society, this version went, you will not be able to reform or "modernize" its administration.[27]

We agree with Latouche who cautioned against confusing organization culture with the cultural environment that surrounds the organization.[28] The administrative culture of which Kuruvilla writes is truly part of political culture, but it is not the culture of administration. Our main emphasis will be with the values, symbols, and interpretative codes of the Canadian administration.[29] Even so, it is useful to be reminded that such a culture does not exist in isolation from the rest of society. We assume that the evolution of values and interpretations among the population in general, and among the politicians in particular, challenges or reinforces values present in the administration, changes the interpretations of practice and discourse, and informs or detracts from the worth attributed to various symbols.

In conclusion, our subject is the culture of the Canadian federal administration. This culture is a part of Canadian political culture which is, in turn, a part of the wider culture of Canada in general. The culture of the administration is sometimes supported, sometimes challenged by two important subcultures: first, the culture of each department or agency, with its own mandate, interests, client groups, and major professional and occupational components; second, professional subcultures, such as those of accountants, lawyers, economists, engineers, diplomats, and scientists, that cut across organizational boundaries.

2 · The Place of Values

We defined culture as a characteristic way for a group or a society to view the world, to attribute meaning, value, and significance to it. We now need to look more closely at the idea of values and how they may be studied.

While it is no doubt possible to think of symbols and interpretations that have no value attached to them (an airport is full of them), most symbols and significances carry contents closely related to preferred or unwanted states. The latter are what values are all about. If the idea of value is related to notions of trade and exchange, it has been generalized to cover individual and collective preferences. To Christopher Hodgkinson, values are "concepts of the desirable with motivating force."[30] Preferences are not limited to monetary or quantifiable traits; they include what, on the basis of personal judgment, we find to be true, beautiful, or good.[31]

In a social context, according to Boudon and Bourricaud, values "are nothing more than collective preferences which appear in an institutional context and which... contribute to the regulation of this context."[32] The reference to regulation is most opportune, since any guiding principle or control necessarily refers to some value. As Gérard Bergeron has been stressing since the mid 1960s, a control involves the comparison of two elements or terms according to a norm or standard.[33]

We thus define a *value* as a principle or a quality from which may be inferred a norm or standard conducive to ordering or ranking by preference objects, activities, results or people. Values may be personal or collective. Obviously, culture deals with collective values, but an important source of conflict may come when individual members' personal values are at discord with the collective.

A further important distinction is made by Hofstede, who warns against confusing the desired and the desirable.[34] What is in fact desired is in the realm of behaviour, which is observable. What is desirable need not be grounded or evident in behaviour. Hofstede notes two possible contradictions coming from this: one, between behaviour and what is desired (we act so as to achieve what we desire), the other between what is desired and what is desirable (this involves someone else's judgment about what we desire).

Here is the link between value and ethics. Ethics, according to the *Shorter Oxford Dictionary*, is "that which is worthy of esteem for its own sake; that which has intrinsic value." Ethics, as the application of moral principles to conduct, in this case conduct of office,[35] thus carries with it the germs of conflict, for not only may interests and preferences lead to divergent values in social relations, intrinsic values, if adhered to despite the context, may obviously cause friction.[36]

The study of values as reflecting the desired, values as they may be observed, is the domain of anthropology, where whole societies are concerned. That of the desirable relates to moral philosophy. How we might connect the study of the two is the subject of the next section.

THE PLACE OF VALUES IN PUBLIC ADMINISTRATION

As a practical field of knowledge, public administration, like its private counterpart, has always been concerned with values. Any applied science necessarily deals with the achievement of certain goals.[37] One student of the history of management notes that, from their inception, schools of public administration have been used to transmit the values of their parent organizations to new generations of bureaucrats. Students of modern management theory, public and private, have shown that it invariably has an ideological content — and more specifically, a value content.[38]

However, management scientists and public administration specialists have often acted as if their work was value-neutral. There are probably two main reasons for this in public administration.[39] First, there was the desire of the founders (Max Weber in Germany, Woodrow Wilson and Frank Goodnow in the United States) to separate administration from politics, in order to eliminate the influences of patronage and spoils and to provide a foundation for a rigorous approach. In the United States also, there was what Richard J. Stillman has called the "peculiar stateless origins" of American public administration theory.[40] Thinking that the American political system was permanent, American academics did not develop a full theory of the state and how it changes, taking almost a technocratic approach to the study of politics. Second, the desire to be scientific led subsequent generations of management specialists to try to factor out values.[41] From the beginnings in the Scientific Management movement, through the search for principles of public administration between the wars, to the highly sophisticated techniques of rational systems management developed in the 1960s and 1970s, theorists hoped to achieve the status of scientists in the fields of pure and applied science. In policy analysis, this trend took the form of claims to be able to do a rational analysis of any problem and the development of a calculus of political costs and benefits, as if the milieu could be scrutinized and tallied up once and for all, without any capacity to mobilize, intervene, or strike back.[42]

This neglect of values has had an impact on the teaching of public administration. In an international survey of 136 educational institutions undertaken in 1981-2, "values and ethics" were ranked as the third weakest area in their programmes. Among the 17 North American respondents, values and ethics were ranked as the weakest subject area. In this, public administration in North America has not been very different from business administration.[43]

The problem of values and ethics is more acute in public than in private administration, since activity in the public sector is aimed at a wider variety of goals and is subject to greater constraints than those which apply in the private sector. As put by Dwight Waldo:

> Moral complexity increases as memberships in organizations increase; persons in formal organizations in addition to traditional/nonformal organizations face greater moral complexity than those in the latter; those in *public* organizations face more moral complexity than those in non public organizations; and moral complexity increases as responsibilities in an administrative hierarchy increase.[44]

The complex requirements of public service were spelled out by Aaron Wildavsky in this way:

> Civil Servants are faced with conflicting tasks: on one hand they must maintain a separation from society or risk becoming dupes of a particular interest or class; on the other hand, they must still appear to represent society or risk undermining the state as legitimate in the eyes of the public.[45]

In public administration, tension arises because officials are both producers and wielders of public power. In this latter capacity, they apply the revenues raised by taxing individuals and organizations to the implementation of public policies, as found in law, regulation, and governmental directive. They need to be judicious in the use of others' money, but they also must act within the bounds of legality and in conformity with their elected superiors' wishes. The fact that all behaviour cannot be foreseen and controlled by rules leads to the placement of discretionary powers in the hands of public servants.[46]

Since the mid-1970s, these concerns have taken the form of a search for increased accountability, but the problem is as old as administration itself.[47] Ancient Chinese administrative science was preoccupied with the moral education of future mandarins, while the Roman Empire left us with the quandary "Who will guard the guardians?" In our century, the famous debate between Herman Finer and Carl Friedrich emphasized the difficulty of choosing whether to rely on external controls to ensure ethical conduct of public servants, or to try instead to develop moral and professional standards which would lead public servants to control themselves.[48]

As in so many issues in public administration, solutions in the Western world have incorporated some aspects of these two approaches. The recent concern for accountability has spawned administrative codes of ethics and the introduction of ethics into public administration teaching.[49] But our systems do not rely only on the exemplary character of public administrators.

As the dean of Canadian public administration, J.E. Hodgetts, stated: "Public office cannot create virtue, but only put it to severe test...even the most virtuous public administrator requires the salutary restraints imposed by democratically elected actors."[50]

Whatever the merits of these two approaches, we agree with Christopher Hodgkinson's statement that administrators "simultaneously initiate values and practise ethics."[51] We turn now to the question of how values in public administration may be studied.

3 · How to Study Values in Public Administration

Since values have been given little place in the positivist world of much administrative science, they have sometimes had to return in disguise. Cloutier and Paquet see organization culture as the "Trojan horse" that has allowed values to reappear in the management curriculum.[52] In public management, ethics courses have been one place for this rediscovery, administrative law and codes of ethics another. Nevertheless, the problem remains of discovering a basis from which values may be studied in some reasonably objective way. A look at two typologies of ethical values in administrative behaviour and policy analysis will set the stage for three possible approaches to the study of values.

TWO TYPOLOGIES OF VALUES IN PUBLIC ADMINISTRATION

There is a lot of common ground in most statements of administrative values and duties in industrialized countries.[53] The two we present here help to highlight the problems of choosing a single standard by which all others might be judged.

First, borrowing from Andrew Dunsire,[54] we propose a typology of qualities that the public and politicians may look for in public servants:

1 DISCIPLINE. This is the lowest level of expectation. Public servants must do their work diligently and competently, without waste or deviation from the goals assigned to them by democratically elected superiors.

2 STEWARDSHIP. This notion combines leadership with trusteeship. It refers to character, probity, honesty, and rectitude.

3 FAIRNESS. Here the accent is on equity, social justice, non-discrimination, and disinterestedness.

4 CARDINAL VIRTUES. These involve upholding one's duty to the nation, the constitution, and the public interest, and imply that a career in the public service is a vocation.

A second typology comes from Ronald Manzer and involves six criteria for evaluating public policy decisions. In it, Manzer presents two trios of values in ascending importance and gravity, according to whether they are instrumental values or substantive values. They are:

Instrumental Values

1 EFFICIENCY. This well-known criterion involves either producing a given service with minimum cost or maximizing output with a given amount of resources.

2 EFFECTIVENESS. The question here is whether a policy is successful in achieving its goals. The accent has shifted from costs to results and impacts.

3 LEGITIMACY. In instrumental terms, legitimacy refers to the source of a policy. Was it taken in accordance with law, custom, or principle? This is the legal type of legitimacy referred to in Max Weber's theory of bureaucracy.

Substantive Values

1 ACCEPTABILITY. In public administration, policies are not only required to be efficient, effective, and legitimate. They also have to be acceptable in political terms. Many a policy that could claim to be justified on instrumental grounds has had to be abandoned on grounds of political feasibility.

2 AUTHENTICITY. Perhaps the most controversial of Manzer's criteria, it refers to the distinction that policy makers must make among competing demands. Manzer links it to the distinction between wants and needs, but it could just as well refer to the means of ranking the seriousness and importance of various demands for public policy attention.

3 JUSTICE. As Manzer puts it "Justice means proportionality." It allows decisions about whose needs will be met by public action, and which characteristics will be deemed worthy of attention.

Manzer did not offer practical guides to the combination of these criteria, he did not present them as all being amenable to rational or scientific analysis. He argued only that all of these criteria *are* met when policy decisions are being made, albeit not always explicitly. [55]

THE BASES FOR DETERMINING FUNDAMENTAL VALUES

The search for the roots of ethical judgments has been shown to follow two possible paths.[56] They can be founded either on fundamental principles or a reasoned analysis of cause and effect. The first approach, based on the search for the cardinal virtues, is called the *deontological approach*. It seeks to discover a person's duty regardless of the circumstances. Deontological judgements take place in the realm of the desirable, or ethics. On the other hand, the *teleological approach* is based on analyzing the success of a decision in producing a desired effect. While still in the realm of the desirable, this approach pays much more attention to intervening realities on the path to realizing goals or respecting values.

The *deontological approach* can seek its sources in either religion or philosophy. O.P. Dwivedi has for some years been an exponent of an "administrative theology" based on a synthesis of world cultures, religions, and their leaders. Such an attempt follows upon the invitation of Dwight Waldo to survey religion to see "what instruments of navigation it can provide."[57] Dwivedi sees a secular administrative theology as providing guidelines for administrative ethics and the idea of a vocation in the service of the public good. This is tricky ground, for the modern secular state has only with difficulty disengaged itself from the embrace of established religion, which had the effect of placing the spiritual beliefs of some over those of others.

In the world of philosophy, the search for a reasoned basis to morality has tended to revolve about the notion of justice as proportionality. Immanuel Kant proposed the "categorical imperative" which decreed: "Act only according to a maxim by which you can at the same time will that it shall become a general law."[58] This formulation has the dual disadvantage that not all will agree on which rules should be generalized and that it is most likely to be found wanting on the basis of its consequences (or the other, teleological approach). As a practical matter, a great deal of political life involves granting funds, goods or services only to some people on the assumption that not everyone will need them.

From an economic-type philosophy comes another approach to the categorical imperative. In *A Theory of Justice*, John Rawls proposed that each person should have the right to the maximum personal freedom compatible with that of others.[59] In a philosophical version of the merit principle,

Rawls argues that necessary social and economic inequalities will be managed so that they will be of benefit to all of the population, and unequal advantages will derive from positions that are open to all in competition. Once again, as Rosanvallon observes, this is a procedural form of justice which gives no place to the results of its application. He relates it to the "Pareto optimum," a situation which is reached when no change could be made which will make every one better off,[60] but this has clearly taken us over into the realm of results-oriented teleology.

Duty-based deontological approaches have disadvantages apart from the fact that not all agree on their contents. In public administration, difficulties often arise because two or more values are in conflict, such as the sense of patriotism and the obligation to do one's legal and constitutional duty. To test this proposition, let the reader consider her or his reaction to three cases where public servants put their kind of patriotism ahead of these other duties: feeling that the American government was withholding vital information about the Vietnam War, Daniel Ellesberg leaked the "Pentagon Papers" to the *New York Times*; with scorn for Congressional limitations, and as a "good soldier" following his Commander-in-Chief's orders, Oliver North arranged secret illegal arms deals with the government of Iran, and applied some of the proceeds to helping the "Freedom Fighters" in Nicaragua; during the Canadian constitutional referendum campaign of 1992, unknown Québec public servants leaked dossiers to the magazine *L'Actualité*, which indicated that some officials had advised Premier Robert Bourassa against accepting several parts of the Charlottetown Accord.[61] A reader who approves all three actions may be classified as an anarchist!

The likelihood of conflicting values brings one inevitably to consider the consequences. The person who adheres rigidly to principle without regard for the consequences is at best a "difficult" person,[62] at worst a dangerous fanatic. Carol Gilligan has suggested that men are more likely to stick to rules, whereas women are more pragmatic and more attentive to feelings and relationships.[63] What principle other than practical considerations would allow us to discriminate between these two positions? Lastly, let us note that great spiritual leaders have tended not to be rule-bound, but to apply deep intuition to the problems they addressed, often to the puzzlement of their followers.[64]

The *teleological approach* has its basis both in philosophy and policy analysis. The most relevant school of philosophy, utilitarianism, took as its slogan "the greatest good of the greatest number." As Kernaghan and Langford have pointed out, such an approach gives little help in deciding when the rights of the larger number may be invoked to limit those of the few, nor does it give consideration to the means to achieve a desired end.

In this latter respect, its defect is the mirror image of the deontological approach, which was all method and no result.

But we are familiar with this kind of reasoning in public administration and policy analysis. It is our bread and butter. As Herbert Simon long ago pointed out in the defence of his form of positivism, most values in public administration are only intermediate values on the route to something more sublime. This position has allowed many policy analysts to feel at ease with the question of values, since they considered that they could contribute to the analysis of their coherence and integration, their conformity to certain principles of action, and their likely results.[65]

Experience of policy analysis has somewhat undermined this position and that of teleologists in general. It now seems clear that goals do not exist independent of the means to achieve them, and that what we learn during analysis and implementation informs us about our preferences.[66] Moreover, no amount of refinement in methodology can help us avoid some deontological choices with regard to what Manzer would call the authenticity of various needs and demands and the justice of satisfying some and not others.

A RETURN TO THE CONTEXT OF ETHICAL BEHAVIOUR

If we cannot make an absolutely convincing claim to either a philosophical or religious demonstration of virtue for the public service, and if methods to calculate the consequences also leave this question unanswered, does this mean that we have to accept complete ethical relativism? No; it means that the two elements are necessary for moral analysis in public administration, but that neither can make a decisive claim to ultimate superiority. The necessity of this kind of combination can be seen in the following argument from Aaron Wildavsky:

> An important consequence of the desire for egalitarian policies is that more and more groups are included.... This speaks well of social conscience. But it also speaks poorly of priorities. Because there are now so many categories of the deprived and their numbers grow so large that it becomes difficult to choose among them or to find the resources to aid them all.[67]

This is not to say that Wildavsky is right in his social policy, but he provides a good example of a deontological principle (akin to the moral imperative) coming into collision with its anticipated consequences (a teleological principle).

Fortunately, we do not have to leave the matter there. Moral judgments do not take place in a vacuum. In a phrase that brings us back to our theme of administrative culture, Charles Taylor writes: "Things take on importance against a background of intelligibility." Human life has a "dialogical character" and we define ourselves and reason with respect to some reference group, some "significant other."[68] Amitai Etzioni takes the argument further. His position is that people act simultaneously on the basis of rational calculation of their self-interest and judgements about values and morality. In his "I & We" paradigm, "individuals act within a social context."[69]

The importance of this observation is that a change in the moral horizon may bring about a change in either an individual's preferences or in the acceptability of a previously unacceptable solution. Etzioni gives examples such as legalizing divorce, purchasing on credit, and abortion; these acts are now more acceptable than they have previously been. Some representatives of the neo-institutionalist school of political analysis also stress the importance of institutional structures in shaping the preferences of individual and group actors.[70]

In organizations, Linda deLeon has argued that the "importance assigned (by the administrator) to competing claims is not entirely arbitrary or idiosyncratic but is influenced by the administrator's perception of the organizational structure within which he or she functions."[71] Using two variables, clarity or ambiguity of goals and certain or uncertain knowledge about the means to be used, she obtains four models, three of which are relevant in public administration.[72] They are presented briefly here with their effects on the individual's capacity for moral decisions:

MODEL 1: HIERARCHY (clear aims, clear means). Perceiving one's organization to be of this type lowers personal moral responsibility. The ethic of hierarchy is "discipline, obedience, service."[73] Its pathology is the obliteration of values before the rules.

MODEL 2: PLURALISM (ambiguous goals, clear beliefs about means). This is the world of pluralistic competition, of politics. Chief loyalty in this worldview is to the "rules of the game" and ethics concentrate on "deference to popular sovereignty, accountability and due process." Its unfortunate effects may be to stress process over substance, to reduce the goal to simply beating the competition, and to encourage a conformity to accepted rules ("everyone does it").

MODEL 3: COLLEGIAL OR EGALITARIAN (clear goals, uncertain means). This is the world of professionals, where informed judgment

31

is applied in cases of uncertainty about the best manner to proceed. The main obligation here is to one's colleagues and to professional standards. The less fortunate consequence is resistance to surveillance or criticism by non-professionals.

These three models, with their ethical biases, help to explain how systems may have moral effects that individuals would not necessarily want. Model I has often been castigated as burying personal responsibility under the excuse of "orders." A scathing critique of bureaucracy was thus offered by Hanna Arendt:

> Bureaucracy is the rule of an intricate system of bureaus in which no men, neither one nor the best, neither the few nor the many, can be held responsible, and which could properly be called rule by Nobody.[74]

At higher levels of the hierarchy, where the prevailing style may be perceived as either collegial or competitive, there may be the problem of "dirty hands" which arises when an "individual...feels moral guilt when he is doing his duty."[75]

These examples show at once that one's position and view of the organization condition the "moral horizon" but that they do not suffice to explain or inform the moral judgements of its members. Organizations can frame the actions of their members, but it was long ago pointed out by Luther Gulick that organization alone cannot ensure compliance or coordination.[76] It is this understanding that has led many organizations and governments in recent years to introduce mission and value statements, the former dealing with the organization's objectives, the latter with its "core values."[77]

This brings us full circle to our discussion about administrative culture. While all organizations have shared meanings and values that make up their culture, organization leadership will try to fashion these elements in order to make the members responsive to the priorities of the leadership. In studying Canadian administrative culture, we will be looking both for indications of what the official position on values has been and signs of what other values have aided or interfered with acceptance of that position. True to the teleological perspective, we will also be searching for signs of unintended consequences that may have led the administration away from official objectives.

Geert Hofstede's massive cross-cultural study deals with organizational values and attitudes concerning power, authority, deference, interpersonal relations, work, careers, and rationalistic and intuitive approaches to decision-making.[78] In our context, we are looking for values and meanings dealing with relationships of officials to elected politicians; the public service as a career; bureaucratic versus personal initiative and responsibility; labour relations; and sub-cultures based on department, occupation, sex, and language.

Where will we discover these values? Official values concerning the desirable are to be found in public documents, policy statements, royal commission reports, government statements to the House of Commons, administrative reforms, and the contents of training programmes. Of course, this official culture means little unless we can verify to what degree it has been accepted and adopted by public servants. Short of being able to observe them in action, clues to the presence of other cultures come in the history of employee unions and staff relations, in the evidence given in studies of reform about past obstacles or likely future ones, and in departmental and professional cultures as described in histories and memoirs.

The study of administrative culture includes the study of the learning experiences by which an administrative culture is passed on from generation to generation. These are found in the careers and memoirs of the outstanding public servants of each generation. Furthermore, the study of administrative culture may also lead to a new perspective on the administrative history of a nation. When one talks about the administrative history of Canada, the names of two Canadian scholars stand out: R.M. Dawson and J.E. Hodgetts.

Finally, the study of Canadian administrative culture is not new. Scholars of government and administration, particularly those who have tried to explain why the administrative system of the nation operated the way it did, have been aware of and commented upon it, although they may not have used the term "administrative culture." Among the first generations of Canadian scholars worthy of our acknowledgement are R.M. Dawson, Harold Innis, Alexander Brady, J.A. Corry, J.E. Hodgetts, Taylor Cole, J.R. Mallory, M. Brownstone, Stephen Dupre, and Donald C. Rowat. They all helped us to understand the administrative process at work. Their work and that of those belonging to the second generation is reflected in the sources used for this study.

4 · Conclusion

To sum up, culture refers to the values and symbols that allow members of a group to interpret and evaluate the world in which they live and work. In organizations, we prefer the broad anthropological approach to a narrow vision of "corporate culture" as something which is created and manipulated by top management. However, it is clear that senior management does try to act in this way, and it is important to study its attempts to do so, as well as its successes and failures.

Starting from this basic anthropological approach, we offer a hierarchy of cultures. Political culture is that part of a broader societal culture that refers to government and state activity. Administrative culture is part of political culture, but it also draws directly upon the societal culture for attitudes about work that may have little to do with government. The Canadian administration is at once a unified single culture and a composite of the dozens of organizational cultures that are found in departments and agencies, large sub-units, and occupational groups.

While the study of administrative culture may be done in a detached, relatively objective way, it raises the problem of the best way to treat values. We have argued that the search for first principles — the deontological approach — or the study of the moral consequences of actions — the teleological approach — cannot on their own provide a sure basis for a study that responds to the requirements of social science. However, we can study how the organizational culture shapes the moral horizon of the public servant. We intend to show how different administrative cultures have altered values.

We begin in the next chapter with the sources of administrative culture, its historical roots, and domestic and foreign influences. In Chapter Three we examine the foundations of Canadian administrative culture, both the shared political values and the specific doctrines of merit, neutrality, anonymity, secrecy, and accountability, as well as the guardian institutions created to protect and promote them. Chapter Four considers how the arrival of the administrative state put the classic Westminster model under increasing stress. In Chapter Five, we will see how ideas drawn from management have increasingly been proposed and adopted as solutions to the strains noted in the older culture. In the final chapter, we will evaluate the new administrative culture from the deontological and teleological points of view, with the aid of the contextual or "moral horizon" approach noted above.

Notes

1 On societies and innovativeness, see J. Arnold Toynbee, *A Study of History*, abr. D.C. Somerville, vol. 1 (London: Oxford University Press, 1946) 425; Jean-William Lapierre, *Vivre sans Etat? Essai sur le pouvoir politique et l'innovation sociale* (Paris: Le Seuil, 1977) 172. For individuals, Betty Friedan has summarized a good deal of research in a book on aging, *The Fountain of Age* (New York: Simon and Schuster, 1993) ch.4.

2 Robert B. Denhardt, *The Pursuit of Significance: Strategies for Managerial Success in Public Organizations* (Belmont, Ca.: Wadsworth Publishing Co., 1993).

3 The explosion in articles on organization culture has been documented by S.R. Barley, G.W. Meyer, and D.C. Gash, "Cultures of Culture: Academics, Practitioners and the Pragmatics of Normative Control," *Administrative Science Quarterly* 33 (1988): 32-33.

4 J. Smucker, "La culture de l'organisation comme idéologie de gestion: une analyse critique," *La culture des organisations*, ed. G. Symons (Québec: Institut québécois de recherche sur la culture, 1988) 39-68.

5 Cited by Milton Singer, "The Concept of Culture," *International Encyclopedia of the Social Sciences* (New York: Macmillan and Co. and Free Press, 1968): 527, 537.

6 R. Boudon and F. Bourricaud, "Culturalisme et culture," *Dictionnaire critique de la sociologie* (Paris: Presses universitaires de France, 1982) 133-34. (Trans. Dwivedi and Gow).

7 As in Ruth Benedict, *Patterns of Culture* (Boston: Houghton Mifflin, 1934).

8 Boudon and Bourricaud.

9 Cited by Singer 528.

10 Geert Hofstede, "Culture and Organizations," *International Studies of Man and Organizations* x:4 (1981): 25.

11 G. Morgan, *Images of Organization* (Beverley Hills: Sage, 1986) 121, 132.

12 N. Lemaître, "La culture d'entreprise: facteur de performance," *L'analyse des organisations. Tome II: Les composantes de l'organisation*, ed. J-F Chanlat and F. Séguin (Boucherville, Qué.: Gaëtan Morin, 1987) 419. (Trans. Dwivedi and Gow).

13 Howard E. McCurdy, "NASA's Organizational Culture," *Public Administration Review* 52:2 (1992): 189.

14 G. Symons, "La culture des organisations: une nouvelle perspective ou une mode des années 1980?," Symons 27-28.

15 Barley, Meyer, and Gash 52-57.

16 For the anthropological or sociological perspective see: Morgan 139; Symons; Gerald Britan, *Bureaucracy and Innovation: An Ethnography of Policy Change* (Beverley Hills: Sage, 1981); Daniel Latouche, "La culture organisationnelle du gouvernement: mythes, symboles et rites dans un contexte québécois," *Revue internationale des sciences sociales* 35 (1983): 285-309.

The managerial literature is recalled in Barley, Meyer, and Gash, who cite, particularly in the early 1980s, the commercial successes of William G. Ouchi's *Theory X* (1981), Peters and Waterman's *In Search of Excellence* (1982), and Deal and Kennedy's *Corporate Cultures* (1982). For the Canadian Government, see J. Bourgault, S. Dion, and M. Lemay, "Creating a Corporate Culture: Lessons from the Canadian Federal Government," *Public Administration Review* 53 (1993): 73-80.

17 Our position is similar to that of James G. March and Johan P. Olsen, who write that politics "is symbolic, not in the recent sense of symbols as devices of the powerful for confusing the weak, but more in the sense of symbols as the instruments of interpretive order." James G. March and Johan P. Olsen, "The New Institutionalism: Organizational Factors in Political Life," *American Political Science Review* 78 (1984): 741.

18 Latouche 295.

19 As in the *Report of the Special Committee on the Review of Personnel Management and the Merit Principle* (D'Avignon Report) (Ottawa: Government of Canada, 1979) 47; and Bourgault, Dion and Lemay.

20 G. Bergeron, *Petit traité de l'Etat* (Paris: Presses universitaires de France, 1990) 181 (Trans. Dwivedi and Gow).

21 Carolyn Ban, How Do Public Managers Manage? *Bureaucratic Constraints, Organizational Culture and the Potential for Reform* (San Francisco: Jossey Bass, 1995) 22.

22 J.I. Gow, *Learning From Others: Administrative Innovations Among Canadian Governments* (Toronto: Institute of Public Administration of Canada [IPAC] and Canadian Centre for Management Development, 1994) 63. Although IPAC membership is much wider than the federal public service, the common outlook seems to apply at all levels of government.

23 P.K. Kuruvilla, "Administrative Culture in Canada: Some Perspectives," *Canadian Public Administration* 16:2 (1973): 284-97; esp. 286.

24 See the debate between Jean Mercier and Herman Bakvis over its applicability to Canada: Herman Bakvis, "French Canada and the 'bureaucratic phenomenon,'" *Canadian Public Administration* 21 (1978): 103-24; and Jean Mercier, "'Le phénomène bureaucratique' et le Canada français: quelques donnnées empiriques et leur interprétation" *Canadian Journal of Political Science* 18 (1985): 31-55.

25 Ferrel Heady, *Comparative Public Administration*, 4th ed. (New York: Marcel Dekker, 1991) ch.6; Wallace Sayre, "Bureaucracies: Some Contrasts in Systems," *Indian Journal of Public Administration* 10:2 (1964): 219-29, repr.in *Readings in Comparative Administration*, ed. N. Raphaeli (Boston: Allyn and Bacon, 1967) 341-54.

26 Fred W. Riggs, *Administration in Developing Countries: The Theory of Prismatic Society* (Boston: Houghton Mifflin, 1964).

27 Garth Jones, "Frontiersmen in Search for the Lost Horizon: the State of Development Administration in the 1960s," *Public Administration Review* 36:1 (1976): 99-110; and Abdo Baaklini, "Comparative Administration: the Persistence of an Ideology," *Journal of Comparative Administration* 5:1 (1973): 109-24.

28 Latouche 291.

29 In this, we are closer to J.E. Hodgetts who wrote of administrative culture as "the implicit values or working assumptions that infuse, inspire, colour and constrain the attitudes and behaviours" of both practitioners and students of public administration in Canada. J.E. Hodgetts, "Implicit Values in the Administration of Public Affairs," *Canadian Public Administration: Administration and Profession*, ed. K. Kernaghan (Toronto: Butterworths, 1983) 29.

30 C. Hodgkinson, *Towards a Philosophy of Administration* (Oxford: Blackwell, 1978) 105.

31 As in *Le Petit Robert: Dictionnaire de la langue française* (Paris: Société du Nouveau Littré, 1972).

32 Boudon and Bourricaud 602 (Trans. Dwivedi and Gow).

33 G. Bergeron's theoretical work spans three decades, beginning with *Fonctionnement de l'Etat* (Paris: A. Colin, 1965) and most recently producing *l'Etat en fonctionnement* (Paris and Sainte-Foy: L'Harmattan and Presses de l'Université Laval, 1993).

34 Hofstede 21.

35 This definition comes from D.F. Thompson, "The Possibility of Administrative Ethics," *Public Administration Review* 45 (1985): 455, as cited by O.P. Dwivedi, "Moral Dimensions of Statecraft: A Plea for an Administrative Theology," *Canadian Journal of Political Science* 20:4 (1987): 703.

36 In their article "In Praise of Difficult People: A Portrait of the Committed Whistleblower" *Public Administration Review* 49:6 (1989): 552-61, Philip H. Jos, Mark E. Tomplins, and Steven W. Hays show that many whistleblowers are people of principle who act without regard for the practical consequences of their speaking out.

37 Professor J.A. Corry liked to quote Justice Oliver Wendell Holmes to the effect that "to act is to affirm the worth of an end."

38 André Gingras, *Les fondements du management dans l'histoire* (Chicoutimi: Gaëtan Morin, 1980) 196.

For management in general, see Judith Merkle, *Management and Ideology* (Berkeley: University of California Press, 1980); for public administration, see the typologies of George Frederickson, "The Lineage of New Public Administration," *Administration and Society* 8:2 (1976): 149-73; and Nicholas Henry, *Public Administration and Public Affairs*, 3d ed. (Englewood Cliffs, N.J.: 1986) ch.2.

39 These ideas are developed in O.P. Dwivedi, "Teaching Ethics in Public Administration Courses," *International Review of Administrative Sciences* 54 (1988): 115-30.

40 Richard J. Stillman, *Preface to Public Administration: A Search for Themes and Directions* (New York: St. Martin's Press, 1991) 19.

41 Theodore Lowi, "The State in Political Science: How We Become What We Study," *American Political Science Review* 86:1 (1992): 2; Simcha Werner, *The Self-Moralizing Organization*, SICA Occasional Papers Second Series No.9 (Austin: University of Texas at Austin, 1985).

42 In Canada, the height of this pretension probably came with the eighth annual report of the Economic Council of Canada, *Design for Decision-Making* (Ottawa: Information Canada, 1971).

43 E.A. Engelbert and K. Konig, *International Cooperation for Education and Training in Public Management, A Survey Report* prepared for the International Association of Schools and Institutes of Administration and the German Foundation for International Development (Brussels, 1983). See also Michel Cloutier and Gilles Paquet, "L'éthique dans la formation en administration," *Cahiers de recherche éthique* (1988) 69-90. Dwight Waldo, *The Enterprise of Public Administration: A Summary View* (Novato, CA: Chandler and Sharp, 1980) 109, writes, "Ethics has not had much to say about behaviour in large scale organizations" but that management science has had even less to say. Also, J. Padioleau, "Les 'Business Schools' doivent faire la morale," *Le Monde*, 27 October 1988.

44 Waldo 114.

45 A. Wildavsky, "Ubiquitous Anomie: Public Service in an Era of Ideological Dissensus," *Public Administration Review* 48:4 (1988): 755.

46 John A. Rohr considers "the responsible use of administrative discretion [to be] the most fundamental ethical issue for American bureaucrats." John A. Rohr, "Bureaucratic Morality in the United States," *International Political Science Review* 9:3 (1988): 167.

47 Waldo recalls from E.N. Gladden's *History of Public Administration*, that administration is the second oldest profession, the oldest being shamanism. Waldo, *Enterprise of Public Administration* 3.

48 Herman Finer, "Administrative Responsibility in Democratic Government," *Public Administration Review* 1 (1940): 335-80; and C.J. Friedrich, "Public Policy and the Nature of Administrative Responsibility," *Public Policy*, ed. C.J. Friedrich and E.S. Mason (Cambridge, Mass., 1940).

49 O.P. Dwivedi, "Moral Dimensions of Statecraft" and "Teaching Ethics in Public Administration Courses." Also, Kenneth Kernaghan, "Promoting Public Service Ethics: the Codification Option," *Ethics in Public Service*, ed. Richard A. Chapman (Ottawa: Carleton University Press, 1993) 15-30.

50 J.E. Hodgetts, review of *Exemplary Public Administrators*, T. Cooper and N.D. Wright (Jossey-Bass, 1992), *Canadian Public Administration* 36:2 (1993): 313.

51 Hodgkinson 3. He refers to Simon, Smithburg and Thompson, *Public Administration* (New York: Knopf, 1950) 539, 554.

52 Cloutier and Paquet 79.

53 For example, the *Code of Ethics of the American Society for Public Administration* and the *Statement of Principles Regarding the Conduct of Public Employees of the Institute of Public Administration of Canada* cover many of the same themes in a similar way. The collection of texts made by Louis Fougère in *La fonction publique: étude et choix de textes commentés* (Brussels: International Institute of Administrative Science, 1966) ch.6, shows the long-standing nature of most of these.

54 Andrew Dunsire, "Bureaucratic Morality in the United Kingdom," *International Political Science Review* 9:3 (1988): 179-91.

55 R. Manzer, "Policy Rationality and Policy Analysis: the Problem of the Choice of Criteria for Decision-making," *Policy and Administrative Studies*, ed. O.P. Dwivedi, vol.1 (Guelph, ON: Department of Political Studies, University of Guelph, 1984) 27-40; esp. 37.

56 The distinction that follows can be found in K. Kernaghan and J.W. Langford, *The Responsible Public Servant* (Halifax: Institute for Research on Public Policy and Institute of Public Administration of Canada, 1989) 23-28; Kathryn G. Denhardt, *The Ethics of Public Service* (Westport, Conn.: Greenwood Press, 1988); and Cloutier and Paquet 75-76.

57 Dwivedi, "The Moral Dimensions of Statecraft"; Waldo 109.

58 This rendering comes from Bertrand Russell, *History of Western Philosophy* (London: George Allen and Unwin Ltd, 1961) 683.

59 J. Rawls, *A Theory of Justice*, 2nd ed. (Oxford: Clarendon Press, 1972). Our commentary is drawn from Pierre Rosavallon, *La crise de l'Etat-Providence* (Paris: Editions du Seuil, 1981) 88-96.

60 See Rosavallon; Paul Samuelson and Anthony Scott, *Economics*, 3rd ed. (Toronto: McGraw-Hill, 1971) 757. Lester Thurow calls Pareto efficiency "a fancy term for 'more is better than less,'" *The Zero-Sum Society* (New York: Basic Books, 1980) 218.

61 Jacques Bourgault and Stéphane Dion, "Public Sector Ethics in Quebec," *Corruption, Character and Conduct*, ed. John W. Langford and Allan Tupper (Toronto: Oxford University Press, 1993) 84-85.

62 Jos, Tomplins, and Hays.

63 C. Gilligan, *In a Different Voice: Psychological Theory and Women's Development* (Cambridge, Mass.: Harvard University Press, 1983).

64 J.I. Gow, "The Guru and the Bureaucrat," *Canadian Public Administration* 27:3 (1984): 442-47.

65 H.A. Simon, "Rationality in Administrative Behaviour," *Administrative Behaviour*, 2nd ed. (Glencoe: Free Press, 1957) ch. IV; Michel Bellavance, "Valeurs et politiques: Considérations théoriques et problèmes pratiques," *Canadian Journal of Political Science* 16:3 (1983): 535-76.

66 Charles Lindblom, Inquiry and Change (New Haven: Yale University Press, 1990). M. Trebilcock et al, *The Choice of Governing Instruments* (Ottawa: Economic Council of Canada, 1982) 24-27; and M. Crozier and E. Friedberg, *The Actor and the System* (Chicago: University of Chicago Press, 1980) 191-208.

67 Wildavsky 754.

68 C. Taylor, *The Malaise of Modernity* (Concord, Ont.: Anansi Press) 33, 37.

69 A. Etzioni, *The Moral Dimension: Toward a New Economics* (New York: The Free Press, 1988) 5.

70 Kathleen Thelen and Sven Steinmo, "Historical Institutionalism in Comparative Politics," *Historical Institutionalism in Comparative Analysis*, ed. S. Steinmo, K. Thelen, and F. Longstreth (Cambridge: Cambridge University Press, 1992) 1-32. This is also an important theme in Crozier and Friedberg 167-79.

71 L. deLeon, "As plain as 1,2,3 ... and 4: Ethics and Organization Structure," *Administration and Society* 25:3 (1993): 294.

72 A fourth model, based on uncertainty about both goals and means is not really appropriate in public administration, for at best it is a "live and let live" approach and at worst it is completely self-centred.

73 deLeon 305.

74 H. Arendt, *On Violence* (New York: Harcourt, Brace and Wood, 1969) 38.

75 Richard A. Chapman, "Reasons of State and the Public Interest: A British Variation on the Problem of Dirty Hands," *Ethics in Public Service*, ed. Richard A. Chapman (Ottawa: Carleton University Press, 1993) 91.

76 L. Gulick, "Notes on the Theory of Organization," *Papers on the Science of Administration*, ed. L. Gulick and L. Urwick (New York: Institute of Public Administration, 1937). Reprinted in J.E. Hodgetts and D.C. Corbett, *Canadian Public Administration* (Toronto: Macmillan, 1960) 64.

77 Kenneth Kernaghan carried out for the Institute of Public Administration of Canada a survey of 93 formal value statements produced by Canadian government departments and agencies at all levels, "The Emerging Public Service Culture: Values, Ethics and Reforms," *Canadian Public Administration* 37:4 (1994): 614-30.

78 Geert Hofstede, *Culture's Consequences, International Differences in Work-Related Values*, abr. ed. (Newbury Park, Ca.: Sage Publications, 1984, 1980).

TWO

The Sources of Administrative Culture in Canada

Every society has institutions in place that transmit its key values from one generation to the next. The principal ones are the state, the family, churches, schools, the media, and organized groups such as professions, unions, and bureaucracies. But where do these values and their attendant perceptions come from? Without pretending to cover such a vast subject, we will cite here the influences that seem to be the most important for the Canadian administrative culture.

J.E. Hodgetts has suggested that bureaucratic values are moulded by changing social, economic and political forces — namely the "environment." We look in turn at the physical environment, social values, economic values, and the resulting political culture. However, bureaucracies also generate their own cultures, by means of the division of labour and the creation of professional and institutional loyalties. The link between the two kinds of influence has been neatly summed up by Hodgetts:

> Once organizations are brought into being they begin to create a network of linkages essential to survival and growth: they compete with other organizations for scarce financial and manpower resources; they seek public acceptance and prestige by cultivating their clientele and generally creating an environment congenial to their ongoing functions. In short, the laws of organizational survival compel organizations to enter into transactions with the environment and with other components of the political system.[1]

There is another connection between workplace culture and broader cultural values. Neil Nevitte has shown that attitudes towards authority are linked, whether they refer to authority in the family, the workplace or politics.[2] We must therefore expect that as political, economic and social values evolve, they will produce changes in administrative culture also.

In the following pages, we present the two kinds of indigenous sources of Canadian administrative culture: the external (the physical, social, economic, and political environment) and the internal (sources in the workplace), followed by a short discussion of foreign influences.

1 · The Physical Environment

Our starting point is the country itself: vast, cold much of the year, with severe weather conditions in the heart of the continent. In Canadian culture the themes of space and survival are strong. Space was a preoccupation of the first explorers, and it continued as the search for the Northwest Passage went on. Early economic activity tended to be based on one of the "staple" products desired in Europe: furs, timber, and, later, grain.[3] Communications were vital to the security first of the colony and then of the new nation. The immensities of the task meant that governments were involved in major infrastructure projects: canals, railways, highways, airports, and harbours. When the urgency of this need declined, the status of some of the great public services changed. For example, Ian Lee has shown that so long as the Post Office was considered a vital link in the national communication system, there were no complaints about the cost of the subsidy provided each year by Parliament. As soon as ministers began referring to it as a commercial service, it descended to the level of an ordinary business in the minds of many, and it began to be viewed as a costly bureaucratic service.[4]

Examining Canadian literature, Margaret Atwood found that the theme of survival is one of its characteristic traits.[5] The difficulty for European settlers of adapting to the geographic and weather conditions left a sense of the fragility of the enterprise and the need to cooperate in order to survive. As we see below, these traits left their mark on Canadian political culture.

The size and diversity of the country meant that regionalism has been a strong factor both in politics and in administrative life. The great majority of Canadian public servants have always been stationed outside Ottawa. For a long time, primitive communications meant that many of them enjoyed considerable autonomy and discretionary powers in the exercise of their duties. When the telephone and other modern means of communication made it possible, the headquarters in Ottawa developed centralizing tendencies, but the need to adapt administrative policies to local conditions continually reasserts itself.[6] Strong regional loyalties underlie many demands of the provinces for the transfer of federal responsibilities to them, or at least increased provincial influence on the way federal policies are developed and defined.

Another geographical fact that defines Canadian culture in all its forms is that it has only one immediate neighbour, and that a giant. We will see specific examples of the influence of the United States in the following sections. It is well to remember that the United States was, from the Revolutionary War until the twentieth century, a real or potential threat to Canadian territorial integrity and security. Now, America has become Canada's closest ally, its biggest trading partner, and the most important source of influence over its culture.

2 · Social Values

There seems little doubt that Canadian society has been guided by the Judeo-Christian tradition. The latest census, taken in 1991, shows that Catholics are the largest religious affiliation at 45.7 per cent, Protestants follow at 36.2 per cent, 12.5 per cent claim no religious affiliation, followed by non-Christian Eastern religions at 2.8 per cent and Judaism at 1.2 per cent of the total population. Nevertheless, in all provinces, Protestants outnumber all religious affiliations except for Québec and New Brunswick, where Catholics predominate.[7]

Comparatively, Nevitte's analysis of the 1990 World Values Survey shows that 50.6 per cent of Canadian respondents said that God was important in their lives. This is considerably less than the 70 per cent of Americans who say so, but substantially more than the European average of 34.9 per cent. In terms of regular attendance at church, Canada at 27 per cent is practically identical with the European average, but well below the US figure of 44 per cent.[8]

The real question is what this means for Canadian society and government administration. Two major international comparisons dealing with organizations and management culture both found Catholic countries resistant to modern management. Hofstede found that managers in Catholic countries demonstrated low individualism and low tolerance for ambiguity and high adherence to authority and to masculine values. Managers in Protestant countries showed greater acceptance of uncertainty, more individualism, less insistence on rank, and less adherence to exclusively masculine values such as competition, power, and success. In his study of the reception given to three major management approaches in four countries, Guillen concludes that Catholicism places general emphasis on community, self-actualization, paternalism, and organicism, while Protestantism emphasizes individualism, instrumentalism, independence, and contractualism.[9]

What should we conclude if we argue, as we do below, that Canada has always had a more collectivist approach to politics than the United States?

Does this mean that Catholic values predominated in Canadian political and administrative life? No, because there was also a split between tradition and modernity, as Hofstede points out.[10] It is obvious that the Catholic religion is more rooted in traditional values. What is not always appreciated is to what extent modern management ideas are linked to Protestant values.[11] While Nevitte does not directly address the Catholic-Protestant split in his discussion of values at work and in politics, he writes that "people who have traditional conceptions of political authority are also more likely to have traditional notions about authority in the workplace" and the same holds true for people who have non-traditional orientations towards authority.[12] The decline of deference in various areas of life would seem to undermine values based on an authoritarian theology.[13]

Our own view is that the more collectivist orientations of Canada, as compared to its neighbour, are due to some combination of the effects of its size, climate, religion, and the influence of the United Empire Loyalists. Certainly Canadian politics in the nineteenth century and much of the twentieth involved a careful balancing by the prime minister of the competing claims of Catholics and Protestants.[14] But Canadian literature and memoirs about the frontier are full of accounts of doors left unlocked, lights left in windows, and meals given to passers-by without question. That this tradition was undermined by urbanization is one of the reasons for state intervention in the twentieth century. J.A. Corry wrote that Canadians were not afraid of the state: the power that distributed homesteads and timber concessions did not inspire fear and mystery as did the Crown in England.[15]

Another form of collectivism led Canadians in the twentieth century to accept, if not to unanimously embrace, such instruments of cultural self-defense as the Canadian Broadcasting Company, the National Film Board, the Canada Council, and the Canadian Radio and Television Commission (which enforces rules about Canadian content of programmes in radio and television).

We maintain that Canadian values are solidly rooted in the Judeo-Christian tradition, but that this tradition splits into camps stressing collectivity, authority, and traditional values on the one hand, and individualism, competition, and achievement on the other. It seems clear that the latter tendency has been gaining ground, at least in undermining the tradition of deference. Of course, with regard to other aspects of the Protestant ethic, the elites of two of the three traditional parties have been preaching its neo-liberal ethos for the last decade and a half, a point to which we return below.

3 · Economic Culture

Economic culture consists in a society's view of producing and distributing goods and services. As a staple-producing society, Canada has always depended on trade for many of the essentials of living. Perhaps the main debate that had to be resolved was that of free trade or protection of local industries and producers. Though there was a considerable movement for what was then called reciprocity during the period of the United Provinces (1840-1867), the debate was settled for a century by Sir John A. Macdonald's National Policy of 1879, which determined to use tariffs on manufactured imports to promote the development of indigenous industry. However, after World War II, successive Canadian governments moved closer to free trade, first through the General Agreement on Tariffs and Trade (GATT) and its recent successor organization, the World Trade Organization, and then through the Free Trade Agreements with the United States (1989) and the North American Free Trade Agreement with Mexico and the United States (1994).

We have already mentioned that the size of the country necessitated government intervention. One of the principal goals of the new nation was economic development and inter-regional trade and communications. British Columbia agreed to join Confederation under condition that a transcontinental railway would be built; it was completed in 1885. The Intercolonial Railway linking Atlantic and Central Canada was completed in 1876. Later, other economic infrastructures continued to connect all regions of the country, such as the creation of the Canadian Broadcasting Company in 1936 and Trans-Canada Airlines (now Air Canada) in 1937. The Trans-Canada Highway opened in 1962, joining Canada by road, and the C.N. Tower, in 1975, connected Canada through telecommunications. Then and now, economic development undertaken by government has provided both physical and symbolic dimensions of national unity.

In addition to major infrastructure programmes and tariff protection, Canadian business was traditionally eager for other forms of government assistance. Most railway construction was done by private enterprises, but with public subsidies. Provincial governments used their control of the public domain to encourage development by private enterprises of natural resources: timber, mining, and hydro-electricity. In the twentieth century, fiscal policy used exemptions, rebates, and early amortization as ways to encourage economic development, scientific research and development, mineral exploration, and so on.

Over time, business and labour have organized to promote and defend their respective interests. From the adoption of the Trade Unions Act in 1872, which legalized their existence, trade unions have developed in size and experience. Union membership in Canada has remained higher—35 per cent of the labour force in 1992—than in the United States, where in recent years it has fallen to below 20 per cent. The largest union federation in Canada is the Canadian Labour Congress, which intervenes in many debates on public policy. One of its larger component unions is the Canadian Union of Public Employees, a union of 413,685 members (in 1991) drawn from all levels of government. The public sector is much more unionized at all levels of government than is the private, the current rate being almost 80 per cent. As we will see later, federal employees had their own associations from the beginning of the twentieth century.

Business groups have an older connection with Canadian governments, dating back to before Confederation.[16] While associations like the Canadian Manufacturers' Association (1871) and the Canadian Chamber of Commerce (created in 1929) were multi-purpose representation groups, in recent decades business groups have appeared whose main purpose is to influence the federal government. For example, in 1971, the Canadian Federation of Independent Business (CFIB) appeared, representing small and medium-sized businesses; then, in 1976, an elite organization, the Business Council on National Issues (BCNI)—composed of the 100 largest companies in Canada—was set up. The BCNI states that it is "dedicated to the development of public policy in the national interest."[17] As Paul Pross puts it, its membership is small, but they "wield great economic power."[18] While Canadian governments have a tradition of elite accommodation with organized interests, the influence of business groups is clearly greater than that of labour. Many ministers of the Canadian government have come from the business world, or pass into it after their political careers are over. The same is true of many senior public servants. Canada has never embraced the European tradition of a separate state sector; it has inter-locking elites who know each other and who want to work together. The most important royal commissions and study groups of the last forty years reflect this tendency of government to seek to reflect the values of the business community.[19]

As we show below, from 1940 to 1970 the Canadian government put in place a version of the welfare state that has been popular with the public. Beginning with the election of the short-lived Progressive Conservative government of Joe Clark in 1979, Canada has joined other developed countries in putting a stop to the expansion of the role of government. Where possible, there have been cutbacks. Since the election of the government of Brian Mulroney in 1984, Canadian governments have made deficit reduction a priority. While it is not clear how far the Canadian people will follow the attempts of their political elites to reduce the role of the state and increase that of market forces, it is clear that those who are attached to Canada's universal social programmes are at present on the defensive, in the face of a concerted discourse of globalization and the need for increased competitiveness in a world of free trade.

4 · Political Culture

Political culture is defined by Robert Jackson and Doreen Jackson as "the broad patterns of individual values and attitudes toward political objects." The "political objects" refer to images of power such as government institutions or national symbols.[17] In our treatment of this topic, we begin with the institutions that provide the framework for political life, then pass to political practice, before considering the resulting political culture.

The original Canadian constitution, the British North America Act of 1867, did not provide much written guidance for public servants. It could not serve, as John Rohr thought a constitution should, "as a source of a list of regime values for administrators,"[18] because the main components of the Canadian system were customary parts of the British tradition: the role and powers of the Crown, the Rule of Law, the selection of the Prime Minister, the collective and individual responsibilities of ministers, and the amendment of the constitution by unanimous consent of the federal government and all of the provinces. Until the adoption of the Charter of Rights and Freedoms in 1982, the principal features of the relationship between the elected government and its public service were present in the constitution only in customary form, with all the ambiguity that such a situation implies. A succession of Civil Service Acts provided the framework for this relationship.

What the written constitution did supply, however, were two principles of government that were not easily compatible with each other: parliamentary government and federalism.[19] In Britain there are few judicial limits to laws adopted by parliament, which, since 1909, has essentially meant the House of Commons. In Canada, the division of powers between the federation and the provinces led to numerous court cases in order to determine which level had jurisdiction in areas of taxation, spending, and powers. The existence of a Senate based more on provincial than on popular representation has limited impact on the Canadian government, so long as senators are appointed by the government of the day, but it has led to the recent demand from the West for an elected, equal, and effective senate. Such a triple-E senate would raise interesting problems for the tradition of responsible government based on the governing party's majority in the House of Commons.

Out of this combination of constitutional features and the other environmental features already discussed have come some political practices that deserve mention. First, there is the tradition of regionalism in many activities of government. The Canadian cabinet has often been larger than necessary, in order to accommodate regions or provinces that would otherwise be left outside the government. Regional considerations are present in most major issues affecting economic development, such as scientific research and development, location of federal facilities, and federal purchases. Since the provinces first met in conference at the invitation of Honoré Mercier in 1887, the twentieth century has featured a vast amount of "federal-provincial diplomacy."[20] From the beginning of Confederation, the federal government provided a per capita subsidy to each province. From the end of World War I to the late 1970s, it used the powers granted to it by the constitution to spend for the purposes of "peace, order and good government," to entice the provinces into joint programmes in areas of provincial jurisdiction such as natural resources, education, culture, highways, etc. Also, from 1952, the federal government began paying equalization payments to the provinces that fall below a national standard of wealth, in effect using taxes from the richer provinces to subsidize the poorer ones. Unlike the joint programmes, these grants are unconditional.

Many observers have noted that federalism as practised in Canada prevents the federal state from having a strong role in orienting and directing social and economic life.[21] It has risen to clear pre-eminence in times of crisis, like the two World Wars and the Great Depression of the 1930s, but in peacetime, the provinces have tended to have more importance, as they have jurisdiction over natural resources, labour, education, culture, welfare, and health — most of the concerns that affect people directly in their daily lives. This trend was so pronounced after 1960 that it was called "province-building," although that was an exaggeration, since province-building had been going on since 1867.[22] It has produced what Alan Cairns has called a "fragmented state with a fragmenting impact on Canadian society."[23]

Another aspect of political practice is leadership. It influences administrative culture in two ways. First, the example of a leader may inspire his or her employees. Second, many leaders put in place structural reforms that change the parameters or the moral horizon of the administration. When one of us polled the members of IPAC in 1987, a question was included asking who had influenced respondents, either by example or by ideas. We expected answers naming many former mandarins, the visible elite of the public service whose passage leaves its imprint on their colleagues. While many people mentioned present or former colleagues, four of the top eight people named were politicians: Pierre Trudeau (by far the most cited, with 38 people, or 4.9 per cent of the respondents naming him), Jacques Parizeau, Lester B. Pearson, and René Lévesque. Two academics were cited, J.E. Hodgetts and Kenneth Kernaghan, while only two mandarins were named, R.B. Bryce and Roch Bolduc (the latter had spent his career in the Quebec public service).[24]

With this in mind, we present in Table 2.1 a brief summary of the institutional legacy of Canadian prime ministers of the twentieth century. Not all prime ministers have been intimately interested in the management and operation of the public service. Some, like Louis Saint-Laurent and J.G. Diefenbaker, are most remembered in this connection for the royal commissions they created. Writing in 1971, J.G. Mallory observed that "of all the Prime Ministers of Canada, only Sir Robert Borden displayed any interest in civil service reform...He found it [the civil service] an antiquated structure distinguished by no discernible operating principles. He left it a service modeled on scientific methods for the management of government in a modern democracy."[25] Table 2.1 makes it clear, however, that Lester Pearson and, above all, Pierre Trudeau also have claims to be remembered as major public service reformers. The trend continued with later prime ministers, who became more involved with these questions, through reducing the size of administration rather than reforming it.

These practices already reveal much about the Canadian political culture. Canadians have long lived easily with parliamentary government. There has been little sign, except in Western Canada, of the kind of populism that brought to so many American states the practice of direct democracy in the form of the initiative, the referendum, and the recall.[26] The joint programmes that gave Canada its welfare state and the equalization payments are evidence of the collectivism that we spoke of earlier. What other key values and perceptions can we identify?

An essay by D.B. Dewar identifies four major Canadian values:

- The peaceable kingdom. Canadians have not been revolutionaries, nor have they adopted a militant brand of patriotism. Indeed, the United Empire Loyalists fled revolutionary America to remain loyal to Britain.

- Fairness and equity.

- Community and mutual help.

- Civility and gentleness; tolerance, minding one's business, and not rocking the boat.[27]

If we look at the empirical evidence collected by Ronald Manzer, Canada has been one of the less violent nations. While there have been and continue to be many inequalities among its citizens, he found that

TABLE 2.1: **CANADIAN PRIME MINISTERS AND THEIR INFLUENCE ON THE PUBLIC SERVICE REFORMS**

PERIOD	PM	CHALLENGES	REFORMS
1911-20	Sir Robert Borden	Politically neutral, patronage appointments, and independent Civil Service Commission	Civil Service Act of 1917/1918 introduction of merit system
1921-30 & 1935-48	William Lyon Mackenzie King	Professionalism and Position-classification, management of budget, need for welfare state	Introduced Keynesianism increased the hiring of intellectuals. Established the Royal Commission on Administrative Classification (Gordon Commission)
1930-35	R. B. Bennett	Great Depression, Fiscal Accountability	Fiscal conservative, stringent controls, consolidated Revenue and Audit Act, balanced budget
1948-1954	Louis St. Laurent	Demand for governmental intervention in economy and society	Gordon Commission on Canada's Long-Term Economic Prospects
1957-63	John Diefenbaker	Demand for social expansion, managing administrative state	Critical of Public Service, Established Royal Commission on Government Organization (Glassco Commission) which emphasized management within government

they were roughly the same as those suffered by citizens of other developed countries. On the other hand, tolerance has not been a prominent virtue; Manzer discovered a "strong streak of intolerance in Canadian public opinion."[28]

There is also evidence that, compared to Americans, Canadians place more importance on order and less on personal freedom. However, as we saw above, since 1980, Canada has joined in the trend to increasing distrust of government and a decline in deference to authority in politics, family life, and at work.[29]

Equally important are the representations that Canadians made of themselves and their country. C.E.S Franks has taken from Margaret Atwood the idea that survival has been a major theme not only of Canadian literature, but of Canadian politics.[30] There have been two consequences of

TABLE 2.1: **CANADIAN PRIME MINISTERS AND THEIR INFLUENCE ON THE PUBLIC SERVICE REFORMS (CONT'D)**

PERIOD	PM	CHALLENGES	REFORMS
1963-68	Lester B. Pearson	Demand for trade union rights in the civil service, equal status for French language, rights of women	Introduced collective bargaining legislation for public servants, Royal Commissions on Bilingualism and Biculturalism, and Status of Women
1968-79 & 1980-84	Pierre Elliott Trudeau	Francophone representation in the public service, government by management, gender issue	Political management, improved the Cabinet Committee System, Official Languages Act passed, Charter of Rights and Freedoms
1979	Joe Clark	Desire to contain growth of state	Policy Expenditure Management System (PEMS)
1984-93	Brian Mulroney	Neo-conservatism, restraining government operations	Nielson Task Force, downsizing, deregulation, privatization, PS 2000 Task Force
1993	Kim Campbell	Downsizing government operations	Initiative in downsizing and restructuring government to eight broad functional areas
1993 —	Jean Chrétien	Restructuring, doing more with less human and financial resources, privatization	Expenditure Management System replaces PEMS, fiscally-driven downsizing of government, program review, and deficit management.

Source: O.P. Dwivedi and Richard W. Phidd, "Public Service Reform in Canada," *Public Service Reform*, ed. John Halligan (Canberra: University of Canberra, 1998) 50-51.

this: first, both English and French Canadians have tended to cast themselves as victims, the former at the hands of the British imperial authorities, the latter at the hands of the English Canadians. Second, according to Reg Whitaker, Canadians have taken a "Hobbesian" view of the state, and presumably of the state of nature. In his view, their colonial experience disposed Canadians to accept the use of extraordinary powers, as in the War Measures Act.[31]

However this may be, Canadians were not in a hurry to be rid of the status of a colony. The independence that was achieved by the cession to the status of Dominion under the Statute of Westminster in 1931 was not the result of any mass demand, nor was it known to most citizens. It was considered an act of autonomy that Canada made its own declaration of war in 1939, but at the time of the Suez crisis in 1957, the Conservative Opposition made a scandal of Prime Minister St. Laurent's declaration that the days of the supermen of Europe were over. In 1964 there was a long and acrimonious debate in Parliament about the adoption of a Canadian flag in place of the British Union Jack.

All of this supports the view of D.B. Dewar that Canadians have not had an aggressive or jingoistic nationalism. Or, as Whitaker puts it, Canada was not a nation state. Until after World War II, Canada did not have a strong identity or a strong state as Europeans would understand it. As a result, the country was held together by patronage, which not only secured the support of its beneficiaries, but also provided a form of arbitration among competing groups.[32]

Canada did not have a tradition of a strong, bureaucratic state, but it did have an interventionist state, the purpose of which was to build a national economy.[33] The answer to the apparent contradiction between the two observations lies in the form of an aid to business. Tariff protection, grants for railway construction and other economic activities, leasing of mineral, timber, and water resources at favourable terms, and provision of basic public infrastructures (constructed under contract by private enterprises)— none of these activities required large bureaucracies. But they did give the Canadian state a more interventionist cast than that found in the United States, a fact that has led to descriptions of the Canadian tradition as "Red tory," "private enterprise at public expense," and "the corporate welfare state."[34]

The dominant political tradition in Canada during its first fifty years (since 1867) was this Tory tradition. At the policy level the chief opposition came from the Liberals, but their policy of free trade with the United States was defeated in the general election of 1911 and was not revived until the Macdonald Royal Commission of the 1980s and the implementation of the idea by the Mulroney government in 1989.

During these first fifty years, the principal conflicts with which the ruling coalition had to deal were those between French and English: the language question in Manitoba and Ontario, the treatment of Louis Riel and the *Métis*, and conscription in World War I. In the 1920s, however, new forms of dissent based on class and occupation became important. There were United Farmers' governments elected in Ontario (1919-1923) and Alberta (1921-1935). The Progressive Party (a farmers' party in favour of free trade) held the balance of power at Ottawa from 1921 to 1926.

With the Depression of the 1930s, radical protest linked farmers and labour in the Cooperative Commonwealth Federation (CCF), founded in 1933. Although this party and its successor, the New Democratic Party, have never been in power nationally, they have made a substantial contribution to Canadian political culture. Since the 1920s, Canada has not returned to the two-party system that prevailed beforehand. Moreover, the election of the CCF in Saskatchewan in 1944, and its strong showing in Ontario at the end of the war, pushed the Liberal government at Ottawa to adopt social policies based on Keynesian thinking.[35] In the decade from 1941 to 1951, the federal government introduced unemployment insurance, family allowances, and old age security. Hospital insurance followed in 1957, the Canada Pension Plan in 1965, the Canada Assistance Plan in 1966, and health insurance in 1968.

As a result, Canada has a number of universal social programmes to which Canadians are evidently attached.[39] In typical Canadian fashion, the Canadian welfare state is a mixed regime, more collective than that of the United States, but less socialistic than those of many European countries.[40] For Boismenu, this puts Canada along with Britain and the United States in the pluralist camp, as compared to higher degrees of corporatist social-economic organization in Europe.[41]

The consequences of this political cultural tradition for the administration have been several. First, the strong and tenacious tradition of political patronage has affected the public service in its recruitment, promotion, and disciplinary practices. As discussed in Chapter 3, the decision to eliminate patronage coloured most aspects of personnel administration after 1918. The obsession with patronage influenced both management policies and the desire of public servants for institutionalized protection from arbitrary discipline or dismissal. Moreover, the authoritarian tradition kept public sector unionism at bay until the 1960s.

Then, in an excellent example of how an institutional change can provoke a change in political culture, the inclusion of the Charter of Rights and Freedoms in the Constitution Act of 1982 dramatically changed the situation. At one stroke, it ended the supremacy of parliament in matters of federal jurisdiction, allowed citizens to challenge the constitutionality of laws, and allowed women and ethnic and religious groups to intervene on the grounds of discrimination.[42] If we consider also the policies of bilingualism, equal opportunity for women, and multiculturalism adopted in the late 1960s and the early 1970s, much of the unspoken unanimity in which the administration operated until 1960 no longer exists.[43]

5 · Internal Causes: Workplace Sources of Administrative Culture

Up to this point, we have spoken about sources of administrative culture that are outside of the administration. They penetrate the administration via its contacts with the political, economic, and social systems, and because public servants do not leave their perceptions and their values at the door when they enter their offices to work. However, there are parts of the administrative culture that come from the workplace itself.

The main reason for this is the division of work, which creates specialization and, it is hoped, greater efficiency. Adam Smith brought this idea to the world's attention in 1776 in *The Wealth of Nations*, but some 112 years later Emile Durkheim suggested that such a division of tasks also produced *anomie*, a state where the sufferer lacks moral judgments.[41] Also, we saw earlier that a critic like Hannah Arendt considered that the very precise division of labour in a bureaucracy renders no one responsible for the outcome of its decisions.[42]

The division of labour gives one a task for which one is supposedly qualified and a set of well-defined responsibilities. In doing so, it also creates a common cause with those who work in the same organization. One sign of common cause is the strong criticism that falls on people who criticize their organization in public, the "whistleblowers."[43] Another is the way in which departments and agencies resist attempts to compel them to share their power and responsibilities.

The division of labour has two other important consequences for our concerns here. First, by bringing specialists into the organization, it leads them to establish links with others of their kind. Aside from those who continue to keep in touch with others of the same legally recognized profession (e.g., lawyers, accountants, agronomists, doctors), many others join associations of people who do the same thing they do: for instance, the Canadian Comprehensive Auditing Society or the Canadian Evaluation Society. Organizations like the United Nations and the OECD give these specialists a chance to meet with their counterparts from other countries, and in many cases obtain support for their status or their work in their home organization.[44]

Second, specialized units in government administrations also have strong links to their own client groups. While this has been the case since before Confederation, the increasingly complex organization of contemporary society has led analysts to speak of "policy communities" in which specialized services establish durable links with established groups in their field of activity. Opinions differ on their importance: some simply include in them all durable and interested organizations, while others see them as being formed by the dominant interest groups, becoming "sub-govern-ments" and representing a form of sectoral corporatism.[45] We take it as a postulate that these links between a specialized service, other members of the same specialization, and their client groups strengthen the tendencies towards a separate organizational culture.

6 · Foreign Sources of Influence

Foreign influences are particularly important in the Canadian case, because there are few political traditions and even fewer academic traditions within the country to which practitioners and academics can turn for inspiration. In particular, as compared to Americans, we have no literature which looks back to the Constitution as a crucial text, nothing comparable to the Federalist papers which still elicit much comment and debate, and no land-mark introductory text such as the article written by Woodrow Wilson for the *Political Science Quarterly* in 1887.[46] Without any well-known text of founding fathers to refer to, Canadians might have adopted R.M. Dawson's *The Civil Service of Canada* (London, 1929) as the starting point of modern public administration thinking, but there are no references to the book in current textbooks.[47] In the absence of any enduring historical references, Canadian public servants and professors have tended to follow debates else-where, particularly in the United States, to inform their thinking on Canadian public administration problems.

As we saw above, Canada's constitution followed the British parliamen-tary system, with a minimum of written rules and a great many conventions that are being continually reinvented by politicians and judges. Until World War I, the predominant administrative ideas came from Britain also. When the government of 1911 felt itself overloaded with work, it turned to a British investigator, Sir George Murray who, much like Lord Durham sev-enty years before him, left a short and lucid report after a brief visit.[48]

Since World War I, however, administrative influence has been largely American. The development of Scientific Management by Frederick Taylor had, as we will see, profound influences on personnel administration in the federal government. As the study and practice of management pro-gressed in the United States, Canada usually followed after a short delay. A study of fifteen major administrative innovations introduced by the federal government and the provinces between 1960 and 1990 found that ten of them showed direct evidence of American influence (e.g., the Planning, Programming and Budgeting System, the Zero-Base Budgeting System, Freedom of Information, Deregulation, the Administrative Procedure Act, affirmative action programmes).[49] The sheer importance of American tech-nical services means that many Canadian administrative practices follow the lead of the United States in matters like toxic substances, consumer protection, military technology, and so on.[50]

Having similar political systems, Commonwealth countries tend to watch each other for workable solutions to current issues. The United Kingdom, with the arrival to power of Margaret Thatcher in 1979, influenced Canada and many other countries with a series of innovations designed to reduce the importance of the state and to introduce business-like practices to the remaining administration. Privatization of public corporations, executive agencies with considerable autonomy from central government, results-based management, the Citizen's Charter, and clear performance standards — all of these have had their impact at Ottawa. Among others, New Zealand has been influential as an example, first in being the first Commonwealth country to adopt the Ombudsman (1962) and then in the 1980s by vigorous action to reduce its deficit and its public debt. From Australia came the ideas of a major reduction in the number of government departments, the transformation of the head of each department into a chief executive officer, and the creation of many autonomous administrative units. Along with the United States, these countries have been leaders in the New Public Management Movement.[51]

Of other individual countries, Sweden has probably been the most influential. From it came the ideas of the Ombudsman and Access to Information laws. Moreover, its practice of decentralizing small government departments and all major operations to autonomous agencies has been known to Canadian officials for a long time, and it inspired the British Executive Agencies.

As we noted earlier, in recent years, international organizations like the United Nations and the OECD have provided experts with many forums to meet and exchange ideas. For example, if today there is a generally accepted way of examining government finances in national accounts on a comparative basis, it is because of their influence. Public administration never really was a strictly national phenomenon in Canada, but in the last thirty years, it has become more and more open to ideas of "best practices," wherever they are found.

7 · Conclusion

The argument of this chapter can be summed up by the following quote from J.E. Hodgetts:

> Canada's administrative culture consists of the British heritage of institutions and conventions mingled with American ideas and practices, with adaptations of both to meet indigenous features of a federal state, overlaid by regional and cultural factors.[55]

We found that the country has a tradition of state intervention, but not one of a strong state or administration. Aside from giving considerable support to Canadian businesses and producer groups, the tendency to collective action gave rise to the creation of a welfare state between 1940 and 1970. Since 1980, the parties in power have been trying to reverse or reduce this tendency. While there is no indication that the general public is ready to abandon any important social programme, there are signs that the public is less trustful of government and its administration then they were in the past.

For the first fifty years, the main preoccupation of the administration was its ambiguous relationship to the party in power. After 1918, it became much more bureaucratic and isolated itself progressively from political storms. Since 1960, however, new pressures have been exerted on it by economic leaders, social groups, cultural minorities, and the opening of Canada to world trade. These are issues to which we will be returning in later chapters.

Notes

1 J.E. Hodgetts, *The Canadian Public Service: A Physiology of Government* (Toronto: University of Toronto Press, 1973) 17, 20.

2 Neil Nevitte, *The Decline of Deference: Canadian Value Change in Cross-National Perspective* (Peterborough, On.: Broadview Press, 1996) 267-80.

3 H.A. Innis, "Transportation as a Factor in Canadian Economic History," Hodgetts, *Canadian Public Service* 62-77; and Ralph Heinzman, "Political Space and Economic Space: Quebec and the Empire of the St. Lawrence," *Journal of Canadian Studies* 29:2 (1994): 19-63.

4 Ian Lee, *The Canadian Postal System: Origins, Growth and Decay of the State Postal function, 1765 to 1981*, diss. Carleton University 1989.

5 Margaret Atwood, *Survival: A Thematic Guide to Canadian Literature* (Toronto: Anansi Press, 1972). The trend continued in the bestseller of the 1990s by Jane Urquhart, *Away* (Toronto: McClelland and Stewart, 1993). It is also present in French Canadian literature, most notably in Louis Hémon's *Maria Chapdelaine* and F-A. Savard's *Menaud, maitre draveur*, but the theme of survival here was directed at the foreigners who had come to take over their land.

6 Paul Brown, "Decentralization and the Administrative Ecology of the National State in Canada," *International Review of Administrative Science* 53:4 (1987): 641-56.

7 Statistics Canada, *Religions in Canada: The National 1991 Census* (Ottawa: Supply and Services, 1993) 8, 14.

8 Nevitte 210-11.

9 Hofstede, *Culture's Consequences* 137, 172-73, 204; Mauro F. Guillen, *Models of Management, Work, Authority and Organization in a Comparative Perspective* (Chicago: University of Chicago Press, 1994) 297.

10 Hofstede, *Culture's Consequences* 172.

11 Jeanne Siwek-Pouydesseau, "La critique idéologique du management en France," *Revue française de science politique* 19:5 (1974): 966-93.

12 Nevitte 268.

13 Peter C. Newman, *The Canadian Revolution From Deference to Defiance* (Toronto: Penguin Books, 1996) 35-36, gives some of the figures of the many cases of sexual abuse brought against priests and ministers in the 1980s. He says more than 115 priests and pastors have been convicted and sent to jail for such abuse.

14 A.R.M. Lower, *Colony to Nation* (Toronto: Longmans Green, 1946) 364-69.

15 J.A. Corry, *The Growth of Government Activities Since Confederation*, A Study Prepared for the Royal Commission on Dominion-Provincial Relations, mimeograph (Ottawa: 1939) 3-4.

16 Michael M. Atkinson and William D. Coleman, *The State, Business and Industrial Change in Canada* (Toronto: University of Toronto Press, 1989); and W.T. Stanbury, *Business-Government Relations in Canada. Grappling With Leviathan* (Toronto: Methuen, 1986).

17 Donald J. Savoie, *The Politics of Public Spending* (Toronto: University of Toronto Press, 1990) 307-08.

18 A. Paul Pross, *Group Politics and Public Policy*, 2nd ed. (Toronto: University of Toronto Press, 1992) 93.

19 John Porter, *The Vertical Mosaic* (Toronto: University of Toronto Press, 1965); Dennis Olsen, *The Canadian Elite* (Toronto: McClelland and Stewart, 1980); Wallace Clement, *The Canadian Corporate Elite* (Toronto: McClelland and Stewart, 1975).

For relevant royal commissions and studies, see the Glassco Royal Commission on Government Organization (1962-1964); Independent Review Committee of the Office of Auditor General (1978); Lambert Royal Commission on Financial Management and Accountability (1979); Macdonald Royal Commission on the Economic Union (1985); and Neilsen Task Force Programme Review (1986).

20 Robert H, Jackson and Doreen Jackson, *Politics in Canada: Culture, Institutions, Behaviour and Public Policy*, 2nd ed. (Scarborough: Prentice-Hall Canada, 1990) 81-2.

21 John Rohr, *Ethics for Bureaucrats* (New York: Marcel Dekker, 1978) 67, as cited by Katherine G. Denhardt, *The Ethics of Public Service* (Westport Conn.: Greenwood Press, 1988) 20.

22 Douglas Verney, *Three Civilizations, Two Cultures, One State: Canada's Political Traditions* (Durham NC: Duke University Press, 1986).

23 Richard Simeon, *Federal-Provincial Diplomacy: the Making of Recent Policy in Canada* (Toronto: University of Toronto Press, 1972).

24 Donald V. Smiley, *The Federal Condition in Canada* (Toronto: McGraw-Hill Ryerson, 1987) 22.

25 R.A. Young, Philippe Faucher and André Blais, "The Concept of Province-Building: A Critique," *Canadian Journal of Political Science* 17:4 (1984): 783-818; and Gow, *Histoire de l'administration publique québécoise, 1867-1970* (Montréal: Les Presses de l'Université de Montréal and IPAC, 1986) 378.

26 Alan Cairns, "The Embedded State: State-Society Relations in Canada," *State and Society: Canada in Comparative Perspective*, ed. K. Banting, vol. 31: Royal Commission on the Economic Union Studies (Toronto: University of Toronto Press, 1986) 56.

27 Gow, *Learning From Others* 51.

28 Mallory, *The Structure of Canadian Government* (Toronto: Macmillan, 1971) 152-53.

29 Seymour Martin Lipset, *Continental Divide: The Values and Institutions of the United States and Canada* (New York: Routledge, 1990) 31. In 1996, British Columbia adopted a law providing for initiatives and recall.

30 D.B.Dewar, "Public Service Values: How to Navigate in Rough Times," *The Dewar Lectures* (Ottawa: Canadian Centre for Management Development, 1994) 9.

31 R. Manzer, *Canada: A Socio-Political Portrait* (Toronto: McGraw-Hill Ryerson, 1974) 74-84, 257, 319.

32 Stephen Brooks, *Canadian Democracy: An Introduction* (Toronto: McClelland and Stewart, 1992) 61-66; R. Van Loon and M. Whittington, *The Canadian Political System*, 2nd ed. (Toronto: McGraw-Hill Ryerson, 1976) 80-81; and Lipset 36, 37.

An Angus Reid poll published in *The Gazette* (Montreal) 29 June 1996, found a majority not very or not at all likely to trust the federal government. Moreover, in a list of seven kinds of institutions, the federal government placed last with 47 per cent who were somewhat or very likely to trust it.

33 C.E.S. Franks, *The Myths and Symbols of the Constitutional Debate in Canada* (Kingston ON: Queen's University Institute of Intergovernmental Relations, 1993) 11-25.

34 Reg Whitaker, "Images of the State in Canada," *The Canadian State*, ed. L. Panitch (Toronto: University of Toronto Press, 1977) 42.

35 Whitaker, *Images of State* 46; Whitaker, "Between Patronage and Bureaucracy: Democratic Politics in Transition," *A Sovereign Idea* (Montreal and Kingston: McGill-Queen's Press, 1992) 261-64; Atkinson and Coleman 56.

In addition, see S.L. Sutherland, "The Canadian Federal Government: Patronage, Unity, Security and Purity," *Corruption, Character and Conduct,* eds. John Langford and Allan Tupper (Toronto: Oxford University Press, 1993) 126; Edgar McInnis, *Canada, A Political and Social History* (Toronto: Rinehart and Co., 1947) 346; *Report of the Royal Commission on Bilingualism and Biculturalism,* Book III: *The World of Work* (Ottawa: Queen's Printer, 1969) chap. 6A; and Lower 364-69. For Lower, however, after 1885, Canada experienced "the limits of opportunism" (380).

36 Alexander Brady, "The State and Economic Life in Canada, " *Business and Government in Canada: Selected Readings,* eds. K.J. Rea and J.T. McLeod (Toronto: Methuen, 1969) 67.

37 Whitaker, "Images of the State" 42-43; H.V. Nelles, *The Politics of Development: Forests, Mines and Hydro-Electric Power in Ontario, 1849-1941* (Toronto: Macmillan, 1974) 491-92. While this latter book refers only to the largest province, the theme was used for all of Canada by David Lewis, leader of the New Democratic Party, during the 1972 election campaign. His attack was on what he called the "corporate welfare bums."

38 Yves Vaillancourt, "Le régime d'assistance publique au Canada: perspectives québécoises," diss. Université de Montréal, 1992.

39 Roger D. Voyer and Mark G Murphy, *Global 2000: Canada* (Toronto: Pergammon Press, 1980) 119.

40 Jean-Philippe Thérien and Alain Noël, "Welfare Institutions and Foreign Aid: Domestic Foundations of Canadian Foreign Policy," *Canadian Journal of Political Science* 27:3 (1994): 547-48.

41 Gérard Boismenu, "Systèmes de représentation des intérêts et configurations politiques: les sociétés occidentales en perspective comparée," *Canadian Journal of Political Science* 27:2 (1994): 318, 328.

42 Alan Cairns refers to these citizens as Charter Canadians in his *Disruption: Constitutional Struggles From the Charter to Meech Lake* (Toronto: McClelland and Stewart, 1991). For a debate on his theory, see Ian Brodie and Neil Nevitte, "Evaluating the Citizens' Constitution Theory," *Canadian Journal of Political Science* 26:2 (1993): 235-60, and the reply from Cairns in the same journal issue: 261-68.

43 Leslie A. Pal, "The Role of the State: Canada and the Contradictions of Political Cohesion," *Un Etat réduit? A Down-Sized State?*, eds. R. Bernier and J.I. Gow (Quebec: Les Presses de l'Université du Québec, 1994) 389-407.

44 Emile Durkheim, *De la division du travail social* (1888; Paris: PUF, 1967).

45 Arendt 22.

46 Philip H. Jos, Mark E. Tompkins and Steven W. Hays "In Praise of Difficult People: A Portrait of the Committed Whistleblower," *Public Administration Review* 49:6 (1989): 552-61. Also, Michael Winerip, "H.U.D. Scandal's Lesson: It's A Long Road From Revelation to Resolution," *New York Times* 22 July 1990: E20.

47 The Canadian Auditor General in the 1970s was a member of the United Nations Board of External Auditors. The Independent Review Committee on the Office of the Auditor also cited in its report the Seventh International Congress of Higher Institutions of Control of Public Finance, 1971 (Gow, *Learning From Others* 152-53).

48 For the first position, see Joan Boase, *Shifting Sands: Government-Group Relationships in the Health Care Sector* (Montreal and Kingston: McGill-Queen's Press and IPAC, 1994) 3-6.

For the conflicting view see, in order, Pross 118-30; A. Cawson (ed.) *Organized Interests and the State: Studies in Meso-Corporatism* (Beverley Hills: Sage, 1985); and G. Lembruch, *Patterns of Corporatist Policy-Making* (London: Sage, 1982) 6-8.

49 For recent texts, see the "Forum on Public Administration and the Constitution," *Public Administration Review* 53 (1993): 237-67; Fred Riggs, "Bureaucracy and the Constitution," *Public Administration Review* 54 (1994): 65-72: and Theodore J. Lowi, "The State in Political Science: How We Become What We Study," *American Political Science Review* 86 (1992): 1-7. Also, Woodrow Wilson, "The Study of Administration," *The Academy of Political Science* (1887), repr. *Political Science Quarterly* LVL (1941): 481-506.

50 There are references to Dawson's *The Government of Canada* in G.B. Doern and Richard Phidd, *Canadian Public Policy: Ideas, Structure, Process* (Agincourt: Methuen, 1983) and in V.S. Wilson, *Canadian Public Policy and Administration: Theory and Environment* (Toronto: McGraw-Hill Ryerson, 1981), but these deal with principles of the constitution and not specifically with the public service. Wilson does refer to another work of Dawson, *The Principle of Official Independence* (London: P.S. King and Son, 1922), but no other current author does to our knowledge.

51 Sir George Murray, *Report on the Organization of the Public Service of Canada* (Ottawa: Sessional Papers #57A, 1913). On the influence of the Durham Report, see J.E. Hodgetts, *Pioneer Public Service* (Toronto: University of Toronto Press, 1955) 12-23.

52 Gow, *Learning from Others* 104.

53 For example, a study of two cases, Urea-formaldehyde Foam Insulation (UFFI) and the MEME silicon breast implants, found politicians, public servants, professional groups, and pressure groups all following developments in the US, at the Food and Drug Administration and The Consumer Product Safety Board, as well as in court. Walid El-Ayoubi, "Démocratie, Etat et groupes: La réglementation des produits toxiques: Les cas de la MIUF et de la MEME," diss. Université de Montréal, 1996.

54 Donald J. Savoie, *Thatcher, Reagan, Mulroney: In Search of a New Bureaucracy* (Toronto: University of Toronto Press, 1994; Peter Aucoin, *The New Public Management: Canada in Comparative Perspective* (Montreal: Institute of Research on Public Policy, 1995), esp. 2-5; and Denis Saint-Martin, *Institutional Analysis of Recent Machinery-of-Government Reforms in Australia, Britain, France, and New Zealand* (Ottawa: Consulting and Audit Canada, 1993).

55 Hodgetts, "Implicit Values" 472.

THREE

The Foundations of Canadian Administrative Culture

In the last chapter, we saw that Canadian administrative culture has its roots in geography, in social and economic values and perceptions, in the political culture, and in the workplace itself. Our task in this chapter is to present the basic concepts and values that have been the foundation of the Canadian administrative system in the twentieth century.

This system operates within the framework of the following main features: (1) a parliamentary system of government based on liberal-democratic ideals and representation; (2) a federal system of governance; (3) fundamental freedoms and human rights as found in the Charter of Rights and Freedoms; and (4) the rule of law.

We begin with the constitutional conventions of greatest importance to the Canadian administration, those of the rule of law, of responsible government, and of ministerial responsibility. We then look at the classic regime values, particularly merit, neutrality, anonymity, secrecy, and accountability. Next, we turn to the right of employees to association and collective bargaining. Finally, we discuss the central and autonomous agencies that have been created as guardians of the system. In later chapters we will see how this system has been strained by the advent of the administrative state and how the New Public Management claims to bring solutions to these problems.

1 · Constitutional Conventions and Canadian Public Administration

As we saw in the previous chapter, much of Canada's constitution is made up of customary rules. Of particular importance to the administration are the rule of law, responsible government, and ministerial responsibility.

THE RULE OF LAW

One of the basic tenets of the British parliamentary system of government is the concept of rule of law, which means a system of governance based on law. The expression derives from A.V. Dicey's book *The Law of the Constitution*, which says of Great Britain: "... when we speak of the 'rule of law' as a characteristic of our country,... [we mean] no man is above the law, but ... that here every man, whatever be his rank or condition, is subject to the ordinary law of the realm and amenable to the jurisdiction of the ordinary tribunals."[1] The rule of law also means that no person is punishable unless the law has been broken and is proven to have been broken in the ordinary courts of the land. An important consequence of the rule of law for the administration is the fact that, with very few exceptions, no rules, decrees, orders-in-council or regulations may be adopted by the executive without authorization from a law.[2] There is no sector of public affairs reserved to regulation by the executive without authorization by parliament. The rule of law also assumes that there exists a set of governing institutions that are capable of formulating laws and regulations to provide public order and security.

The ideal — that government is subordinate to laws applied by the ordinary courts of the land — has been sorely strained by the need to delegate powers to the executive to make rules and to apply them through administrative tribunals. That is the subject of the following chapter.

RESPONSIBLE GOVERNMENT AND MINISTERIAL RESPONSIBILITY

The collective responsibility of ministers for government policy and their presence in parliament mean that the electorate has clear knowledge of what group is to receive praise for its successes and blame for its failures, errors, and omissions. The voters do not need a scorecard to keep track of how their member of parliament has voted, for most votes follow the party line. Moreover, it is much less likely that government bureaus, pressure groups, and certain legislators may form "iron triangles" in the pursuit of common objectives, because both the bureaus and the members of the legislature are linked by their obligation and need to respect responsible government.[3]

This is one of those constitutional conventions of which we spoke in the previous chapter. The British North America Act merely states (s.9) that the "Executive Government and Authority of and over Canada is hereby declared to continue and to be vested in the Queen." The present-day convention owes its origins to the acceptance by the British government in the 1840s of the notion that the executive council of the day should have the support of the majority of the legislative assembly. This came in the wake of prolonged strife between successive governors and the assembly, culminating in the rebellions of 1837 in Upper and Lower Canada.[4]

Since Confederation, therefore, the Queen's representative, the governor general, picks the prime minister, although he or she must have the support of the majority of the House of Commons. The interpretation of this rule is flexible; many governments are defeated on particular legislative measures or on resolutions without having to resign.[5] Nevertheless, the rule exists, and governments sometimes have to resign, the most recent cases being those of John G. Diefenbaker in 1963 and Joe Clark in 1979. A government may overcome a temporary setback, but it cannot survive an enduring situation of minority government without support from some third party to keep its majority.[6] This rule has great consequence for the administration, since the central agencies created to serve the government (like the Privy Council Office and the Treasury Board) have the authority that comes from speaking for a government representing the majority of the House of Commons. There is a balance of authority and responsibility in this system that is not always present in presidential and other regimes.

For most public servants, the rule that concerns them most is that designating a member of the government as their minister, responsible for policy and administration in their department. The concept, developed in Britain, has been a parliamentary tradition in Canada. As noted by A.V. Dicey, the doctrine implies "the legal responsibility of every minister for every act of the Crown in which he takes part."[7] It means that a minister is accountable to parliament for anything he or she or the department does or for anything they have powers to do, whether they personally do it or not. As Herbert Morrison explained in the 1950s,

> if a mistake is made in a Government Department, the Minister is responsible even if he knew nothing about it until, for example, a letter of complaint is received from an M.P., or there is criticism in the press, or a question is put down for answer in the House; even if he has no real personal responsibility whatever, the Minister is still held responsible.[8]

The only exception to the rule is the case where a public servant acts deliberately outside or contrary to the policy of his department.

As is the case with other constitutional conventions, however, practice has meant something different. Both in Britain and in Canada, while resignations of ministers have been common, the number of ministers who have in fact resigned over errors or misdeeds by their officials has been very small.[9] The realistic interpretation of the rule seems to be that the minister must resign if the prime minister decides that the matter is too embarrassing to the government or that the minister has become a liability.

In recent decades many ministers and observers have been challenging this doctrine: the ministers because they do not like being held responsible for the acts of public servants over whom they have no immediate control,[10] and the observers because it seems increasingly unrealistic to try to maintain this fiction. Nevertheless, successive Canadian governments have adhered to the principle of ministerial responsibility. In a submission of 1977 to the Lambert Royal Commission on Financial Management and Accountability, the Privy Council Office wrote:

> Ministers are responsible for all the actions taken under their authority. Although it is true that the degree in which they will be required to answer for the action of officials will depend upon the political circumstances and whether an official has, for example, acted in a clearly unacceptable manner of which the minister had no knowledge, the fact remains that the minister is constitutionally responsible and this is essential in determining who answers for what to whom in the system.[11]

The official position has varied little over time: this document was reissued by the PCO in 1993. The Lambert Commission noted a curious ambivalence in those who testified before it. Commissioner J.E. Hodgetts later said that many ministers and senior civil servants who appeared before the Commission "spoke disparagingly of the 'myth' of ministerial responsibility, even though they were the first to decry any recommendations that seemed to ignore that myth."[12]

2 · Classic Regime Values of the Canadian Administration

From these constitutional conventions we turn to the major rules that have found their way into legislation. A convenient starting point is the list of traditional public service values identified by Public Service 2000, given in table 3.1.

TABLE 3.1: **VALUES OF THE PUBLIC SERVICE**

---

1 Service to Canada and to Canadians

2 Loyalty to the duly elected Government

3 Honesty, integrity and non-partisanship

4 Prudence in the use of taxpayers' money

5 Faithfulness to the principles of fairness and impartiality

6 Professionalism in carrying out their duties

7 Respect for Ministers, other Parliamentarians, members
of the public, and other members of the Public Service.[13]

This list is generally appropriate, but it must be said that the first value, concerning service to Canada and to Canadians, has often been taken for granted in the past. Some other values deal with the relationships between public servants and their political masters, while the rest are about efficiency and economy. In the past, the relationship between public servants and ministers was dominated by the patronage system. In order to understand the changes that were introduced by the reforms of 1908 and 1918, we must emphasize the values of merit, political neutrality, anonymity, secrecy, and accountability — values that lie at the heart of this relationship.

MERIT

While the United Kingdom and the United States had set up civil service commissions to administer examinations to candidates for the public service in 1855 and 1883 respectively, the Canadian system was slower to evolve. Although the Act of Parliament that established the federal public service in 1868 included a provision to create a Board of Examiners to consider and appoint the nominees of ministers, this regulation was ignored by successive governments. The patronage system spread rapidly throughout the public service, and for the next fifty years, large numbers of public servants worked actively for their political bosses in order to secure job continuity, promotions or other favours. In the words of one member of parliament: "patronage in this country is one of the worst things that exists today in the civil government. It is one of the most corrupt methods of canvassing for votes."[14]

In 1882, an amendment to the Civil Service Act required that candidates for a large number of positions in Ottawa pass qualifying examinations set by an examining board. The minister was still empowered to appoint the candidate of his own choice from a list of eligible candidates created by the examining board. In 1908, a Royal Commission (established in 1907) concluded that the quality of the Public Service had actually declined in the twenty-five years during which the system had operated.[15] The Royal Commission also reported how protégés of influential politicians secured a greater share of federal government vacancies, while other suitable candidates, often more competent than those appointed, were rejected. It also suggested that civil service salaries were inadequate in the face of the constant increase of the cost of living, having not been increased over the past several decades. Finally, the existing rudimentary classification system produced an inequitable compensation system, and the promotion procedure favoured mostly those who were experts in office politics. The commissioners concluded that the efficiency and morale of the civil service had generally deteriorated.

As the Leader of the Opposition, Sir Robert Borden had made the quality and performance of the public service a major election issue. It was therefore not surprising to see reforms instituted shortly thereafter. As Hodgetts and associates wrote in the *Biography of an Institution*:

> By August [1907] of that same year the Conservative Party, under the leadership of Robert Borden, significantly added to its party's platform, as a major policy plank, the need to eradicate patronage in the Civil Service of Canada. This was the first time in Canadian history that a party elevated civil service reform to the front rank of its policy pronouncements.[16]

The Civil Service Act of 1908 created a Civil Service Commission that was to set examinations for many posts in the "inside" service (employees in the departments in Ottawa); similar reform in the "outside" service was to come later. The Civil Service Commission was given independent tenure similar to that of the judiciary, and recruitment was to be based on competitive examination in future. The 1918 Act also provided that the tenure of the three commissioners would be for a term of ten years, contingent upon good behaviour.[17]

In 1918, sweeping administrative reforms, patterned after the American experience, were implemented. A new Civil Service Act (1918) placed the entire civil service under the Civil Service Commission, stripping the

Treasury Board and departments of any formal power to control the selection, organization, remuneration, grading, or career development of their staffs. The Civil Service Commission now would operate under two principal branches. The Examination Branch dealt with recruitment, examination and placement, and to an extent with promotions. The Investigation and Organization Branch dealt with questions such as the need for new positions and replacements, the classification for positions, rates of pay, and procedural methods and organization. But the passage of the 1918 legislation incited a jurisdictional battle between the Civil Service Commission, as it was then called, and the Treasury Board.

In Canada, as in the United States, reform of the public service came about as the result of pressures for reform and the availability of new theories of scientific management. From the late 1880s, Frederick Winslow Taylor had been expounding his method of the scientific study of work, with the result that Taylorism became one of the names for the new science of management.

In the wake of this movement, American experts had developed new and very precise methods for describing classification positions. Whereas Canada had, until 1918, followed the British tradition of broad classifications based on rank rather than on task, the newly reinforced Civil Service Commission found in the American system a way to overcome patronage. When the qualifications for a job are very precisely defined, it is much easier to determine which candidate is best qualified.

As a result of its contacts with the National Assembly of Civil Service Commissioners (an American association), the Commission appointed in 1918 the firm of Arthur Young and Company of Chicago to study the feasibility of a position classification system for Canada. The new classification system was presented to Parliament in June 1919; the immediate reaction was not very positive. The report, consisting of 678 pages, recommended the creation of 1700 separate classes for the federal civil service, with lines of promotion clearly demarcated and a salary schedule appended to each class.[18]

By 1965, the federal civil service had 138 000 positions, 700 classes, 1700 grades, and 320 salary ranges.[19] It was the most complex position classification system in operation after the American federal civil service system. Its difficulties were addressed by the Public Service Reform Act of 1992, which introduced the notions of appointment to level and deployment to regain some flexibility in personnel management.[20] Following 1918, however, the system was adopted by Canadian provinces and by many municipalities. In one stroke, the human resources management system of the Canadian government adopted an emerging American style. It was the beginning of a trend.

While the personnel management system introduced in 1918 lasted without major change until 1967, it is important to note that it never applied to all federal employees. For one thing, the act only applied to civilian employees of departments and agencies who were recruited by the Civil (Public) Service Commission; these departments and agencies received their budgets from funds voted by parliament. It did not include the employees of crown corporations, the armed forces, or the RCMP, with the result that just over one-third of all Canadian government employees have been covered by the act.[21] This situation allowed successive governments to leave certain categories of employees (for example, local post office employees) outside the system, so that in 1936, R.M. Dawson complained that "political patronage is still the great enemy of civil service efficiency in Canada."[22]

The need to respect the merit system slows down the administration of personnel. In the mid-1990s, there were 21 steps in a competition, with four more if there was an appeal. The average competition took 119 days.[23] Those responsible for personnel administration believe that hiring and promotions procedures in the public service would be comparable to the private sector were it not for the obligations to publish advance notice of competitions and to allow for a period of appeals.[24]

Even within the positions covered by the new civil service system of 1918, exceptions were made from the start. The soldiers who fought in World War I in Europe demanded recognition of their sacrifice upon their return. The government's fear (or gratitude) sparked them into offering special privileges. For example, when the federal Civil Service Act was adopted in 1917, a special provision was introduced to provide "absolute preference" to war veterans. This means that, if a candidate belongs to this category, then although he/she may be at the bottom of the eligible list, he/she moves to the top of the list when appointment letters are issued. This federal provision was also incorporated in various provincial public services of Canada; for example, Ontario, Manitoba, and Nova Scotia introduced absolute veterans' preference about the same time.

Thus parliament denounced inequality while providing veterans with preferential status.[25] Questions did not arise then as to the impact this would have on the merit principle of recruitment and advancement in the public service. This preference was also given after World War II and the Korean War, so that from 1945 to 1962, 27 per cent of all those appointed to the federal service — 45 per cent of the men — benefited from it. At the time of the Glassco Commission inquiry, 40 per cent of the entire federal public service consisted of war veterans.[26] It has been alleged that the presence of veterans had a significant impact on the attitude of the federal service — that it may have made them less interested in collective bargaining than they might otherwise have been. As far as we know, this has not been documented.

Another group of public servants has always fallen outside the scope of the merit system. These are the appointments to the very top positions of confidence in the administration that, by common accord, have been left to the decision of the prime minister of the day. They include the positions of deputy minister, ambassador, and chair and members of various federal boards and commissions. In recent years, the number of these appointments is about 3500 (out of a federal public service of 220,000). In actual numbers, this means Canada has proportionately more political appointees than the United States, where President Clinton had about 9000 appointments to make in an administration of about two million. However, the US has proportionately more key positions in the central administration to be filled in this way, whereas most of the Canadian positions are in boards and commissions on the periphery of the administration.[27]

Merit was intended to apply at initial selection and at subsequent appointments. The adoption of the American position classification plan meant that public servants had no automatic career path as they would have had in Europe, but that they had to compete for important promotions with others who were eligible for the same posts. However, when tempered with the provision that appointments should be made, whenever possible, from within the service, merit laid down the basis for a service made up of professional career-oriented personnel.[28] To make this plan a reality, however, other values or principles were needed.

THE CONCEPT OF POLITICAL NEUTRALITY

If appointments and promotions in the public service were not to be made on the basis of political loyalty, it was necessary to convince ministers that the public service would loyally and impartially serve them. At the same time, if public servants were not "depoliticized," the normal functioning of the state machinery would be greatly affected whenever there was a change in the governing party, raising concerns that the demand for services could be interpreted in a partisan manner. In order to provide an objective service and fair treatment of all members of the public, the traditional method has been to segregate public servants from partisan politics. A number of the values specifically mentioned in PS 2000 (Table 3.1) seem to call for it.

Public servants are required to serve the government of the day regardless of its political leanings. As one British author observes:

> If the Government changes overnight, they (public servants) are
> expected to serve the new Government of the day as loyally and effi-

ciently as they did its predecessor. They are thus required to be political chameleons, and there are strict rules to prevent them becoming
political animals: the logic of the constitutional convention is that a
political chameleon can never be a political animal.[29]

It is a very curious convention, and one that flies in the face of common
sense: in reality, there are no neutral persons. But what the convention has
required is the combination of zeal and detachment peculiar to the public
service. In one sense, public servants in the career service must be "promis-
cuously partisan," they must faithfully serve whatever party the electorate
has returned to office.[30] On the other hand, their situation is very different
from that of political appointees. While their duty is to serve the government faithfully, they have other obligations to the system. They must give
their advice to the minister

> ... without fear or favour, and whether the advice accords with the
> minister's or not; and once the minister has made a decision, it is the
> duty of civil servants loyally to carry out that decision with precisely
> the same energy and good will, whether they agree with it or not.[31]

Moreover, they must remind ministers of the limits set upon their actions
by the law and other rules of fairness and equity.
    Neutrality has in fact been sought by restricting the political rights of
public servants. J.E. Hodgetts elaborates this doctrine:

> Accordingly, even at risk of transforming public servants into political
> underprivileged citizens, draconian legislation and crushing penalties
> were imposed to prevent all civil servants from engaging in open par-
> tisan politics or for standing for elective public office.[32]

The 1908 Civil Service Act restricted all public servants in the exercise of all
their political rights except the right to vote. These restrictions did not alter
greatly in the next forty-five years. Although an Order-In-Council passed
in 1960 which allowed public servants to participate in and be elected at
municipal elections, the revised Civil Service Act of 1961 still forbade public
servants from engaging in partisan work in connection with any federal or
provincial election, and to contribute, receive, or in any way deal with any
money for the funds of any political party.[33]
    The punishment for those found guilty of violating these restrictions was
dismissal. This Act was the last victory for those who insisted on a completely politically neutral public service; within six years, this emphasis was
relaxed. On the basis of the recommendations of a Joint Committee of the

Senate and of the House of Commons on employer-employee relations in the public service of Canada, the Pearson Government agreed to loosen these restrictions. The 1967 Public Service Employment Act marked the first step away from the belief that a politically neutral public service requires the denial of most political rights to all public servants and toward the understanding that political inactivity by all public servants is not necessarily prerequisite to their efficiency and loyalty.

The 1967 Act granted two types of political activity to public servants: the right to attend political meetings and to contribute to the campaign coffers of candidates.[34] The rationale behind this change was apparently that such acts were usually carried out without publicity and would not affect the reputation of the public service for political neutrality. While the Act was not perfectly clear about what partisan activities were forbidden, in granting public servants the right of political attendance and donation, the government departed from the trend of the previous fifty years.

Then, in 1991, in a case brought under the Charter of Rights and Freedoms, the Supreme Court of Canada declared Section 33 of the Public Service Employment Act invalid. Excepting deputy ministers, Canadian public servants now faced no legal restrictions on their political activity — except that before becoming candidates for federal and provincial elections, they must obtain prior permission and leave of duty, and they must resign if elected.[35] In the same case, the Supreme Court recognized the existence of a constitutional convention calling for a nonpartisan permanent public service.

While there have been criticisms of various governments in recent years for politicizing the public service, official doctrine still adheres to the principle of neutrality. *Public Service 2000* states that "those who advise (governments) must be without partisan associations," and that this is one of the conditions of having a career public service.[36]

CIVIL SERVICE ANONYMITY AND SECRECY

The doctrine of ministerial responsibility as a cornerstone of the parliamentary system of government meant that civil servants were to observe two rules: maintain political neutrality and remain anonymous. As we saw, the tradition has meant that ministers would take public responsibility for administrative decisions (good or bad) made by civil servants. Thus, civil servants were protected from public scrutiny of their actions, particularly by parliamentary committees, but elsewhere as well. In return, they felt free to provide advice to their ministers regardless of party, without fear of being exposure to public criticism. Similarly, ministers had the right to accept or reject the advice of their civil servants without defending their actions in public. J.E. Hodgetts thus described this complex situation:

> The public servant benefits because he is not forced out into the open
> to debate the challenge to his political over-lords. His anonymity pre-
> serves the constitutional fiction of his political non-commitment,
> without which he would be unable to remain in office whenever a
> change in political party control occurred at the top.[37]

Associated with anonymity and political neutrality is the notion of official
secrecy. From 1889 to 1939, the British Official Secrets Act applied to
Canada. However, in May 1939, under conditions of increasing international tension, Canada adopted its own Official Secrets Act. Public servants
with office responsibilities must take the Oath of Office and Secrecy, which
binds them not to reveal publicly anything that they may have learned in
the course of their duties.[38]

The desire for greater access to information led to a long campaign by
certain individuals and groups for an Access to Information Law.[39] The
1982 law provides for access to certain documents upon demand. A series of
exemptions concern cabinet papers, security matters, relations with other
countries, and commercial secrets. Nevertheless, the act reduces government secrecy considerably by setting out the matters that may remain secret
and by providing for the appointment of an Access to Information
Commissioner, an independent officer who reports to parliament and not
to the government, to oversee its application.[40] The act has not changed the
situation of public servants, however. They are not free to divulge documents in their possession. The procedures provide for a much more formal
process that does not concern them.

It would be practically impossible for ministers in a parliamentary
system to carry on collective responsibility for government decisions, if the
process by which they reach decisions were public knowledge.[41] Parliament
and its committees are the fora for public debate; the public service is not.
The Federal Court accepted this position when it rejected the action
brought by the Auditor General of Canada for access to cabinet documents
surrounding the purchase of Petrofina by Petro Canada in 1981.[42]

In 1987, the PCO issued guidelines to all public servants who might be
called upon to testify before parliamentary committees, reminding them
that they do so in the name of the minister and not on their own behalf.[43]
However, since then, *Public Service 2000* challenged some very basic foundations upon which the Canadian public service is based, including the
concept of civil service anonymity. The Task Force on Service to the Public
observed that "the federal public service must become more engaged, more
visible, more open and consultative in its relationship with the public."[44]
Task Force chair Bruce Rawson stated, "Anonymity and invisibility are dis-

appearing. The public is demanding communication with a senior public service with names, faces, and telephone numbers they can call."[45]

Anonymity and official secrecy are part of a complex equilibrium that allowed the Canadian political system to operate since 1918 with a career-oriented public service and political direction by elected governments. Recently, relaxations have been introduced to these rules, as we shall see below. How far they can go without undoing the system of which they are a part is not known to anyone at this time.

PUBLIC SERVICE ACCOUNTABILITY

The effectiveness of any governing process depends upon how those in authority account for the manner in which they have fulfilled their responsibilities, both constitutional and legal. "Accountability is the fundamental prerequisite for preventing the abuse of delegated power and for ensuring instead that power is directed toward the achievement of broadly accepted national goals with the greatest possible degree of efficiency, effectiveness, probity, and prudence."[46] A breakdown in the process of accountability is liable to lead to ineffective, corrupt, and irresponsible rule. Consequently, at the very root of democracy lies the requirement for public responsibility and accountability of ministers and public servants. However, when discussing how to hold these two groups accountable, the tendency is to use two different connotations: i.e., ministers are to be "responsible" and public servants "accountable."

The classic mode of accountability was part of the hierarchic bureaucratic model: orders and rules emanated from the top of the pyramid, and discipline was applied to ensure that subordinates obeyed. In this process, there is a tendency for the rules to become the main object of attention of public servants, at the expense of concern for achieving public service objectives.[47] Incentives and punishments are closely related to these rules, so obeying them becomes the chief way to protect one's career.

As we shall see below, the trend in modern management has been to delegate more responsibility to managers and to make them accountable for the results they achieve. This kind of accountability cannot be imposed on managers if they have not been given authority over such important matters as finance and personnel. The question remains, in the words of J.E. Hodgetts: "Who is accountable? For what? To whom? How?"[48]

The Task Force on Public Service Values and Ethics (1997) contributed useful distinctions among four related concepts. First, "responsibility" refers to the authority that is attributed to elected or appointed officials to act in a given field. Second, "accountability" is "the means of enforcing or explaining responsibility." It involves giving account of one's exercise of responsibility and accepting personal consequences for it. Third, "answerability" means providing information and explanation, but does not include accepting personal consequences (the Task Force gives as examples public servants appearing before parliamentary committees and ministers answering for crown corporations in parliament). Finally, "blame" involves disciplinary consequences when an office holder has caused a problem or ought to have taken steps to prevent it. If such distinctions were generally accepted, the debate about accountability would be more serene.[49]

One of the problems in the public service is that there are several objectives to be pursued at one time. Many of these are the responsibility of central agencies that insist on their application by managers and their employees. One example concerning merit comes from a former public service commissioner, John Edwards:

> staffing goes beyond the straight prerogative of management and must serve other values and interests, such as the need to have a Public Service that is representative of Canadian society, the need to ensure that employees and those seeking employment are treated visibly with equity and so on. Thus our tradition has been to create a staffing activity that is a blend of management function and other broader considerations.[50]

A list of all the centrally imposed rules and standards would be lengthy. The federal public service does not have a unified set of standards of conduct listed in one document, but these can be found in such places as the Canadian Charter of Rights and Freedoms, the Public Service Act, the Oath of Office and Secrecy, the Conflict of Interest and Post Employment Code for the Public Service, the Access to Information Act, the Criminal Code, the Security Policy of the Government of Canada, the Official Languages Act, the Public Service Staff Relations Act, and the Master Agreement between the Treasury Board (as the employer) and the Public Service Alliance of Canada (as the union representing the majority of federal public servants), as well as individual departmental professional conduct booklets. In the Master Agreement, subject matters such as restriction of outside employment (after office hours), leave, holidays, severance pay, call-back pay, shift premiums, suspension and discipline, performance review, health and safety, and other related aspects concerned with working conditions and terms of employment are listed. The Master Agreement states that upon written request "… an employee shall be provided with a complete and current statement of the duties and responsibilities of his or her position … and an organization chart depicting the position's place in the organization." It also states that "employees shall not be restricted in engaging in other employment outside the hours they are required to work for the Employer"[51] unless the employer considers that outside employment constituting a conflict of interest situation. But standards governing the responsible, professional, and ethical performance of duties are not mentioned.

In October 1995, for the first time in the history of the federal public service, the Treasury Board of Canada issued a series of booklets under the general heading "Quality Services," intended for "departments, and the government as a whole ... to provide Canadians with quality services that are relevant, responsive, accessible and affordable." A Declaration of Quality Services Principles has been made by Art Eggleton, the President of the Treasury Board of Canada:

> The Government of Canada is committed to delivering quality services to Canadians. Our clients can expect to receive service that:
>
> · is prompt, dependable, and accurate;
>
> · is courteous, and respects individual rights, dignity, privacy, and safety;
>
> · is good value for money, and is consolidated for improved access and client convenience;
>
> · reflects a clear disclosure of applicable rules, decisions, and regulations;
>
> · respects the *Official Languages Act*;
>
> · is regularly reviewed and measured against published service standards, and these reviews are communicated to clients;
>
> · and is improved wherever possible, based on client suggestions, concerns, and expectations.[52]

The above Declaration is a "statement of tenets"; departments and agencies are authorized to mould these guidelines to fit their own needs to assist the augmentataion of their quality service initiatives. One of these sets Service Standards the purpose of which is to emphasize the shift of the administrative culture of the federal public service from bureaucratic culture to "client-oriented culture." Furthermore, "in this client-oriented culture, all unnecessary forms, rules, and bureaucratic thinking should be eliminated."[53] Only time will tell how realistic this statement is. This declaration is focused on improving the service delivery functions of government departments rather than the performances of individual public servants.

As mentioned earlier, standards of behaviour of individual employees are not listed in any master agreement or in any general guidebook published by any central agencies of government, including the Treasury Board and the Public Service Commission. However, there are some departments — such as Revenue Canada and Correctional Services Canada — that have created their own "standards of conduct" or "code of discipline." For example, the *Standards of Conduct* booklet issued by Revenue Canada includes employees' responsibilities (such as making comments on behalf of the Department, appearance, dress, conflict of interest, receiving gifts or favours, political activities, confidentiality and security of information, smoking and consumption of intoxicants, and the use of government property); the responsibilities of the department (with respect to unions, discrimination and harassment, abuse, threats and assaults); and other legal responsibilities. When each Revenue Canada employee receives a copy of this booklet, he or she signs it, and the original copy is kept in the employee's file; this indicates that the employee has received and read the booklet.[54] Correctional Service Canada, has also issued a booklet — *Standards of Professional Conduct* — that is given to each employee. The employee is expected to sign an agreement to maintain "the standards of professionalism and integrity" set forth in it. Six kinds of professional standards are listed: (1) responsible discharge of duties; (2) conduct and appearance; (3) relationship with other staff members; (4) relationship with offenders; (5) conflict of interest; and (6) protection and sharing of information.[55] Similar codes are found in the armed forces and the RCMP.

Although they do not guarantee compliance, written standards help employees to understand their rights, responsibilities, and limitations, and assist them to approach their work in a manner of high ethical and professional conduct.[56]

While the above illustrations anticipate the discussion which follows in later chapters about the new management philosophy, we note that in terms of accountability, it means that a new emphasis is placed on the obligations of public services to citizens and groups outside of the government. At the same time, these "new" service standards include many traditional values.

In conclusion, accountability can be a viable instrument of control to the extent that (a) public servants understand and accept their assigned responsibilities (both legal and moral) for the results expected of them; (b) public servants have authority commensurate with their responsibility; (c) acceptable measures of performance evaluation are available and are used; (d) results of such evaluations are communicated both to managers and to the person concerned; and (e) appropriate, equitable, and timely measures are enforced in response to results achieved and the manner in which they are achieved.[57]

EMPLOYEES' ASSOCIATIONS AND COLLECTIVE BARGAINING

Historically there have been three routes available to public servants through which they could convey their ideas, opinions, and grievances to management. These were political action, internal grievance and appeal procedures, and conventional industrial action. The first of these was only available to individuals by putting their neutrality at risk. The second depended upon hierarchical decisions, even after appeal rights had been largely transferred to the Civil Service Commission. The path to collective defense of rights and interests lay through collective bargaining.

While there have been associations for the defense and promotion of the interests of civil servants' interests since 1907,[58] collective bargaining was not accepted by the government until sixty years later. Here was a major challenge to the tradition of cabinet government, since the government was required to negotiate with public sector unions before having parliamentary approval for its policy.

Why did it take so long to achieve collective bargaining? Hodgetts cites two major reasons: the fragmenting effects of the 1919 position classification plan and the philosophies of the public sector union leaders.[59] According to Frankel, there were two other principal reasons for the delay: first was the slow growth of the membership in the associations, which was particularly retarded by the depression years of the 1930s. Equally important, however, was the effect of the example of the British Whitley Councils, created in the 1920s.[60] These councils were advisory, but the practice was that if both sides agreed, the government was committed to the decision; in cases of disagreement, the British government accepted arbitration. From their inception, they exercised a strong attraction in Canada. While the government of the day was prepared to study the question, a change of government and the Great Depression put an end to the first initiative in this direction. However, in 1944, the government created the National Joint Council, which it intended to be a counterpart to the Whitley Councils. However, because the government insisted on treating the Council as an advisory body not automatically committed to action, and since it refused to discuss wage levels in the Council, it did not have the same effect. The autonomous powers of the Civil Service Commission were also found to be an impediment to direct collective bargaining.

By the early 1960s, the civil servants' associations no longer believed in the NJC as the way to achieve collective bargaining. In the interval, they had strengthened their position by some key mergers. In 1958, the Civil Service

Association of Ottawa merged with the Amalgamated Civil Servants of Canada, giving the new Civil Service Association of Canada a membership of 28,000 in a public service of about 200,000. Then, in 1966, the CSAC merged with the Civil Service Federation, to form the Public Service Alliance of Canada, creating a new union with 115,000 members.[61] In addition, the unstable political situation in 1962-63 gave the public service unions the leverage they needed to obtain a commitment in favour of collective bargaining from the new Liberal government in 1963.

The government appointed a committee presided over by former mandarin Arnold Heeney to make proposals for a collective bargaining system. In its report, the Heeney committee recommended collective bargaining without the right to strike, saying that it did not believe that public servants wanted that right. Almost simultaneous with the publication of the report came a strike of postal workers, leading Mr. Heeney to recognize the justice of an editorial entitled "Famous last words!"[62]

In 1967 the Public Service Staff Relations Act effectively changed the relationship between the Federal Government and its employees from a traditional concept based on paternalism to one based on equality of both sides. The Act gave the public servants the right to negotiate wages and conditions of employment and set out procedures for certifying bargaining agents, negotiation procedures, and dispute settlement procedures. That same year the Treasury Board was identified as the employer for the public service. Accordingly, these public servants now had a focus for their movement to influence management decisions with respect to their careers and working conditions. We shall see in chapter 4 how the law worked.

3 · Guardian Institutions

In any large-scale organization, the values that are truly respected are assigned to some person or organization to ensure their observance. In the case of the government of Canada, there are guardians whose job it is to see that the will of the government is carried out, always within the law. There are other guardian institutions, usually independent of the government, that report directly to parliament on the respect given to values created by law.

For our purposes, the chief central agents of the elected government are the Privy Council Office and the Treasury Board. The chief independent agencies are the Public Service Commission, the Public Service Staff Relations Board, and the Auditor General. We will briefly sketch here their roles and functions, but many details will have to be taken up in subsequent chapters.

The prime minister's department is called the Privy Council Office. The PCO provides the secretariat for the cabinet and its committees, but it also helps the prime minister manage the government.[63] It advises her or him on the appointment of deputy ministers and other top-level political (order-in-council) appointments, and provides options to meet the prime minister's preferences about the machinery of government.

The PCO performs massive coordination and communication functions as the link between cabinet and departmental officials. This role has given the PCO a considerable influence over departmental people in the preparation of memoranda to Cabinet and in the interpretation of its decisions. Within the PCO, the Clerk of the Privy Council and Secretary to the Cabinet performs the most pivotal role in Canadian bureaucracy. The Clerk is the most senior public servant in the federal government and has "important responsibilities in providing a role model for deputy ministers and public servants, establishing standards of behaviour for the public service, and ensuring that minister-deputy minister teams are working satisfactorily."[64] Another sensitive role for the Clerk is as chair of the Committee of Senior Officials that evaluates the performance of all deputy ministers and makes recommendations to the prime minister regarding appointments, assignments, and performance rating.

In the past, these Clerks, acknowledged as the head of the federal public service, set the tone of administration, and by example provided standards of behaviour that were emulated by others. This role has been formalized under the Public Service Reform Act, which states that "The Clerk of the Privy Council and Secretary to the Cabinet is the Head of the Public Service,"[65] and is required to submit a report on the state of the public service to the prime minister. In the first annual report, Paul Tellier, Clerk of the Privy Council stated: "It [the report] reflects the values and traditions of the Public Service as I understand them. It speaks to problems and challenges as I see them before us."[66]

Another central agency that acts as a government guardian of public service standards is the Treasury Board, which is composed of two distinct parts. It is a committee of cabinet, with powers to act on its behalf in many matters dealing with finance, personnel, and administrative reform. As we saw, the Treasury Board is the employer of public servants for the purposes of collective bargaining, and as such it is responsible for government wage and benefits policy. It is also responsible for systems of evaluation, both of programmes and of public servants, and it sets the overall policy for government contracts. The Board is served by a permanent staff of public servants who — along with the staff of the PCO, the department of Finance, and the Department of Foreign Affairs and Trade — make up the elite of federal public servants.

The third central agency traditionally responsible for acting as guardian of public service values is the Public Service Commission. Under the Civil Service Act of 1917, which remained in force with minor changes until 1967, it was responsible for all aspects of personnel management. Its main task was, as mentioned by the Royal Commission on Administrative Classifications in the Public Service, 1946, to be "the guardian of the merit principle,"[67] and to ensure a career service governed by uniform standards. It succeeded in putting an end to political patronage and nepotism in the part of the federal service that came under its jurisdiction. In order to achieve this, it was granted a high degree of autonomy under the act. Commissioners were appointed with the consent of parliament for fixed terms and could only be removed with parliament's approval. As parliament's agent, the Commission took a defensive stance by erecting legislative and procedural barriers against abuse.[68] At the same time, it was the government's principal source of expert advice on personnel matters. This ambiguous position as government adviser and independent controller was frequently criticized. Thus, when the Public Service Employment Act of 1967 introduced collective bargaining and changed the structure of central personnel management, it was no surprise to find that the new Public Service Commission kept staffing and appeal functions, while the major responsibility for personnel management was transferred to the newly constituted central agency, the Treasury Board Secretariat.

In addition to these three central agencies, one should include four other autonomous public service institutions in this list of guardians:

1 The Public Service Staff Relations Board, created in 1967 to handle all the work around certification of unions, arbitrations, and determination of essential services.

2 The Office of Auditor General, who reports to parliament on the government's accounts and its financial management. While the Auditor General has no authority to impose values on public servants, his annual and special reports attract public and parliamentary attention to questions that he considers important. Recent Auditors have laid particular stress on such questions as accountability and value for money.

3 The Official Languages Commissioner, responsible for protecting the language rights of individuals under the Official Languages Act of 1969 and monitoring all federal agencies to ensure proper application of the legislation. His annual reports deliver public praise and blame to departments and agencies.

4 The Canadian Human Rights Commission, established in 1977 to investigate complaints of discrimination on grounds of race, religion, ethnic origin, gender, age, etc.

In terms of the priorities of public servants, the central agencies that speak for ministers (the PCO and the Treasury Board) obviously come first. However, the autonomous agencies, especially the Public Service Commission, all contribute to shaping the public servant's moral horizon. The PSC has jurisdiction that may directly change the course of personnel administration in departments and agencies, either by recruitment, evaluation, training or other services it provides, or by the surveillance function it has over departmental management. The Auditor General and the Official Languages Commissioner have the right to force the administration to provide it with information, but not to compel correction. Their weapons are publicity and parliamentary support. The Human Rights Commission not only advises the government on human rights issues, but it may also initiate court action against offenders in the public service.

4 · Conclusion

Peter Aucoin observes that "There is clearly a tension between the twin pillars of the modern Westminster model: responsible government and the career public service."[69] Responsible government concentrates power over policy and management decisions in the hands of elected ministers. The career public service, however, has been built on the principle of insulating most personnel operations from the interference of ministers, instead handing it over either to an independent agency, the Public Service Commission, or to career public managers in the departments and agencies. For the fifty years following the reforms of 1918, the tension was managed by an equilibrium that allowed ministers to be responsible for their departments' destinies but granted public servants a career based on selection by merit, political neutrality, anonymity, secrecy, and accountability. From early in this century, public servants wanted more than individual protection, but they did not achieve collective bargaining until 1967.

We turn in the next chapter to the ways in which the administrative state increased the pressure under the Canadian version of the Westminster model operates.

Notes

1 A.V. Dicey, *Introduction to the Study of Law of the Constitution*, 10th ed. (1893; London: Macmillan, 1961).

2 For further elaboration, see, Ronald Manzer, *Public Choices and Political Development in Canada* (Toronto: University of Toronto Press, 1985) 100-102. There are a few customary exceptions to this rule based on what remains of the royal prerogative. See Daniel Mockle, "La réforme du statut juridique de l'administration fédérale: observations critiques sur les causes du blocage actuel," *Canadian Public Administration* 29:2 (1986): 282-303.

3 In Canada, as in the United States, we do have "policy communities" and "sub-governments" associated with each major policy field, but, as Paul Pross points out, "subgovernments in Canada lack the cohesion and authority of the American." Pross 237.

4 Hodgetts, *Pioneer Public Service* 21-3, 271-4.

5 Mallory 57-63; and Louis Massicotte, "Government Defeats in the Ontario Legislative Assembly, 1867-1995," manuscript, Department of Political Science, Université de Montréal, 1996.

6 Such a situation existed from 1972 to 1974, when NDP support allowed the Liberal Government of Pierre E. Trudeau to survive; otherwise, he would have had to resign.

7 Dicey 303.

8 Herbert Morrison, *Government and Parliament*, 2nd. ed. (London: Oxford University Press, 1959) 321.

9 For Britain, S.E. Finer, "The Individual Responsibility of Ministers," *Public Administration* 34 (1956): 377-96; and Geoffrey Marshall, "Ministerial Responsibility," *Political Quarterly* 34 (1963): 256-68; for Canada, S.L. Sutherland, "Responsible Government and Ministerial responsibility: Every Reform Is Its Own Problem," *Canadian Journal of Political Science* 24:4 (1991): 91-120.

10 K. Kernaghan, "Power, Parliament and Public Servants in Canada: Ministerial Responsibility Re-examined," *Canadian Public Policy* 5(1979): 366-82.

11 Canada, Privy Council Office, *Responsibility in the Constitution*, Submission to the Royal Commission on Financial Management and Accountability (1979; Ottawa: Supply and Services, 1993) 72.

12 J.E. Hodgetts, "Government and People: the Quest for Accountability," Annual Conference of the Canadian Political Science Association, Halifax, 27 May 1981: 4-5.

13 Canada, *Public Service 2000* (Ottawa: Supply and Services Canada, 1990) 13.

14 Quoted in R.M. Dawson, *The Civil Service of Canada* (London: Oxford University Press 1929) 93. To Dawson, patronage was the dominant fact of the life of the Canadian public service (252).

15 R.M. Dawson, *Government of Canada*, 5th ed. (Toronto: University of Toronto Press, 1970) 251.

16 J.E. Hodgetts et al., *Biography of an Institution* (Montreal and London: McGill-Queen's University Press, 1972) 19.

17 Hodgetts et al., *Biography of an Institution* 104.

18 Alasdair Roberts, *So-Called Experts: How American Consultants Remade the Canadian Civil Service, 1918-21* (Toronto: IPAC, 1996). Also, Hodgetts et al., *Biography of an Institution* 76.

19 Hodgetts, *et al.*, *Biography of an Institution* 68-9.

20 See below, Chapter 5.

21 For example, in 1960, only 131,953 persons out of a total federal employment of 344,362 were under the protection of the merit system.

22 R.M. Dawson, "The Canadian Civil Service," *Canadian Journal of Economic and Political Science* 2 (1936): 291, as cited by W.D.K. Kernaghan," The Political Rights and Activities of Canadian Public Servants," *Public Administration in Canada: Selected Readings*, ed. W.D.K. Kernaghan and A.M. Willms (Toronto: Methuen, 1971) 386.

23 Remarks by Mary Santero, Public Service Commission of Canada, at the Symposium on the Future of the Career Public Service, held by APEX at Ottawa, 5 June 1996.

24 Conseil du trésor, *Guide du gestionnaire* (Ottawa: Conseil du trésor, 1982) 26.

25 Hodgetts, *et al.*, *The Biography of an Institution* 462-63.

26 Canada, *Report of the Royal Commission on Government Organization*, vol. 1 (Ottawa: Queen's Printer, 1962) 346. From 1945 to 1954, 66 per cent of men appointed were veterans, Hodgetts *et al.*, *Biography of an Institution* 470.

27 Sharon Sutherland, "The Canadian Federal Government," *Corruption, Character and Conduct*, ed. J.W. Langford and A. Tupper (Toronto: Oxford University Press, 1993): 121-4; and Bruce Smith, "The United States Higher Civil Service in Comparative Perspective," in his *The Higher Civil Service in Comparative Perspective: Lessons for the United States* (Washington: the Brookings Institution, 1984) 7-10, found that Canada was the most stable country in terms of the balance between career and administrative appointments, while the US was the least stable.

28 Kenneth Kernaghan, "Career Public Service 2000: Road to Renewal or Impractical Vision?" *Canadian Public Administration* 34:4 (1991): 353.

29 Rob Shepherd, "Is the Age of Civil Service Neutrality Over?" *Public Administration* (UK) 65:1 (1987): 69.

30 The expression comes from Aucoin 43, who has adapted it from Graham K. Wilson, "The Prospects for the Public Service in Britain. Major to the Rescue?" *International Review of Administrative Science* 57:3 (1991): 328.

31 Shepherd 72.

32 Hodgetts, *The Canadian Public Service* 316.

33 Canada, *The Civil Service Act, 1961*, Section 61:1.

34 Canada, *The Public Service Employment Act, 1967*, section 32. On the issue of political rights of public servants during the 1960s see O.P. Dwivedi and J.P. Kyba, "Political Rights of Canada's Public Servants," *Contemporary Issues in Canadian Politics*, ed. Frederick Vaughan, Patrick Kyba, and O.P. Dwivedi, (Toronto: Prentice-Hall, 1970): 230-39.

35 W.D.K. Kernaghan and David Siegel, *Public Administration in Canada* (Toronto: Nelson Canada, 1995): 337; and *Osborne v. Canada* (Treasury Board, 1991) 2 SCR.

36 *Public Service 2000* 34, as quoted by Kernaghan, "Career Public Service 2000" 560.

37 Hodgetts, *The Canadian Public Service* 48.

38 Canada, *Report of the Royal Commission on Security*, abr. (Ottawa: Information Canada, 1969) 75; Public Service Act, Revised Statutes of Canada, chap. P-33, Schedule III.

39 Gow, *Learning From Others* 165-69. Professor Donald Rowat of Carleton University and Conservative MP Gerald Baldwin were the leaders of this movement, along with the Canadian Bar Association.

40 For a recent appraisal, see Donald C. Rowat, "Access to Information: Australia and New Zealand Compared to Canada," Bernier and Gow 279-90.

41 For the classic position in Britain, see J.H. Robertson, a memorandum submitted to the (Fulton) Committee on the Civil Service, *Report*, Volume 5:2 (London: HMSO, 1968) 1039-40. For Canada, see Mitchell Sharp, *Which Reminds Me* (Toronto: University of Toronto Press, 1994) 71-84.

42 *Auditor General of Canada v Minister of Energy, Mines and Resources*, 1 F.C. 719 (1985). The judge ruled that the Auditor General has the right to information concerning expenses, but not to Cabinet documents.

43 See below, Chapter 4.

44 Canada, PS 2000, *Service to the Public: Task Force Report* (Ottawa, October 12, 1990) 81.

45 Bruce Rawson, "Public Service 2000 Service to the Public Task Force: findings and implications," *Canadian Public Administration* 34:3 (Autumn 1991): 500.

46 Canada, Royal Commission on Financial Management and Accountability (Lambert Commission), *Final Report* (Ottawa: Supply and Services, March 1979) 21. Hereafter cited as the *Lambert Report*.

47 Robert King Merton, "Bureaucratic Structure and Personality," *Social Forces* 17 (1940): 560-68; repr. *Reader in Bureaucracy*, ed. R.K. Merton *et al.* (New York: Free Press, 1952): 361-71.

48 J.E. Hodgetts, "Government Responsiveness to the Public Interest: Has Progress Been Made?" *Canadian Public Administration* 24:2 (1981): 229.

49 Canada, Privy Council Office, *A Strong Foundation: Report of the Task Force on Public Service Values and Ethics, A Summary* (Ottawa: Privy Council Office, February 1997) 3.

50 John Edwards, DREE seminar on the Canadian System of Government, Notes for Speech, Ottawa, 27 June 1979: 7.

51 Canada, Treasury Board Secretariat, *Master Agreement (PSAC): Agreement between the Treasury Board and the Public Service Alliance of Canada* (Ottawa: Supply and Services, 1989) Article M-32: 75; Article M-13: 15.

52 Canada, Treasury Board Secretariat, *Quality Services: An Overview*, Statement by Art Eggleton, President of the Treasury Board (Ottawa: Supply and Services, October 1995) 1, 3.

53 Canada, Treasury Board, *Quality Services: Service Standards*, Guide VII (Ottawa: Supply and Services, October 1995): 1. (emphasis added).

54 Canada, Revenue Canada, *Standards of Conduct* (Ottawa: Revenue Canada, January 1995).

55 Canada, *Standards of Professional Conduct* (Ottawa: Correctional Service, March 1993).

56 K. Kernaghan, "Promotion of Public Service Ethics: the Codification Option," *Ethics in Public Service*, ed. Richard A. Chapman (Ottawa: Carleton University Press, 1993) 15-30. One of the earliest Canadian texts on this topic was O.P. Dwivedi, "A Code of Conduct for Civil Servants," *Dalhousie Review* 4:1 (1964-65): 452-458. More recently, the Tait Task Force on Public Service Ethics also supported the idea of a general code; see, Privy Council Office, *Discussion Paper on Values and Ethics in the Public Service* (Ottawa: Privy Council Office, December 1996) 70-3.

57 O.P. Dwivedi, "On Holding Public Servants Accountable," *The Administrative State in Canada*, ed. O.P. Dwivedi (Toronto: University of Toronto Press, 1982) 163.

58 S.F. Frankel, *Staff Relations in the Civil Service: the Canadian Experience* (Montreal: McGill University Press, 1962) ch.2. J.E. Hodgetts notes the existence of an earlier association in the "outside service:, that of the Letter Carriers, chartered in 1891." *The Canadian Public Service* 322-40.

59 Hodgetts, *Canadian Public Service* 323-24.

60 Frankel ch.3.

61 Hodgetts, *The Canadian Public Service* 325.

62 O.P.Dwivedi, "Staff Relations in the Public Service of Canada," *Government Labour Relations in Transition*, ed. Keith Ocheltree (Chicago: Public Personnel Association, 1966) 21-27.

The Heeney report was the *Report of the Preparatory Committee on Collective Bargaining and Arbitration* (Ottawa: Queen's Printer, 1965). Mr. Heeney's reaction to the strike was given in "Some Aspects of Administrative Reform in the Public Service," *Canadian Public Administration* 9 (1966): 224.

63 The authors are grateful to Ivo Krupka for notes he provided on the functions of the Privy Council Office. Also, J.R. Mallory, *The Structure of Canadian Government*, rev. ed. (Toronto: Gage, 1984) 117-22; and Richard French, *How Ottawa Decides* (Toronto: James Lorimer and Company, 1980) 4-8.

64 Gordon Osbaldeston, *Keeping Deputy Ministers Accountable* (Toronto: McGraw-Hill Ryerson, 1989) 55.

65 Canada, *Public Service Reform Act*, 1992, section 40, sub-section 1.

66 Canada, *First Annual Report to the Prime Minister on Public Service of Canada* (Ottawa: Supply and Services, 30 June 1992) 1.

67 Canada, *Report of the Royal Commission on Administrative Classifications in the Public Service* (1946), quoted in J.E. Hodgetts and David C. Corbett, ed. *Canadian Public Administration* (Toronto: Macmillan, 1960) 255.

68 See, the A.D.P. Heeney Report, *Personnel Administration in the Public Service* (Ottawa: Queen's Printer, 1958); repr. Hodgetts and Corbett 265.

69 Aucoin 44.

FOUR

The Administrative State in Canada: The Westminster Model Under Stress

Over time, the relatively simple model of government that Canada inherited from Britain suffered pressure and distortion. The political and administrative values introduced with the administrative state were at odds with those of the prevailing political culture in several ways.

In this chapter, we begin with a definition of the administrative state, and the major steps in its introduction into Canadian politics are outlined. Following this, its main components are discussed in light of the strain they put on the Canadian version of the Westminster model of government: administrative discretion and accountability, deficits and cost control, politicization, collective bargaining and representative bureaucracy. Finally, we will see what these changes reveal about the Canadian administrative culture as actually practiced by the political system.

1 · The Advent of the Administrative State

The "Administrative State" refers at once to the growth of the state administration and to the extension of its powers. Specifically, it denotes,

> a system of governance through which public policies and programs affecting almost all aspects of public life, are influenced by the decisions of public officials. Consequently, the administrative process becomes an instrument in the formulation and implementation of a highly expanded public agenda.[1]

Looking at what has happened to the various institutions of political life in modern times, J.E. Hodgetts observed that the administration has changed far more than have parties, legislatures, interest groups, and courts:

in retrospect and in comparison, the public service more than any other institution has shown itself to be the barometer of societal pressures and the innovator of structural and procedural devices for meeting these changing demands.[2]

Aside from very few programmes of purely symbolic nature, the growth of the modern state is reflected in the growth of the administration, for each new programme is attributed to an administrative bureau or agency for its implementation. Not all programmes have the same impact on the administration, however. Some involve the production of goods or services directly by the administration: for example, providing defense services or, until recently, air traffic control in major airports. Others involve the transfer of funds to provinces, municipalities, universities, corporations, or people; but relatively few people are needed to transfer very large amounts of money. The same is true when the government contracts for a service, something it has been doing more frequently recently.

TABLE 4.1: **GROWTH OF FEDERAL PUBLIC SERVICE EMPLOYMENT, 1946-1995 (SELECTED YEARS)**

Year	No. of Civil/ Public Servants
1946	120 557
1951	124 580
1961	135 922
1971	216 488
1977*	282 788
1986	217 223
1991	218 618
1995	212 097

* 1977 was the peak year for federal public service employment

Source: Data from 1946 to 1971 are from J. E. Hodgetts and O. P. Dwivedi, *Provincial Governments as Employers* (Montréal and London: McGill-Queens University Press, 1974) 188. Data on remaining years are from annual reports of the Public Service Commission for respective years.

Finally, an item that takes up a considerable part of the expenditure budget (almost 30 per cent in 1996) is the debt service, the paying of interest and commissions on the consolidated debt of the Canadian state. Here again, the numbers of public servants involved are very small compared to the amounts involved.

The consequence is that only about 20 per cent of federal programmes are actually provided by the federal public service.[3] Tables 4.1, 4.2, 4.3, and 4.4 give an idea of the growth of the federal employment in terms of numbers (between 1946 and 1995), proportion to population and labour force (1951 to 1995), and the cost of their upkeep (wages/salaries) as a proportion of government current general expenditure (1981-1995). Table 4.1 illustrates the growth and decline of federal civil/public service employment since 1946; it should be remembered that the number of federal government

TABLE 4.2: **PROPORTION OF THE FEDERAL GOVERNMENT PUBLIC SERVICE EMPLOYMENT TO POPULATION AND LABOUR FORCE, 1951-1995 (SELECTED YEARS)**

Year	Employees	Population ('000)	Labour Force ('000)	Ratio of Employees per 1000 population	Ratio of Employees per 1000 labour force
1951	124 580	13 980	5 223	8.9	23.8
1961	135 922	18 201	6 521	7.5	20.9
1971	216 488	21 568	8 104	10.1	26.7
1977	282 788	23 258	9 648	12.2	29.3
1981	215 643	24 900	9 700	8.7	22.2
1991	218 618	28 120	10 574	7.8	20.7
1995	212 097	29 606	10 996	7.2	19.3

Source: For public service employment data, see table 4.1. For population and labour force (civilian employed above 15 years of age) see Canada Year Book of various years.

employees under the jurisdiction of the Public Service Commission constitute only a portion of the total government employment. In 1995, there were 497,516 people working for the federal government (including 96,600 in the armed forces, 17,941 RCMP, 142,499 in public enterprises, and 28,322 other employees). Thus, those belonging to the jurisdiction of the Public Service Commission constitute only 42.6 per cent of the total federal government employment universe.[4] Among the three levels of government, provincial government employment has registered a high growth rate while the federal government has shown a decline (see Table 4.4). In Table 4.2, we show how the federal government public service employment has registered growth and then declined when compared to its proportion to population and the labour force; for example, while there were 9 federal public servants for every 1000 Canadians in 1951, by 1977 their number rose to 12; in 1995, they were down to 7. A similar pattern can be seen in their proportion to the labour force. In Table 4.3, we have shown how the proportion of the federal government wage bill to the current general expenditure has declined from 18.4 per cent in 1981 to 9.4 per cent in 1995. This is another indication of government downsizing.

Let us make three observations: (1) the growth of federal government employment continued until 1977, when it reached its peak at 282,788 persons under the federal Public Service Commission jurisdiction, and its subsequent levelling off and decline; (2) greater growth in provincial government employment; (3) at the federal level, the share of wages in cur-

TABLE 4.3: **COST OF FEDERAL GOVERNMENT EMPLOYMENT: 1981, 1991, AND 1995**

Year	Federal Gov't Wages & Salaries (in millions $)	Current General Expenditure (in millions $)	Proportion of the Wage Bill to Current General Expenditure (%)
1981	13 154	71 387	18.4
1991	16 291	160 801	10.1
1995	16 185	172 399	9.4

Source: Statistics Canada: wages and salaries are from Public Sector Employment and Remuneration as well as from Public Sector Employment and Wages and Salaries, 1995, Cat. #72-209-XPB, Table 2.3 (Ottawa: Minister of Industry, 1996) 34. Data on government current expenditures are from Canadian Economic Observer (Historical Statistical Supplement), 1995/96, Cat. #11-210-XPB (Ottawa: Minister of Industry, 1997) 15, 17.

rent general expenditure started declining after 1981, and by 1995 it came to half of its level in 1981. (see Table 4.3)

These quantitative elements help to explain why there was a reaction against the growth of the state in the 1970s, details of which we will see in this and the following chapter. However, we are more concerned with the qualitative changes that occurred as the modern state intervened in more areas of Canadian life. The nature of these changes is summed up by Kenneth Kernaghan:

> The subject matter of many laws passed today is very technical (eg., atomic energy) and very complex (eg., tax reform). Moreover, the implications of major laws are widespread and their full consequences are unpredictable. As a result of this situation, our elected representatives are obliged to pass laws which are written in very general, and sometimes very vague language and to delegate to public servants the authority to interpret, implement and enforce these laws. Thus government employees — who are appointed, not elected — possess powers of both a legislative and a judicial nature.[5]

The challenge to the Westminster model, and especially the principles of responsible government, ministerial responsibility and the Rule of Law comes from this fact that the bureaucracy in Canada (as elsewhere) has encroached on domains previously reserved to cabinets, legislatures, and courts. As we will show in greater detail, governments were obliged to turn

TABLE 4.4: **GROWTH OF GOVERNMENT EMPLOYMENT,
ALL LEVELS (1981, 1986, 1991, 1995)**

Level of Government	1981	1986	1991	1995	Percentage Change
Federal	430 859	379 270	417 879	371 015	− 13.9
Provincial	477 921	494 576	1 054 645	1 004 721	110.2
Local	276 680	303 348	490 526	473 192	71.0
All	1 185 460	1 177 194	2 348 411	2 275 133	91.9

Source: For public service employment data, see table 4.1. For population and labour force (civilian employed above 15 years of age) see Canada Year Book of various years.

over much of their organization and functions to central agencies run by public servants. The growth of administrative regulations to complete the provisions of legislation was largely their work. That this activity was by nature legislative is recognized by two expressions for regulations widely used in Canada: "delegated legislation" and "quasi-legislative" powers or acts. Likewise, many services, boards, and tribunals render acts that in earlier times would have been left to the courts. These are the "quasi-judicial" powers.

Some of the acquired powers of the administrative state concern the running of the administration itself. As Brian Chapman observed many years ago, the modern administration may be compared to a profession, in that some members control the selection and advancement of the others and also disciplinary processes, whereas these functions all belonged to the government in earlier times.[6] On the other hand, some powers are those which would traditionally have belonged to one of the other functions of government. Gérard Bergeron has summed up these two movements: first, the introduction of rules and processes that make government more bureaucratic; and second, the assembly within the administration of extensive information necessary for governing, thus making it more technocratic.[7]

Max Weber's theory of bureaucracy contained two elements: first, that bureaucracy as a way of organizing was technically superior to "all collegiate, honorific, and avocational forms of administration." Second,

> The more complicated and specialized modern culture becomes, the more its external supporting apparatus demands the personally detached and strictly 'objective' *expert* in lieu of the master of older

social structures who was moved by personal sympathy and favor, by grace and gratitude.[8]

Insofar as the Westminster model approximated the Weberian model of the bureaucracy, the challenge presented by the rise of the administrative state is precisely that of accommodating political arrangements worked out for the most part in the nineteenth century to this new complex and technically sophisticated administration.

2 · The Administrative State in Canada

If one wished to chart the introduction of the administrative state in Canada, it would be impossible to pick a single decisive moment. However, there are several key events that contributed to its formation.

1857: The Civil Service Act formally recognizes the existence of the deputy minister, thus codifying the practice developed after the introduction of responsible government in the 1840s of having a single elected head of each department, aided by a permanent, non-elected official.[9]

1908/1918: The creation of the Civil Service Commission, to recruit and appoint by open competitive examinations candidates to the Inside Service (those at Ottawa, 1908) and to the Outside Service (1918).[10]

1931: The creation of the post of Comptroller General in the Consolidated Revenue and Audit Act, to see that no money would be paid by departments and agencies unless there was a parliamentary vote authorizing the expenditure and sufficient funds to cover it and any other known requirements in the current year.[11]

1938-1945: The organization of the Privy Council Office under A.D.P. Heeney who, after being appointed Principal Secretary in the Prime Minister's Office in 1938, became the first holder of a new position created in 1940, combining the existing post of Clerk of the Privy Council with the new one of Secretary to the Cabinet. The secretary and his personnel staffed not only meetings of Cabinet, but also those of Cabinet Committees, the most important being the War Committee.[12]

1951: The Financial Administration Act for the first time delegates to the Treasury Board final decision-making authority on matters concerning the execution of financial policy decisions, including the power to approve contracts. Although the Treasury Board had been gradually assuming new tasks since its creation in 1869, this was the first time that it had received full delegated powers from the larger Cabinet to which it had previously made recommendations. It continued to serve as adviser in expenditure policy matters, including the preparation of the Estimates.[13]

1967: The introduction of collective bargaining in the public service has three impacts which promoted the Administrative State.[14] First, the government from this period on would have to negotiate salaries and other conditions of work, which previously it had been able to determine on its own. Second, the government needed to designate the authority that spoke for it in negotiations concerning wages, working conditions, and related matters. The decision to attribute this role to the Treasury Board increased its powers and responsibilities, most notably at the expense of the Public Service Commission that, as the Civil Service Commission, had previously been responsible for such policy matters as advice on salary levels and position classification. Finally, the creation of the Public Service Staff Relations Board meant that the government had now to submit to an administrative body in disputes over employee status, salary arbitration (if the employees' union chose this path of negotiation), and arbitration of grievances.

1968-79: The reorganization of Cabinet with standing committees under Pierre Trudeau leads to significant growth of the Privy Council Office (PCO). A three-tiered system of planning is developed, centred in turn on the PCO, the Treasury Board, and the Department of Finance.[15]

1969: The introduction of programme budgets under the Planning, Programming and Budgeting System (PPBS) represents an attempt to make the planning of government expenditures more rational by directing attention to their objectives and the costs associated with meeting them.[16]

1969: The Official Languages Act creates the obligation for the administration to serve the public in two official languages, at headquarters and where numbers warranted it elsewhere, and to promote linguistic equity within the public service. By creating also the post of Official Languages Commissioner, the act also established the first position that resembled that of an Ombudsman, albeit for this matter only.

1974: Adoption of the first programme designed to promote the equal representation of women in the public service. Purely voluntary, it was followed in the 1980s by more binding measures. By the late 1980s, representation of cultural minorities became the object of positive action programmes.

1977: Introduction of comprehensive auditing with the Auditor General Act. A new mandate is given to the Auditor General to verify the three E's: economy, efficiency, and effectiveness. Henceforth the Auditor General is to scrutinize not only whether each department or agency that he investigates buys cheap and keeps its production costs low, but also whether it has put in place appropriate evaluation systems to determine that it is effective in meeting its objectives.[17]

1977: Creation anew of the Office of Comptroller General. The previous post had been eliminated in 1969 as part of the decentralization movement started by the report of the Glassco Royal Commission on Government Organization. The new office did not re-establish centralized control over commitments and spending, however. The new Comptroller was to advise the government and its departments on systems of financial reports and something new, internal audit and programme evaluation.[18]

1982: The Access to Information Act adopts, with many exceptions, the principle that bureaucratic information should be available to the public, and creates another ombudsman-type position, that of Access Commissioner, to act as an administrative tribunal in contentious cases.[19]

Thus we see that whether it was to better run the machinery of state, or to better supervise and control it, there has been since before Confederation a trend of transferring new functions and powers to the federal administration. Indeed, many of the innovations were adopted in response to previous extensions of the administrative state. We now turn to three areas requiring more detailed scrutiny: administrative discretion and accountability, financial rationality and economy, and increasing politicization.

3 · Administrative Discretion, the Rule of Law, and Administrative Accountability

The problem of increasing discretionary powers in the hands of ministers and public servants was posed long before such problems as administrative rationality, value for money, and good management were prominent. The initial steps towards the welfare state involved regulation of economic and social activity that, while not as demanding of financial and human resources as the social programme would be, transferred powers to ministers and to the administration that challenged the traditional powers of both parliament and the judiciary.

These concerns are evident in the mandate and report of one of the earliest studies on this question, that of the British Committee on Ministers' Powers (the Donoughmore Committee) of 1932. The two types of power studied by the committee were delegated legislation and judicial or quasi-judicial decisions. While noting that the British constitution had never embraced a complete separation of powers, the committee added that like it or not the practice of delegating both legislative and judicial powers to ministers, local authorities, and other agencies was inevitable. Nevertheless, it held that both the sovereignty of parliament and the rule of law were altered by these new practices, since the latter required that the law would be administered by the ordinary courts. The committee's recommendations were concerned with ensuring that when the administration or the political executive exercised such powers, they should do so in ways that offered legislators and citizens as many safeguards as possible.[20]

In Canada, a study by the Law Reform Commission in 1975 allows a precise measurement of discretionary powers in the Revised Statutes of Canada in 1970. It found almost 15,000 discretionary powers in these laws, which it divided into four groups: administrative (2933), inquiry (1298), judicial (5938), and regulatory (3467).[21] These regulatory powers represent delegated legislative powers, but so do some of the administrative powers that have a widespread impact but are not strictly speaking regulations. Patrice Garant has noted that the regulations of the federal government which were codified in one revised version in 1978 were 1624 in number and covered 14,420 pages.[22]

The concerns over these powers were of three kinds. The first were voiced by jurists about the eclipse of the courts by administrative activity. The second took the form of measures by members of parliament to keep watch over the exercise of delegated legislative powers. Finally, and most recently, legislators and others have shown determination to make public servants directly accountable to parliament.

Our interest here is with the problems caused by the increased powers given to administrators with the growth of regulations. At the same time, there were increasing objections — particularly from businessmen and economists — based on the perception that excessive regulation was harming both enterprises and markets.[23]

JUDICIAL CONTROL OF ADMINISTRATIVE DISCRETION

Prior to 1960, practically the only question which preoccupied Canadian specialists of administrative law was judicial review of administrative action.[24] Most felt, as did J.A. Corry, that "(t)he great threat to the Rule of Law is wide-reaching discretionary power."[25] As John Willis pointed out, Canada had never been a true *laissez-faire* state, so the controversy about the rule of law was not as vivid here as it was in Britain or the United States. It was the appearance of regulatory commissions and other regulatory powers characteristic of state interventions in the early part of this century that generated concern here, since they combined legislative, administrative and judicial powers.[26] Moreover, in the case of autonomous bodies, political control by ministers and members of parliament was reduced by their independence.[27]

Curiously, the problem arose because legislatures went along with governments in their desire to remove the agencies from judicial surveillance. Under the Constitution Act of 1867 (BNA Act), parliament could "render any agency immune from judicial review" so long as it did not contravene the division of constitutional powers between the federal government and the province.[28] In order to prevent a flood of cases emanating from new regulatory agencies, many laws tried to render their findings final. The device used for this purpose was the privative clause.[29] For example, the *Public Service Staff Relations Act 1966-1967* (RSC.P-35) provides in article 100 that there shall be no review or appeal from decisions of arbitrators, nor shall any of the common law writs (such as injunction, prohibition, certiorari) be admitted against them.

The reason for this wording was that the courts had always found ways to review the actions of agencies.[30] As Willis noted, the ordinary courts reserved to themselves the right to determine whether an agency had exceeded its powers. By and large, the courts accepted limits set on rights to appeal the facts of a case settled by an administrative commission or tribunal, but they maintained the right to verify that such a body had stayed within the limits of its mandate and its powers, that it had not made an error of law, nor acted in bad faith. Since discretionary powers were deemed to be beyond the reach of the courts, the latter were particularly sensitive to any procedural safeguards contained in the law. A whole jurisprudence arose based on distinctions of different kinds of acts: regulations and administrative acts were not likely to be annulled if they were carried out within the scope of the law. On the other hand, acts of a quasi-judicial nature were closely scrutinized. The two defining characteristics of a quasi-judicial power were the determination of citizens' rights and duties and a requirement to act in a judicial manner. Not only were procedural safeguards strictly enforced, but if the law was silent, the courts enforced the rules of "Natural Justice," such as a person's right to know an accusation against him or her, and the right to be heard on one's own behalf.[31]

This was the reaction of one of the policy community groups whose task it was to supervise the exercise of discretionary powers by ministers and the administration. Such a situation engendered much work for the courts, particularly the Supreme Court, which heard many appeals both from federal administrative tribunals and from the Exchequer Court (the court in which actions could be brought against the federal government). At the initiative of the Department of Justice in 1971, parliament created the Federal Court in order to "relieve the Supreme Court of Canada of the burden of hearing routine appeals from the Exchequer Court and certain federal administrative tribunals and secondly, to strengthen judicial review of federal administration."[32]

This important adjustment to the growth of administrative powers pales in comparison to the coming into force of the Charter of Rights and Freedoms in 1982. From that point on in Canada, there were individual freedoms that were above ordinary laws and all acts of the administration.[33] Overnight, the respect of the Charter became a constraint upon public administrators' actions.[34] For instance, the Charter was invoked to successfully challenge article 32.A of the Public Service Act of 1967, which previously had forbidden activity of a partisan nature during a federal or provincial election. While the courts had refused to recognize attempts to exclude them from overseeing the exercise of numerous discretionary powers, government initiatives in creating the Federal Court and the Charter of Rights and Freedoms were much more radical moves in defining the normative limits of bureaucratic action and in determining what agency would ensure their respect.

LEGISLATIVE SURVEILLANCE OF ADMINISTRATIVE DISCRETION

When a parliamentary committee looked into the question of regulations in 1968-69, it referred to the Donoughmore Committee report of 1932, but also to the new movement spearheaded in Canada by Donald Rowat and aimed at reducing government secrecy.[35] The McGuigan report noted that the only existing requirement in law about the regulatory process was the obligation to publish, established by the Regulations Act (1950). As a result of the report, a new law, the *Statutory Instruments Act*, was adopted, providing among other things for a joint committee of the House of Commons and the Senate to supervise the exercise of delegated powers of regulation. The committee has done useful work in examining and discussing government regulations, but the government has not necessarily acted on its reports.[36] For this reason, presumably, the McGrath committee of 1985 recommended that the House of Commons adopt a mandatory procedure for affirming or disallowing regulations made in execution of legislation.[37] This procedure has never been adopted.

Parliamentary scrutiny of delegated legislation is not limited to the Joint Standing Committee. Since the 1960s the House of Commons has specialized its work through the creation of standing committees responsible for functional areas such as defense and foreign affairs, health and welfare, and citizenship and immigration. The McGrath Committee reminded members that these committees have used their mandates to look into the content of regulations that fall into their jurisdiction.[38]

POLITICAL ACCOUNTABILITY

While the supervision of delegated legislation is important in terms of the traditional notion of the rule of law, the question of holding public servants accountable for their exercise of discretionary powers is much broader. The reform of the public service had removed from members of the House of Commons such influence as they traditionally had had in the control of public spending, appointments, and public works.[39]

The problem went much deeper than this, however. The growth of the administrative state and its powers and responsibilities meant that politicians, both ministers and members of parliament, saw their influence declining. According to Maurice Lamontagne (academic turned minister in the Pearson government), the "twilight of the ministers" had begun as early as the end of World War I and had reached its height in the wake of the Glassco report on government organization.[40] Lamontagne predicted that the twilight of the civil service was beginning, that in turn it would see its influence over policy challenged by political parties, parliament, and the information media. Whether or not this influence was to decline in the future (and today it appears that Lamontagne was right), it was clear in the 1960s and early 1970s that the public service had grown in power at the expense of elected politicians.

The response to this trend occurred at several levels. Ministers of the Liberal governments of the 1970s began reinterpreting the doctrine of ministerial responsibility by publicly blaming public servants or by criticizing their work. Moreover, an increasing number of journalists and academics as well as politicians had come to believe that the doctrine was obsolete.[41]

It was in this context that the Auditor General James J. Macdonnell reported in 1976 that elected politicians were on the point of losing control over public expenditures, if they had not already done so.[42] The Lambert

Commission, which was created as a direct result of this stand by the Auditor General, wrote on this subject:

> While we have no wish to dispute the principle of ministerial responsibility, there can be little doubt that today the degree to which a minister really has the effective management and direction of his department is open to question.... The twin assumptions that the Parliament had clout as well as information to exact a relevant accounting, and that the departments can be managed and directed by ministers, do not hold as they once did.[43]

Similar views had been voiced by a committee of senior officials reporting on the concept of the ombudsman, and would be endorsed by the McGrath Report on reform of the House of Commons.[44]

The result was an attempt to make senior public servants directly accountable to parliament. The Lambert Report in particular drew up a list of subjects on which it thought that deputy-ministers should be held to account before the appropriate parliamentary committee: these include financial and personnel administration and the responsibilities imparted by the Official Languages Act. The McGrath report proposed to extend these accountability issues to virtually all policy implementation.[45]

Since 1982, as a result, the rules of the House of Commons have been changed to allow for more interrogation of senior officials by members in committees. The operation has created a strain on the system, however, for it is far from clear where the lines of responsibility lie. Attempts have been made to sharply delineate accountability. The Privy Council Office stated,

> Public servants should (and do) of course appear before House of Commons on behalf of their Ministers to answer questions or to provide other sorts of information that Ministers could not be expected to provide personally. Public servants are not, however, directly accountable to the House of Commons for their actions nor for the policies and programs of the Government.[46]

The deputy ministers interviewed by former Clerk of the Privy Council Gordon Osbaldeston were of the same opinion. They felt that "Deputy Ministers are accountable only to those individuals and groups with whom they have a direct authority relationship based on legislation or convention."[47]

The trouble is that the members of parliament do not have the same understanding of this accountability relationship. Sharon Sutherland and C.E.S. Franks have documented cases in which members have attacked

TABLE 4.5: **GROWTH AND IMPORTANCE OF THE CANADIAN DEFICIT (AS % OF GROSS DOMESTIC PRODUCT)**

Years*	1951	1961	1971	1981	1991	1998
Revenues	16.5	16.0	16.6	15.5	17.6	17.7
Programme expenditures	12.8	15.5	15.6	16.7	16.0	12.6
Debt service	2.2	2.0	2.1	3.4	6.3	4.7
Total expenditures	15.0	17.5	17.7	20.1	22.3	17.3
Budget surplus/ deficit (-)	1.5	-1.5	-1.1	-4.6	-4.7	0.4
Consolidated net debt	56.2	35.1	22.5	29.2	57.6	71.2

* (ending 31 March)

Source: Ministère des Finances, Tableaux de référence financiers, octobre 1996 (Ottawa: Ministère des finances, nov. 1998) Table 2.

deputies personally, without regard for the convention.[48] The culmination of this conflict would seem to be the parliamentary hearings on the Al-Mashat affair, where it was revealed that senior public servants were accorded none of the traditional procedural rights of natural justice, but instead were accused and judged without any protection from the government and without any lifting of their obligations to that government.[49] It seems to have been overlooked that parliamentary committees, like parliament itself, are partisan forums, not given to detached, judicial analysis, nor is that their role.

THE PROBLEMS OF DEFICITS AND COST CONTROL

While the pressures placed on the system by discretionary powers provoked a search for solutions, particularly in the case of the courts, the problems associated with the growth of the public service and public expenditures in purely quantitative terms have occupied the forefront of the administrative stage since the mid-1970s. At that time, Canada entered into an era of deficits that contributed to the rapid rise of public debt.

Earlier in the chapter, we presented a glimpse of the growth of government employment in Tables 4.1, 4.2, 4.3, and 4.4. In Table 4.5, we present summary figures showing various facets of Canadian public finances as compared with the gross domestic product. Such comparisons permit us to appreciate the weight of these activities in Canadian economic life. They show that in spite of a heavy net debt as a result of wartime borrowing, federal revenues exceeded expenditures in 1950-51. The share of GDP that went to federal expenditures increased rapidly in the next three decades. Programme expenditures have declined since 1980 to the levels of the 1950s, but the cumulative effects of deficits put the total spending bill (programmes plus debt service) much higher. In 1998, the Liberal government achieved the first surplus in thirty years. As a result, consolidated net debt has begun to decline in relative terms: it passed the 1950-51 level in 1990-91, but at 66.9 per cent of GDP in 1997-8, it remains well below the high levels of World War II, which left the federal government with a net debt of 103.5 per cent of the GDP in 1946-47.

The reaction to growing expenditures in the late 1970s occurred for three reasons. As we have already seen, the Auditor General drew considerable attention to his view that federal expenditures in the mid-1970s were out of control. Moreover, in 1978, Prime Minister Trudeau returned from a meeting in Bonn of heads of member governments of the Organization for Economic Cooperation and Development convinced of the need to reduce or at least cut the rate of growth of public expenditures. At the same time, the federal government began to experience a series of substantial budgetary deficits that continued for two decades. The net public debt went from 20.5 per cent of the Gross Domestic Product in 1970-71 to 74.0 per cent in 1995-96.[50]

That much of the shortfall was due to flagging revenues, and that these were at least partly due to increasing use of tax concessions and other "fiscal expenditures" to stimulate the economy, has made little difference to the attitudes of political leaders in Canada.[51] Since Pierre Trudeau's attendance at the Bonn summit in 1978, the dominant discourse of Canadian political leaders on budgetary questions has been one of cost control.[52]

We have seen that the desire to control public expenditure was behind the creation of the post of Comptroller General in 1931. The autonomy granted to the Treasury Board under the Financial Administration Act of 1951 was another step in this direction. With its new responsibilities for collective bargaining and administration, the Treasury Board became a department of government (1967). Moreover, at this time it was working on the famous Planning, Programming and Budgeting System (PPBS) which was introduced in 1970. While we discuss this question further in the following chapter, let us recall here that the system was designed to give decision-makers and members of parliament a view of proposed expenditures which would inform them about the purposes of these expenses rather than which service or agency was spending how much on what kinds of things. The system was supposed to include evaluation of the results achieved in terms of the objectives set out, but when the Auditor General made his campaign in the mid 1970s, it was clear that the evaluation function had not been developed with anything like the energy and determination which had been put into developing new programmes.

Thus it was that the Liberal government in 1977 created anew the post of Comptroller General, with special responsibility for programme evaluation. Then, in 1979, the government of Joe Clark introduced the Policy and Expenditure Management System (PEMS), which aimed at grafting on to the PPBS system — which was considered to be based on initiatives rising from the bottom of the administration — a top-down approach aimed at restoring government control. The idea was to set the overall limits of government spending and to allocate to the specialized committees of the cabinet envelopes within which they were to make their policy choices.[53] Although it was considered by two American experts to be the one innovation of note in public financial management in the 1980s,[54] the system was abandoned by Prime Minister Brian Mulroney in 1989 precisely because it was not succeeding in its main task of controlling spending.[55] After its election in 1993, the Liberal Government of Jean Chrétien attacked the problem with its Program Review, in which every government programme was evaluated to see if its purpose was still valid, if another government or social actor should be doing it, and whether there were better ways to deliver the product or service.[56]

Since 1978, the governments of Canada have used a variety of techniques to reduce public spending.[57] They have been successful in keeping programme expenditures from running deficits, but until recently this has been overridden by the costs of the public debt charges, transfers to the provinces, and unemployment insurance. There is much to be learned about the culture of the administration of Canada from an examination of the history of public expenditure management and control. We return to this question in the concluding portion of this chapter.

4 · The Politicization of the Administration, From Above, From Below, and From Without

While the classic version of the Westminster model that evolved in Canada was based on the political neutrality of public servants, much has happened over the years to politicize it. We look in turn at how the Canadian administration has been politicized from above, from below, and from the outside.

POLITICIZATION FROM ABOVE

The prime minister has always had a free hand in appointing deputy ministers, heads and members of boards and commissions, ambassadors, and other senior officials.[58] It is an important part of the Canadian tradition that most of these appointments are made from among the senior ranks of the public service.[59] By the early 1970s a practical division of labour in the services available to the prime minister was in place. The Privy Council Office, headed by the Clerk, was non-partisan, operations-oriented, and politically sensitive, whereas the Prime Minister's Office, headed by a Principal Secretary, was partisan, policy-oriented, and sensitive to operational considerations.[60] Prime Minister Trudeau appeared to many to have broken this equilibrium when he chose Michael Pitfield to be Clerk of the Privy Council and Secretary to the Cabinet in 1975. Pitfield was a career federal servant and had experience in the Privy Council Office. His appointment was controversial, however, because, at 37 years of age, he was relatively young for the job, and he was considered by many in Ottawa to have received the appointment because he was a close friend of the prime minister.[61] Joe Clark continued the trend by appointing Marcel Massé as Pitfield's successor. Massé had also been working in the Privy Council Office prior to his appointment, but he had acquired his reputation while working as secretary to the cabinet under premier Richard Hatfield of Nova Scotia, and was "hand picked" by Mr. Clark.[62] The previous custom has been restored in recent years, however. In 1986, Brian Mulroney accepted the advice of outgoing Clerk Gordon Osbaldeston and appointed Paul Tellier in spite of the reservations of many Conservatives about this long-time mandarin.[63] Prime Minister Chrétien also kept custom by appointing Jocelyne Bourgon to this post.

Prime Minister Mulroney chose to politicize the top echelon of each department by creating the position of Chief of Staff to replace that of "executive assistant." While the new title might appear to be symbolic, it clearly indicated the desire of the Progressive Conservative government to reinforce the political dimension of the minister's private staff, by creating a sort of political deputy minister.[64] Created in an atmosphere of suspicion of the public service, these posts allowed for the appointment of relatively young chiefs of staff, averaging 35 years of age, aiming at a better control of the administration. By the early 1990s a *modus vivendi* had been attained with the top levels of the administration, but the Liberal government of Jean Chrétien abolished the position after its election in 1993.

These were relatively minor matters compared to the change that was observed by Campbell and Szablowski in 1979. After studying the elite group of public servants in the central agencies at Ottawa (the Privy

Council Office, the Treasury Board, the Department of Finance, the Federal-Provincial Relations Office), they concluded that these officials were in many cases political bureaucrats, not because of the way they were appointed or because of their past history, but because of their work. They were so closely associated with their political masters, even to the extent of sitting in for them at meetings of the numerous cabinet committees, that there was a symbiosis of mentalities: "Senior officials long ago have evolved from faithful servants of the Crown to full-fledged political administrators who participate collegially in executive functions."[65] It had long been known that public servants did more than merely execute the will of the government. Writing a decade before Campbell and Szablowski, senior mandarin Gordon Robertson stated, "Any civil servant above clerical or stenographic grades who has spent any substantial time in a job without contributing to some degree to the policy he administers should be fired."[66] What was new was the extent of the administrative support apparatus and the degree to which ministers depended upon the officials of central agencies.

Officials in policy-making and implementation positions had long been exposed to another form of politicization, that of interest groups. Around each department and often around major programmes arise "policy communities," groups of interested organizations which are recognized by the administration as legitimate and even necessary interlocutors.[67] The result has been a style of administration that has been called "elite accommodation," meaning that public servants prefer to propose policies and apply them in ways that are acceptable to their powerful clients.

This is evidently a delicate situation for a senior bureaucrat. As Osbaldeston and Bourgault and Dion have shown, ministers do not as a general rule like their deputy ministers to take the limelight.[68] Nor do they want government policy to be subverted by intimacy between public servants and interest groups. It is therefore the duty of public servants to be close to their organized clients, but not too close. The situation is further complicated by the possibility of collusion between a government official thinking of retiring or leaving the public service and an enterprise doing business with him or her. While Canada has not known either the phenomenon of the "pantouflage" of career French civil servants, nor that of Washington, where this practice is common, it has been prevalent enough to give rise to regulations adopted by the Treasury Board in 1985 forbidding public servants from taking employment with any firm with which they have done business until at least one year has passed after their leaving the public service.[69]

Just as public servants give policy advice to governments, they also do political work, whether by their proximity to ministers if they work in central agencies, as deputy ministers, on loan to a minister's private office staff, or by their contact with client groups. Indeed, systems analysts have pointed out that public servants sift out from among the many demands on departments those deserving of attention and identify the legitimate spokespersons for these groups.[70]

POLITICIZATION FROM BELOW: COLLECTIVE BARGAINING

When the government introduced legislation in 1966-67 after intense bargaining with the public sector unions, it proposed a curious dualistic system. Each union would have to decide, before entering into a round of negotiations, whether it wanted to have any impasse in negotiations solved by arbitration by the new Public Service Staff Relations Board, or whether it preferred to retain its right to strike. As was anticipated, at the beginning of the new regime, the great majority of associations chose the arbitration route. In 1970, 100 of the associations recognized in 114 bargaining units chose arbitration, and they represented 80 per cent of the 198,000 eligible employees. By 1976, however, the proportions had almost been reversed, with 37 units representing 70 per cent of all eligible employees choosing conciliation with the right to strike. In 1991, the percentage was even greater: 90 per cent of employees and 54 per cent of units were in the conciliation column.[71]

While their experience of the early 1970s made the unions more radical, governments have suspended the rules governing the system three times since 1967. From 1975 to 1978 agreements fell under the supervision of the Anti-Inflation Board. Then, in 1982-83, the government used legislation to extend existing collective agreements and impose limits on wage increases of 6 per cent in 1982 and 5 per cent in 1983.[72] Finally, in the critical years of increasing financial problems and the recession of the early 1990s, the government again suspended the right to collective bargaining and imposed virtual wage freezes for three periods of two years each from 1991 to 1997.

Public sector unionism and collective bargaining have politicized the public service in at least two ways. First, and most obvious, through collective bargaining and strike action, it has embroiled itself and governments in confrontations which drew much public attention. As a general rule, the public has not been sympathetic to public sector strikes.[73] Less spectacular but nonetheless important was the effect of giving employees representatives who could speak out on a number of issues without being accused of breaching their duties of obedience and discretion. For example, in July 1987, the Professional Association of Foreign Service Officers criticized what it called the abusive recourse by the government to political nominations, making the diplomatic corps "the personal senate of Brian Mulroney."[74] In 1992, Daryl Bean, President of the PSAC said that civil servants who were being increasingly the objects of abuse and violence on the part of the public were in fact paying for frustration caused by government policies. In 1994, the Alliance called for whistleblower legislation, which would allow public servants to denounce cases of waste and fraud. Similarly, while the Professional Institute of the Public Service of Canada welcomed the change of government in 1993, a few months later they announced that a poll showed the morale of their members to be low, and that they felt that their views had no effect when they were consulted.[75] Public sector unions frequently take positions on behalf of their members before parliamentary committees.

POLITICIZATION FROM WITHOUT: REPRESENTATIVE BUREAUCRACY

From the outset, the Canadian administration has had close relations with certain client groups. For the first fifty years of its existence, recruitment, the letting of contracts, and other routine matters of administration were profoundly affected by political patronage.[76] Then, under the combined effects of political reform and scientific management, the administration was supposed to be impersonal and neutral. More recently, pressures have been exerted to make it more representative of the Canadian public.

In the 1960s, under the stimulus of the wave of *Créditiste* members elected from Quebec in 1962, and then with the rise of the separatist movement in Québec, came the demand for more French-speaking Canadians in the public service. In spite of the view of the majority of the Royal Commission on Government Organization that the subject was outside its mandate, commissioner Eugène Therrien issued a minority report calling for recognition of the bilingual character of the public service. For most of the 1960s, the Royal Commission on Bilingualism and Biculturalism was in operation. Its studies revealed that French Canadians had lost ground in the public service since the introduction of the competitive examination system. Following a preliminary report from the Commission, Prime Minister Pearson made a policy statement on 6 April 1966, calling for fair and equitable representation of French Canadians in the federal service.[77]

The final report of the Commission in 1969 was followed shortly by the passage of the Official Languages Act, which adhered closely to the recommendations of the Commission.[78] It was based on two principles: first, that the national administration at Ottawa was to be able to function in both official languages, while in the regions, language of service would depend on the composition of the local population; second, positions would be designated as requiring either English, French, or both. Those appointed to these positions would either have to possess the requisite language skills or acquire them. Although it has not been without controversy, this policy has been notably successful. Whereas the number of French-speaking Canadians in the public service was 21.5 per cent in 1965, by 1997, it was 29.2 per cent. Moreover, in senior positions, which had been at the origin of the controversy from the beginning, their presence rose from 11.5 per cent in 1967 to 25.4 per cent thirty years later.[79] As noted above, the post of Official Language Commissioner was created, thus giving the task of watching over and reporting on the progress achieved in the application of the law to an independent actor.

Contemporary with the launching of the Official Languages Act were the first stirrings of the movement calling for equal opportunity for women. In their history of the Civil Service Commission of Canada, Hodgetts and colleagues observe:

> Until very recently, the Government in general, and the Civil Service Commission in particular, never considered women as employees to be treated on an equal basis with men. Unlike more subtle forms of covert discrimination against French-speaking civil servants, there was never any particular attempt made to hide the discrimination against women which was, and is, built into the very fabric of civil service legislation and personnel practice.[80]

The Bird Commission on the Status of Women reported in 1970. As a result, two initiatives were taken which are of interest to this study. First, the government announced a policy of favouring greater access to employment for women, particularly in the scientific, professional, and executive categories. The second change was the creation of the Advisory Council on the Status of Women. The Council had a much broader mandate than the Office of the Official Languages Commissioner, since it followed all aspects of public policy of interest to women, but, like it, it brought into the administration representation of outside interests. These policies were not compulsory to begin with, but provided guidelines for departments and agencies.

Over time, the federal government has used a variety of programmes to promote equal opportunity, of which certain have been more obligatory for personnel managers. In terms of the presence of women in the public service, progress has been slow, notably at the higher levels. It has nonetheless been steady over the twenty years since the first steps, with the overall presence of women passing from 27.3 per cent in 1967 to 50.0 per cent in 1997, while that at senior levels went from 1.0 per cent in 1971 to 23.0 per cent in 1997.[81]

While other programmes have been created for Native peoples and visible minorities, only the language question and representation for women have had major impacts on the federal service. They changed the composition of the federal service, as we have just seen. They also brought new values and obligations to the attention of managers and they changed the culture of the federal service in ways that are difficult to measure.[82]

5 · The Canadian Administrative Culture as Revealed by the Growth of and the Response to the Administrative State

We have seen how the political and judicial system responded to the growth of the administrative state in Canada. The courts, never willing to surrender their control over administrative action, received new powers with the Charter of Rights and Freedoms. While streamlining itself to better handle more business, parliament took steps to supervise the use of delegated powers of regulation and widened the practice of having senior public servants testify before its committees. Government gave itself central agencies and policies and practices to better coordinate and control what was happening in them.

All of this tells what other actors did. It informs us about the values that they sought to impose upon the administration. It tells us little, however, about the values as held by the various components of the public service. It is to these that we now turn.

ELITE VALUES

Prior to the mid-1950s, the Ottawa elite were few enough in number that most of them knew each other.[83] They were conscious of belonging to an elite, even while they were vulnerable, being personally known to the minister, or even to the prime minister. Highly educated, they had for the most part made government their career, and their relatively small number meant that they acquired a wide variety of experience.

A.W. Johnson has described the curious mix of attitudes and aptitudes that deputy ministers must display. They must be at times active, at times passive. They must be practical, yet have some qualities of the academic; frank, yet willing to carry out policies that they would not choose; take the long view, yet live with limited responsibilities. Above all, "in government, the choices do not involve a single value system — more or less profit; they involve hierarchies of social values, all of which are subjective."[84]

Extensive interviews by Osbaldeston and by Bourgault and Dion have shown that this portrait of the deputy minister is still valid some thirty years later.[85] We will return in the next chapter to the elements that have changed as a result of recent management practices.

Extending our vision to include other top managers in central agencies and departments, we may note two important doctrines that seem to be widely accepted and practised. The first is what Aberbach, Putnam and Rockman called the "energy-equilibrium model" of relations between civil servants and politicians.[86] This model recognizes that bureaucrats have political dealings with client groups, but accepts that the major impetus for change comes from elected governments, whereas senior officials provide the necessary stability and knowledge of the system to allow these changes to be introduced in a manageable way. In matters of administrative management, this model reserves the lion's share of responsibility to senior public servants.[87]

The second doctrine, complementary to the first, has already been referred to: it is the idea of elite accommodation. Our administrative elites have not had an exalted idea of their role of guardians of the public interest, which was to be upheld in the face of the self-interested behaviour of politicians and of interest groups. Instead, they have believed that the best way to run their departments and their program was to work by consensus with those groups or institutions that were under their jurisdiction.[88]

The result of these two traits is that senior officials in Canada (as elsewhere) have a strong attraction to moderation, even to the status quo. In the realm of ideas, they turn up in the centre of ideological scales showing a left-right range of opinions. The history of the Department of External Affairs shows that once the department hit turbulent times of changes of government and rapid expansion, it was almost always found counselling caution to ministers or the prime minister.[89]

A further trait emerges from what we know about senior civil servants. This is their attachment to the department or agency in which they work. This comes out most clearly in budgetary matters. While public servants do not fit the model of the "budget-maximizing bureaucrat" proposed by William Niskanen, they do generally favour higher budgets for their departments.[90] And it is very difficult to get them to suggest cuts. Donald Savoie, who has charted the attitudes and tactics of departmental officials, calls the principal tactic the "musical ride" approach, since when forced to propose spending cuts, officials will try to propose the elimination of a popular program that the government will not want to cut.[91]

The belief in the special nature of their department and its problems has led departmental officials to successfully challenge two policies that might have made them more vulnerable to central control. First, when programme budgets were introduced, instead of adopting a government-wide definition of a programme, the Treasury Board accepted that it was necessary to allow each department to define what the word meant in its context. The result was that the Department of External Affairs, for example, had a single programme for "Representation of Canada's interests abroad," which for many years accounted for about 90 per cent of its expenditures. Now that the Canadian International Aid Agency has merged with the Department of Foreign Affairs and International Trade, there are two programmes that make up 90 per cent of the department's expenditure. Such a broad brush was not what the inventors of PPBS had in mind. Likewise, departments won the right to define their own needs in program evaluation, which has greatly reduced the rigor of the policy introduced in 1977.[92]

The existence of departmental subcultures has as its counterpart the subcultures of the central agencies. These are the elite of the public service: the officers of the Privy Council Office, the Treasury Board, the Department of Finance, the Public Service Commission, and the Department of Foreign Affairs and Trade. They are the "high flyers" who not only have been recognized as people of exceptional talent, they have also entered into a privileged circuit where appointments from one agency to another are common. Their work is intellectual. They do not deliver programmes to citizens or to other institutions, but rather plan, coordinate, evaluate, and control their colleagues. As a result, while they are conscious of belonging to an elite, they are sometimes resented by their colleagues. As is the case all over the world, those with "line" or operational responsibilities frequently view the requirements of central agencies as intrusions on the already difficult work of delivering goods and services to their various groups.[93]

If this seems to be a portrait of a group of self-interested manipulators, the impression is wrong. There are many indications that the elite of the Canadian public service have been and are committed to the idea of public service and to promoting the national interest. This was the attitude of the post-war elite, the "Ottawa men."[94] We think that the contemporary signs of this attitude are to be found in the greater stress laid by federal public service elites than by their business counterparts on the intrinsic qualities of their work. The public servants surveyed by Zussman and Jabes were motivated by the interest of the job itself more than by the material rewards and others that come from the outside world. The difference between the two eras was two-fold. In the 1980s, the system had become huge and much more impersonal. Public servants were trying to cope with difficult financial circumstances, as well as a hostile political environment. They had become "adapters" — people who conform to the demands of their political masters, but without conviction. This tells us something about how institutions shape the moral horizons of all bureaucrats. A major finding of Zussman and Jabes was that disaffection or discontent rose sharply as one moved down the ladder of senior executive positions. Those in close contact with ministers were much more satisfied with their overall working conditions than those three, four or five rungs down the ladder.[95]

Confirmation comes from Campbell and Szablowski's study of the small elite in Ottawa in the late 1970s who worked in central agencies. They found that there reigned among the members of this elite a "competitive collegiality" grounded in high professional and academic achievement, a sense of personal influence based on access to ministers and to privileged information, and the size of the units in which they worked. There is a sense of being members of the elite group, regardless of rank.[96] This phrase anticipated one of Linda de Leon's types of moral environment, as referred to in Chapter 1.

When an elite is in small numbers, most of the mechanisms for transmitting its values are informal. Indeed, it may take an outsider such as an anthropologist to identify and describe these means, since they are so much a part of the elite's way of conducting itself.[97] Over time, as numbers and complexity grew, more institutional solutions were thought to be necessary. One was a system of evaluation of the elite, introduced with the creation of the Committee of Senior Officials by Prime Minister Trudeau to give advice to the Clerk of the Privy Council about senior appointments and evaluation of office holders. The other was the organizing of training programmes for new and aspiring senior officials, first with the Centre for Executive Development, then with the Canadian Centre for Management Development. Both of these came to be instruments in the transmission of a "management philosophy" to which we return in the following chapter.

Believing in serving the public interest and being loyal to one's department are perfectly compatible. To most public servants, the one requires the other. They may agree, for example, that there is room for further staff cuts, but they are certain that there are much bigger savings to be made in other departments than in theirs.[98] One way to limit loyalty to one's department is for central management to rotate managers at regular and frequent intervals. This has in fact been done, but it is part of the management approach, to which we turn in the next chapter.

OTHER EMPLOYEES

There is much less information about federal employees, since their impact on departmental policies is less certain and they are less likely to reveal themselves through memoirs, articles, or talks.

There are several signs that security has long been, in Canada as elsewhere, one of the main motivations of ordinary public servants. Certainly people outside the service see it as the most important reason to work for the government.[99] Also, the law has recognized this value since the creation of the Civil Service Commission in 1908, for seniority has been accepted as a rival value to merit from the beginning. Finally, security has been a major objective of public sector unions in the troubled years since 1980. Numerous statements by public sector union leaders, as cited earlier, also indicate a deep fear of political interference, whether it be in appointments, contracting out, or programme evaluation.

It seems revealing that public sector unions had compulsory arbitration as their main goal from the 1920s until the creation of the National Joint Council in 1944, when they tried to make the new system work in the manner of the Whitley Councils. When it did not turn out this way, they focused on obtaining a full regime of collective bargaining rights. Even so, most unions declared, before obtaining the right to strike, that they would never use it,[100] and when they got it, they generally opted for arbitration as the mechanism for resolving impasses in negotiations. Eventually, experience with the act led many to believe that the version that allowed strikes was more profitable.[101] Quite naturally, employee unions have opposed the pay restrictions and suspension of bargaining rights that have occurred in 1975-78, 1982-83, and 1991-97. As interest has shifted from wages as a prime focus of bargaining, the associations have shown greater interest in other dimensions of working conditions. They complained, for example, of being left out of the preparations and studies that led to the *Public Service 2000* report.[102]

A factor that should not be overlooked in explaining the deference to authority of the employee associations, particularly in the past, is the presence of veterans in the public service. As we saw above, for nearly a generation after World War II, close to half of new appointments of men went to veterans. It is possible that this factor explains the longstanding reluctance among public servants to use the strike against the employer. On the other hand, postal employees have a tradition of militancy that predates the adoption of collective bargaining, so in this case at least, organization culture was stronger than earlier military socialization.

One thing that the rank and file share with the elite is a preference for a slightly improved version of the status quo. Like public servants elsewhere, Canadian bureaucrats are somewhat more likely than other groups to favour state intervention, but once again we are far from the "budget-maximizing bureaucrat."[103] On the other hand, both groups, elites and employees, have shown little sympathy with the claims of outsiders until forced to accept them. Leadership on the language question came from a few politicians before 1960, the principal case being Ernest Lapointe in the King governments of the 1930s. In the wake of the adoption of the Official Languages Act in 1969, there was considerable opposition in the ranks of the public service, the most notorious example being that of the Canadian Air Traffic Controllers Association, both to the introduction of French in their work, and to the creation of a French language association.[104]

In the case of women, neither politicians nor public servants showed any great sympathy with their cause until they were forced to by outside pressure. Rather, the system was manipulated from the beginning to put women at a disadvantage. When women succeeded too well in the first examinations conducted under the 1908 law, deputy ministers were given the authority to limit their numbers in competitions. The requirement that women in all but clerical positions had to resign on marrying was only lifted in 1955, and maternity leave was not recognized as a right until 1962. Once again, it was observed that public sector unions were not eager to include women's issues in their bargaining demands. There were also indications that discrimination was present when dossiers were evaluated by juries.[105] As we shall see in the next chapter, men and women in the public service continue to have very different views of their respective situations.

A telling point in both cases was the absence of statistics about the presence of francophones and women in the public service. When Real Caouette and his *Creditistes*, following their election in 1962, began asking questions about the number of French Canadians in the Canadian bureaucratic elite, there were no ready answers. Similarly, when the Bird Report was published, the Public Service did not regularly publish statistics on the presence of women in all ranks.

6 · Conclusion

In this chapter, we have examined how the growth of the Canadian administration in size, wealth, and power first caused tension, and then reactions from other actors in the political system. We have also considered what these changes and other evidence tell us about the culture of the administration.

The growth of discretionary powers was the first trend that provoked a reaction through judicial review and legislative supervision of statutory instruments. With time, this question extended to the cabinet itself, and for the last twenty years we have been witness to attempts to redefine ministerial responsibility and public servants' accountability.

Greater turbulence has affected the public service in recent years, both in the form of budgetary restrictions and in the demands made on it by outside groups, most notably French Canadians and women. At the same time, public service unions and collective bargaining have altered the traditional version of the Westminster model that has been applied in Canada.

The need for these changes and the reactions to them have revealed a lot about the culture of the Canadian administration. Elites have worked hard for the public interest as seen through the prism of their departments' or agencies' interests. They recognize a role for both politicians and outside pressure groups, but they show a preference for the groups they already know and with whom they deal. They are less ready to consider radical change than are politicians. The major change since World War II has been the passage from a small group of individuals who knew each other to that of a vast administration where even elites became too numerous to have personal knowledge of each other.

The rank and file have been motivated by security and concern for their own well-being, but there is no reason to believe that they do not also wish to do their jobs well. However, they were slow to accept the claims of other groups who asked for better representation in their ranks. In their defense, however, for a long time they were very moderate, and it was only with the Public Service Staff Relations Act in the 1970s that they took a more aggressive union stance in large numbers. As many theorists have said, public servants seem to want to protect themselves as much as possible from the political and economic environment surrounding them,[106] with the result that it sometimes seems like a closed shop.

While the elites were few in number, they could function efficiently in an informal way. With the growth of the administration, more structure was needed to inform the elites' selection, indoctrination, training, and motivation. Pressure from business and the tendency of the mass of the administration to pursue security by conforming to the rules led to the search for new and more efficient ways of managing the public service. It is to the public management movement that we now turn.

Notes

1 V.S. Wilson and O.P. Dwivedi, "Introduction," *The Administrative State in Canada*, ed. Dwivedi, 5. Also, David H. Rosenbloom, *Public Administration: Understanding Management, Politics and Law in the Public Sector* (New York: Random House, 1989) 34-53.

2 Hodgetts, *The Canadian Public Service* 344.

3 Eugene Swimmer, "Six and Five," *How Ottawa Spends, 1984: the New Agenda*, ed. Alan Maslove (Toronto: Methuen, 1984) 240-81.

4 Statistics Canada, *Public Sector Employment and Wages and Salaries,* 1995 (Ottawa: Minister of Industry, October 1996) 74.

5 W.D.K. Kernaghan, "The Role of the Public Service in the Canadian Democratic System," *Bureaucracy in Canadian Government,* 2nd ed., ed. W.D.K. Kernaghan (Toronto: Methuen, 1973) 8.

6 Brian Chapman, *The Profession of Government* (London: G. Allen and Unwin, 1959).

7 G. Bergeron, *Fonctionnement de l'Etat* (Paris: Armand Colin, 1965) 345-60.

8 H.H. Gerth and C. Wright Mills, *From Max Weber* (New York: Oxford University Press, 1964) 214, 216. Emphasis in the original.

9 Hodgetts, *Pioneer Public Service* 91-95.

10 Hodgetts, *et al., The Biography of an Institution* ch. 2 and 3.

11 R.D. Maclean, "An Examination of the Role of the Comptroller of the Treasury," *Canadian Public Administration* 7:1 (1964): 1-136.

12 W.E.D. Halliday, "The Privy Council Office and Cabinet Secretariat," *Canada Year Book* (1956) 62-70; repr.in Hodgetts and Corbett 108-119. Also A.D.P. Heeney, "Cabinet Government in Canada: Some Recent Developments in the Machinery of the Central Executive," *Canadian Journal of Economics and Political Science* 12:3 (1946); repr. *Politics: Canada*, ed. Paul Fox (Toronto: McGraw-Hill, 1962) 145-63.

13 Hodgetts, *The Canadian Public Service* 254-55.

14 Sylvain Cloutier, "Le statut de la fonction publique du Canada: son histoire," *Canadian Public Administration* 10:4 (1967): 500-13.

15 Gordon Robertson, "The Changing Role of the Privy Council Office," *Canadian Public Administration* 14:4 (1971): 487-508; Colin Campbell and George Szablowski, *The Superbureaucrats* (Toronto: Macmillan, 1979) 29-53; and French 18-58.

16 Donald Gow, *The Progress of Budgetary Reform in the Government of Canada*, Special Study No. 17 prepared for the Economic Council of Canada (Ottawa: Information Canada, 1973).

17 J.I. Gow, *Learning from Others: Administrative Innovations Among Canadian Governments* (Toronto: Institute of Public Administration of Canada and Canadian Centre for Management Development, 1994) 152-56.

18 Savoie, *The Politics of Public Spending in Canada* 110-14.

19 Donald C. Rowat, "The Right of Public Access to Official Documents," *The Administrative State in Canada*, ed. Dwivedi, 151-176.

20 UK, *Report of the Committee on Ministers' Powers*, Cmd 4060 (London: HMSO, 1932) 4-7. The committee was set up in the wake of the publication in 1929 of a controversial book by Lord Chief Justice Hewart, *The New Despotism* (London: Benn, 1929).

21 Law Reform Commission of Canada, *A Catalogue of Discretionary Powers in the Revised Statutes of Canada* (Ottawa: Information Canada, 1975). This catalogue underestimates the importance of the powers known traditionally as "quasi-judicial" since it studies only the object of each power and not the way in which they were to be carried out.

22 Patrice Garant, *Droit administratif* (Montréal: Editions Yvon Blais, 1985) 287.

23 Economic Council of Canada, *Responsible Regulation* (Ottawa: Supply and Services, 1979) and *Reforming Regulation* (Ottawa: Supply and Services, 1981).

24 J.A.Corry, "The Prospects for the Rule of Law," *Canadian Journal of Economics and Political Science* 21 (1955): 405-15; John R. Humphrey, "Judicial Control Over Administrative Action With Special Reference to the Province of Quebec," *Canadian Journal of Economics and Political Science* 5 (1939): 351-95; Gerald E. LeDain, "The Supervisory Jurisdiction in Quebec," *Canadian Bar Review* 35 (1957): 788-827; André Gélinas, "Judicial Control of Administrative Action: Great Britain and Canada," *Public Law* (1963): 140-71.

25 Corry, "The Prospects for the Rule of Law," repr. in Hodgetts and Corbett 548.

26 John Willis, "Administrative Law in Canada," *Canadian Bar Review* 39:2 (1961) 251-65.

27 Jean Beetz, "Uniformité de la procédure administrative," *Revue du Barreau* 25 (1965) 245.

28 Willis 252.

29 R. Dussault, *Traité de droit administratif canadien et québécois* (Québec: Les Presses de l'Université Laval, 1974), première partie, deuxième titre; and Patrice Garant, *Droit administratif* 607-614. In the second edition, published with Louis Borgeat, René Dussault notes that Quebec was much more prone to use such clauses than was the federal government, tome III (Québec: Les Presses de l'Université Laval, 1989) 119.

30 Willis 618; Garant 618.

31 J.A. Corry, "Statutory Powers," *Legal Essays in Honour of Arthur Moxon*, ed. J.A. Corry (Toronto: University of Toronto Press, 1953) 127-55; and René Dussault, "Relationship Between the Nature of the Acts of the Administration and Judicial Review," *Canadian Public Administration* 10:3 (1967): 298-322.

32 Peter H. Russell, *The Judiciary in Canada: the Third Branch of Government* (Toronto: McGraw-Hill Ryerson, 1987) 311. Also, John H. Turner, *The Federal Court of Canada: A Manual of Practice* (Ottawa, Information Canada, 1971).

33 Russell 358-62.

34 Kernaghan and Siegel, *Public Administration in Canada* 411-12.

35 Canada, House of Commons, *Third Report of the Special Committee on Statutory Instruments*, Chairman, Mark McGuigan (Ottawa: Queen's Printer, 1969) vii and 7. The article of D.C. Rowat cited was "How Much Administrative Secrecy?" *Canadian Journal of Economics and Political Science* 31 (1965): 477-98.

36 Gary Levy, "Delegated Legislation and the Standing Joint Committee on Regulations and Other Statutory Instruments," *Canadian Public Administration* 22:3 (1979) 349-65; and C.E.S. Franks, *The Parliament of Canada* (Toronto: University of Toronto Press, 1987) 255.

37 Canada, House of Commons, *Third Report of the Special Committee on Reform of the House of Commons*, Chairman James A. McGrath (1985) 36. Hereafter cited as *McGrath Report*.

38 *McGrath Report* 35.

39 See, for example, Vincent Brassard, *Les insolences d'un ex-député* (Montreal: Imprimerie Nationale, 1963) 51, 72-3, 151.

40 M. Lamontagne, "The Influence of the Politician," *Canadian Public Administration* 11:3 (1968): 263-71.

41 Kenneth Kernaghan has charted this trend in "Power, Parliament and Public Servants in Canada," *Canadian Public Policy* 5 (1979): 383-96.

42 Auditor General of Canada, *Report to the House of Commons for the Year 1976* (Ottawa: Supply and Services, 1976).

43 Canada, *Final Report of the Royal Commission on Financial Management and Accountability* (Ottawa: Supply and Services, 1979) 373. Hereafter cited as *Lambert Report*.

44 Canada, *Report of the Committee on the Concept of the Ombudsman* (Ottawa, 1977) 16-17; *McGrath Report* 20.

45 *Lambert Report* 182-84, 374-77. *McGrath Report* 20. These passages are analyzed by S.L. Sutherland, "Responsible Government and Ministerial Responsibility: Every Reform Is Its Own Problem," *Canadian Journal of Political Science* 24:1 (1991): 109-10.

46 Privy Council Office, "Notes on Responsibilities of Public Servants in Relation to Parliamentary Committees," (Ottawa, 1987); repr. S. L Sutherland and Y. Baltacioglu, *Parliamentary Reform and the Federal Public Service* (London, Ont.: National Centre for Management Research and Development, School of Business Administration, University of Western Ontario, 1988) 177-82.

47 Osbaldeston 5.

48 Sutherland 114-17; Franks 245-49.

49 S.L. Sutherland, "The Al-Mashat Affair: Administrative Accountability in Parliamentary Institutions," *Canadian Public Administration* 34:4 (1991): 573-603.

50 See Table 4.5; and Michael J. Prince, "Canada's Public Finances Under Restraint: Has Ottawa Shrunk?" Bernier and Gow 24.

51 David Wolfe, "Les dimensions politiques des déficits," *Les dimensions politiques de la politique économique*, dir. G. Bruce Doern, vol.40: les études faites pour la Commission royale d'enquête sur l'union économique et les perspectives de développement du Canada (Ottawa: Approvisionnements et services, 1985) 137-90. Deputy Prime Minister Erik Nielsen noted, on the presentation of the Review of Government Programs which he directed, that the federal deficit would disappear overnight if these concessions etc. were ended. Task Force on Program Review, *An Introduction to the Process of Program Review* (Ottawa: Supply and Services, 1986) 20-22; and Gazette News Service, "Ottawa is Throwing Away Billions a Year, Nielsen Task Force Reports," *The Gazette* (Montreal) 12 March 1986: A1.

52 Savoie, *The Politics of Public Spending* 152-58, 163-71.

53 R. Van Loon, "Stop the Music: the Current Policy and Expenditure Management System in Ottawa," *Canadian Public Administration* 24:2 (1981): 175-99; Rod Dobell, "Pressing the Envelope," *Policy Options* 2:5 (1981): 13-18; and Jerry McCaffery, "Canada's Envelope Budget: A Strategic Management System," *Public Administration Review* 44:4 (1984): 316-23.

54 Allen Schick, "Micro-Budgetary Adaptations to Fiscal Stress in Industrial Democracies," *Public Administration Review* 48:1 (1988) 532; and Aron Wildavsky, *The Politics of the Budgetary Process*, 4th ed. (Boston: Little Brown, 1984) 275-77.

55 Savoie, *The Politics of Public Spending in Canada* 348-49.

56 Amelita Armit and Jacques Bourgault, ed. *Hard Choices or No Choices: Assessing Program Review* (Toronto: Institute of Public Administration of Canada and Canadian Plains Research Center, 1996).

57 Prince 18.

58 The present version of this rule is found in The Public Service Act (RSC P-33), Art. 32.

59 Jacques Bourgault and Stéphane Dion, "Canadian Senior Civil Servants and Transitions of Government: the Whitehall Model Seen From Ottawa," *International Review of Administrative Sciences* 36 (1990): 152-55; and L.R. Smith, ed., *The Higher Civil Service in Europe and Canada* (Washington: Brookings Institution, 1984) 12.

60 Gordon Robertson, "The Changing Role of the Privy Council Office," *Canadian Public Administration* 14:4 (1971): 506.

61 Christina Newman, "The Whiz Kid of 37 Who's Canada's Top Mandarin," *The Globe and Mail* 4 January 1975: 1.

62 Bob Young, "What Will Massé Do Without Massé-Who?" *The Plain Dealer* (Fredericton) 6 August 1977: 6. Jeffrey Simpson said that Mr. Clark had "handpicked" Mr. Massé. Simpson, "Office Politics: Clark Advisers at the Hub of Ottawa Power Network," *Globe and Mail* 8 September 1979: 1.

63 Bernard Descôteaux, "Le PC et les fonctionnaires: deux solitudes qui se rapprochent?" *Le Devoir* 18 March 1986: 1.

64 Bernard Descoteaux, "Pour contrôler l'appareil, des chefs de cabinet 'politiques' à Ottawa," *Le Devoir* 26 September 1984: 1; Micheline Plasse, "Les chefs de cabinets ministériels du gouvernement fédéral canadien: rôle et relation avec la haute fonction publique," *Canadian Public Administration* 35:3 (1992): 317-38; and Loretta J. O'Connor, "Chief of Staff," *Policy Options* (April 1991): 23-26.

65 Campbell and Szabloswki ch.6.

66 R.G. Robertson, "The Canadian Parliament and Cabinet in the Face of Modern Demands," *Canadian Public Administration* 11:3 (1968): 272.

67 Pross 118-30; Boase 3-6. Whereas Pross sees the policy community as having achieved a "dominant voice" in determining public policy in a particular field, Boase, following other leads in the literature, considers that it refers to all actors or potential actors interested in a particular policy field.

68 Osbaldeston ch. 2; Bourgault and Dion 160-61.

69 Treasury Board of Canada, *Conflict of Interest and Post-Employment Code for the Public Service* (Ottawa: Supply and Services, 1985).

70 Gabriel Almond, "Introduction: A Functional Approach to Comparative Politics," *The Politics of Developing Areas*, G. Almond and J.S. Coleman (Princeton, NJ: Princeton University Press, 1960); and Jean-William Lapierre, *L'analyse des systèmes politiques* (Paris: Presses Universitaires de France, 1973) 92-106.

71 Charlotte Gray, "Striking It Rich?" *Saturday Night* (January 1981): 9-11. Public Service Staff Relations Board, *Twenty-fifth Annual Report, 1991-92* (Ottawa, 1992) 70-1. A short history of this evolution can be found in Gérard Hébert, *Traité de négociation collective* (Boucherville QC: Gaëtan Morin, 1992) 902-14.

72 Swimmer 240-81.

73 According to Gallup poll data published by the Montreal *Gazette* 22 September 1982, Canadians were opposed to strikes in the public sector by 51 per cent in 1981 and by 62 per cent in 1982. From the same source, the numbers of citizens opposed to strikes in essential services rose from 59 per cent in 1978 to 73 per cent in 1981, and returned to 58 per cent in 1987 (*The Gazette* 9 May 1985 and *La Presse* 23 April 1987). When asked to chose one as a source of our troubles, Canadians polled by Gallup over twenty years always put "Big Unions" (1969-78) or "Big Government" (1981-1985) ahead of "Big Business."

74 Michel Vastel, "Le Service extérieur, dépotoir des compères et amis de Mulroney," *Le Devoir* 12 July 1987.

75 Presse canadienne, "Les fonctionnaires fédéraux écopent pour les décisions prises par les politiciens," *La Presse* 30 April 1992.

Jean Chartier, "Les fonctionnaires fédéraux réclament le droit de dénoncer le gaspillage et la fraude," *Le Devoir* 15 September 1994.

Manon Corneillier, "Les fonctionnaires heureux du départ des conservateurs," *Le Devoir* 3 November 1993; and John Ward, "Fonction publique: le moral à plat," *La Presse* 18 March 1994.

76 Jeffrey Simpson, *Spoils of Power: The Politics of Patronage* (Toronto: Collins, 1988) ch. 3 and 4.

77 *Glassco Report* vol.1: 67-77.

In 1966, Taylor Cole noted that the situation had not improved in twenty years: in 1947, French Canadians were "heavily under-represented in the public service... the degree of under-representation increased progressively as one moved upward in the civil service echelons...". The situation was such that it had been unanimously deplored by the Quebec Legislative Assembly. Taylor Cole, *The Canadian Bureaucracy and Federalism, 1947-1965* (Denver CO: University of Denver, 1966) 32.

Canada, House of Commons, *Debates* (6 April 1966) 3915-17.

78 Gow, *Learning From Others*, 178-81.

79 For the overall figures from 1965, see the *Rapport de la commission royale d'enquête sur le bilinguisme et le biculturalisme* vol. III (Ottawa: Imprimeur de la Reine, 1969) 95. For senior public servants in 1967, see the return made by Prime Minister Pearson on 7 December 1966 and published in full by *Le Devoir* 19 January 1967: 5. Also, Commissioner of Official Languages, *Annual Report 1997* (Ottawa: Public Works and Government Services, 1998) 40-1.

80 Hodgetts *et al.*, *Biography of an Institution* 483.

81 André Leblond, *L'action positive dans la fonction publique fédérale et son impact sur l'emploi* (Ottawa: Université d'Ottawa, Faculté d'administration, 1982); Nicole Morgan, *The Equality Game. Women in the Public Service of Canada, 1908-1967* (Ottawa: Advisory Council on the Status of Women, 1988); and Gow, *Learning From Others* 173-77. Also see, *Rapport de la Commission royale d'enquête sur la situation de la femme au Canada* (Ottawa: Information Canada, 1970) 121; and Treasury Board, *Employment Statistics for the Federal Public Service 1996-97* (Ottawa: Treasury Board Secretariat, 1997) 9, 15.

82 An impressionistic version of the differences between francophone and anglophone managers is given by Paul Michaud, "Certains aspects du milieu de l'administration fédérale," *Optimum* 7:2 (1976): 21-28. For the differences between men and women, see chapter 6.

83 J.L. Granatstein, *The Ottawa Men, The Civil Service Mandarins, 1935-1957* (Toronto: Oxford University Press, 1982) ch.9; H.L. Laframboise "Administrative Reform in the Federal Public Service: Signs of A Saturation Psychosis," *Canadian Public Administration* 14:3 (1971): 303-325.

84 A.W. Johnson, "The Role of the Deputy Minister: III," *Canadian Public Administration* (1961): 363-73.

85 See note 62.

86 J. Aberbach, R. Putnam and B. Rockman, *Bureaucrats and Politicians in Western Democracies* (Cambridge Mass.: Harvard University Press, 1981).

87 Gow, *Learning From Others* 95; and also the answers of deputy ministers to the questions of the Lambert Commission.

88 On the notion of the public interest as an administrative doctrine in France, see Jacques Chevallier, "La notion de l'intérêt public," *Revue internationale des sciences administratives* 41:4 (1975): 325-50.

R. Presthus, *Elite Accommodation in Canadian Politics* (Toronto: Macmillan, 1973) found that fully one-half of Canadian Government departments had created or encouraged the creation of at least one pressure group among their clientele. In the marxist view elite accommodation became elite collusion at the expense of the lower classes. See Dennis Olsen, *The State Elite* (Toronto: McClelland and Stewart, 1980).

89 Savoie writes,"It is clear, however, that the biggest disappointment ministers and their staffs have with policy research units is their inability to challenge the status quo in their department." Savoie, *The Politics of Public Spending* 216. Lee Sigelman and W.G Vanderbok, using Presthus's data, found that legislators were more interventionist than public servants. Sigelman and Vanderbok, "Legislators, Bureaucrats and Canadian Democracy: the Long and the Short of It," *Canadian Journal of Political Science* 10:3 (1977): 615-23. That this is a general condition of senior officials in the developed countries is shown by Aberbach, Putnam and Rockman 125-33.

Finally, see John Hilliker, *History of the Department of External Affairs 1946-1968*, vol. 2 (Montreal: McGill-Queen's University Press and Institute of Public Administration of Canada, 1995).

90 André Blais and Stéphane Dion, "Are Bureaucrats Budget Maximizers? the Niskanen Model and Its Critics," *Polity* 22:4 (1990): 655-74; and Blais and Dion, eds., *The Budget Maximizing Bureaucrat. Appraisals and Evidence* (Pittsburgh: University of Pittsburgh Press, 1991).

91 Savoie, *The Politics of Public Spending* 216.

92 R.V. Segsworth, "Downsizing and Program Evaluation: An Assessment of the Experience of the Government of Canada," Bernier and Gow 249-76; Senate of Canada, Standing Committee on National Finance, *The Program Evaluation System of the Government of Canada* (Ottawa, 1991) 20-21; and Gow, *Learning From Others* 194-99.

93 For Canada, this reaction was most vividly put by H.L. Laframboise in "Signs of a Saturation Psychosis."

94 Laframboise; Granatstein.

95 D. Zussman and J. Jabes, *The Vertical Solitude* (Halifax: Institute for Public Policy, 1989) 33; 114; 52 and 107.

96 Campbell and Szablowski 188-89.

97 In the 1960s an outsider who did not fall under their charm wrote an amusing but revealing account of the way junior foreign officers were initiated into their role as members of Ottawa's elites. Louise Cote, "Nos ambassadeurs? des prix de vertu," *Le Magazine Maclean* (Sept. 1965): 20, 42-7.

98 Savoie, *The Politics of Public Spending* 210.

99 A Gallup Poll released on 25 February 1948, found that 73 per cent of those asked gave permanence, pension plans, and benefits as the main reason to work for the government (grouped in the release as "security"), followed by better working conditions (22 per cent). Whereas the private sector was thought to give more chance to get ahead, it was more interesting and less impersonal, and it was free from political influence. See also N. Islam and M. Paquet, "Les étudiants et la fonction publique: étude des perceptions, des valuers et de l'attrait comparatif," *Canadian Public Administration* 18:1 (1975): 38-54.

100 O.P. Dwivedi, "Recent Developments in Staff Relationships in the Public Service of Canada," *Public Administration* (Australia), 24 (December 1965): 359-67. See also, J.E. Hodgetts and O.P. Dwivedi, *Provincial Governments as Employers: A Survey of Public Personnel Administration in Canada's Provinces* (Montreal and London: McGill-Queen's Press, 1974). Chapters 9 and 10 of this book discuss both the federal and provincial public service employers-employees relations until early 1970s. See 149-78.

101 See, Charlottetown Gray, "Striking it Rich?" *Saturday Night* (January 1981): 9-11.

102 Robert J. McIntosh, "Public Service 2000: The Employee Perspective," *Canadian Public Administration* 34:3 (1991): 490-511.

103 André Blais, and Stephane Dion, "Trop d'Etat? Un barometre de l'opinion," *Politique* 11 (1987): 43-72.

104 Canada, *Rapport de la commission royale d'enquete sur le bilinguisme et le biculturalisme*, vol. III (Ottawa: Imprimeur de la reine, 1969) 105-7. Among public servants, the Commission also mentioned one exception, O.D. Skelton, Under-Secretary of State for External Affairs, who made special efforts to recruit francophones in his department. See also, Sandford Borins, *The Language of the Skies* (Montreal and Kingston: McGill-Queen's and IPAC, 1983).

105 Kathleen Archibald, *Les deux sexes dans la fonction publique* (Ottawa: Public Service Commission, 1969) 17-18, 20-21, 227-37; Gow, *Learning From Others* 173-77; Hodgetts *et al.*, *Biography of an Institution* 488; Carolle Simard, *L'administration contre les femmes* (Montreal: Boreal Express, 1983) 67-79.

106 Merton, "Bureaucratic Structure and Personality" 361-371. Also J. Chevallier and D. Loschak, *Traite de science administrative*, vol. II (Paris: Librarie generale de droit et de jurisprudence, 1978) 153-79

FIVE

The New Public Management Movement Comes to Canada

In the previous chapter, we saw how the Canadian administration grew steadily in size and power during the first seven decades of the twentieth century. As it did so, it challenged the system of political and judicial control which had only reached a mature state with the creation of the Civil Service Commission in 1908 and the extension of its coverage to the entire public service in 1918.

While the courts and political institutions reacted to defend their roles and mandates, the administration itself kept growing. The result was a vast, impersonal collection of organizations which, like the giant private corporation, has passed under the direction of its senior employees. As the historian Alfred D. Chandler Jr. wrote of American corporations, the largest ones became so large and complex that no individual or small group could control all their activities, nor know their activities in detail.[1] The result has been the "managerial revolution," in which the government of large organizations has been taken over by groups of specialists.[2]

In the public sector, the idea of management has been seen in recent times as the solution to many of the dilemmas that we studied in the previous chapter. In the following pages, we trace the origins and lineage of the New Public Management movement in the United States, Britain, France, and Canada. We then look at its main applications in the federal administration.

1 · Genesis and Lineage of the New Public Management

In a sense, the idea of management as a professional activity has been present in public administration since Woodrow Wilson's famous article of 1887.[3] It represents the first claim in modern times that administration is an activity that should be left to specialists. The notion got strong support from Frederick Taylor's "scientific management" movement.

As Denhardt has noted, "Managerialism…is essentially the application of market principles and business practices to the management of government."[4] This has been true since that initial essay of Wilson's, which held that "the field of administration is a field of business."[5] That management itself has greatly changed over the last century is evident; whereas it formerly concentrated on narrow issues of efficiency and effectiveness, over time, it became more interested in strategic questions of planning, adaptation, and survival.

It is not easy to say what management is. Some identify it as a doctrine, some an ideology.[6] Many have summed it up by its major components, from the POSDCORB of the 1930s to Plumptre's "plan, organize, motivate, control."[7] Hood finds the New Public Management "a shorthand name for the set of broadly similar administrative doctrines that dominated the bureaucratic reform agenda in many of the OECD group of countries in the 1970s."[8]

Peter Drucker first identified "management" as action aimed at obtaining desired results.[9] This sounds very like Simon, Smithburg and Thompson's definition of "administration" as "cooperative activities in pursuit of common goals."[10] Some writers argue that the only difference between the two definitions is semantic.[11] There is, however, a meaningful difference between management and administration.

Two French academics have given what we think is the best generic definition of management: "the rational combining of human and material means with the aim of meeting objectives in optimal conditions."[12] Certainly the idea of optimizing was present in the mandate of the Lambert Commission to favour "the most efficient use of human resources"[13] and in the declaration by Paul Tellier, former Clerk of the Privy Council, that the government's philosophy was to obtain "the optimal use of human resources to meet the needs and priorities of the Government and the public."[14] The French authors note that managerial thinking carries with it a new kind of rationality that is action- and results-oriented, whereas the older legalistic bureaucratic rationality gave greater stress to order, reliability, hierarchy, and consistency.

"Management" has not always meant the same thing. In North America, the focus of the Scientific Management movement was efficiency — maximizing output at minimal cost. It was essentially a technical discipline.[15] Since the mid-1970s, a New Public Management has taken a more dynamic view. Christopher Hood has identified three sets of core values in public management: efficiency or frugality (values of the kind just mentioned); fairness and rectitude (values that are more related to legitimacy, due process, and legality); and survival values, which have to do with adaptability and security.[16] The first two kinds of values have long coexisted in a somewhat antagonistic relationship. Being fair and stressing equality was thought to interfere with being efficient and effective. The third set of values stresses innovation, strategic planning, and adaptability. While public management is still heavily influenced by efficiency values,[17] one could argue that the addition of survival values is the principal contribution of New Public Management. Another way of approaching it is to note that since the introduction of programme budgets and policy analysis, management has claimed to contribute to policy-making as well as to its implementation.

Contemporary management is simply the expanded version of the idea of seeking the best combination of means to achieve the desired results. In this respect, it is useful to note some of the underlying assumptions on which the idea of public management is based:

1 its ideological foundations lie in competitive individualism as expressed in business ideology;[18]

2 while inclined to be scornful of myths, management science may be based on the "metamyths" that all problems have rational solutions and that the means are more important than the ends;[19]

3 the idea of management seems to depend on restoring the separation of politics and administration, which was present in the early theories of public administration, but has been challenged by practitioners and academics;[20]

4 for the two previous reasons, management science tends to ignore that in the public sector rational methods of analysis have to coexist and sometimes compete with political decision-making methods involving bargaining, compromise, coalition-building, and persuasion. In these cases, there is no clear goal to inform an operative framework, but only an agreement that is acceptable to the principal players.[21]

5 finally, management is a professional ideology that emphasizes the necessity of discretion. In this respect, it favours some organizational actors over others.[22]

The New Public Management movement has been in existence since the late 1970s, as Table 5.1 attests. There is a remarkable similarity in developed countries with regard to policies of improvement. They are:

TABLE 5.1: **THE COMPONENTS OF THE NEW PUBLIC MANAGEMENT**

Authors' Syntheses			Government Reports or Programs
Marceau Long	Christopher Hood	Osborne & Gaebler	UK Next Steps & Citizen's Charter
1) State as enterprise		Enterprising government	
	Accent on results	Results-oriented	Results oriented
	Competition	Market orientation	Market testing
	Managerial autonomy	Decentralization	Executive agencies
	Budgets cuts	Smaller but stronger	Financial management initiative, 1982
2) Participatory state		Participatory management Community Empowerment	
3) Productivity measure	Performance measure	Performance measure	Performance measure Results measure
4) Accent on clients		Customer driven	Citizen's charter
5) Transparent state			Appeal rights
6) Public servants as wage earners	Private sector management styles	Anti-bureaucratic	Performance pay

Sources: Marceau Long, "Réflexions sur l'évolution de l'administration française." *Administrative publique du Canada* 24:2 (1981): .272-94; Christopher Hood, "A Public Management for All Seasons?," *Public Administration* 69:1 (1991): 3-19; David Osborne and Ted Gaebler, *Reinventing Government* (New York: Penguin Books, 1993); Canada, *Public Service 2000* (Ottawa, 1990); Cabinet Office, Efficiency Unit, *Improving Management in Government: The Next Steps* (London: HMSO, 1988); H.M. Government, *Citizen's Charter* (London: HMSO, 1988); Denis St. Martin, *Institutional Analysis of Recent Machinery-of-*

TABLE 5.1: (CONT'D)

Canada. PS 2000	USA. Gore Report	France. de Closets	Japanese Administrative Reform Committee
Innovation	Entrepreneurship	Innovation	Creativity
Results oriented	Accountability for results	Accountability for results	
	Market dynamics		Market incentives
Decentralization	Decentralization	Contractual decentralization	Agencies
	Cutting back to basics		Minimum necessary
Partnership	Labor-Management Partnership	Union-management concertation	
		Users' committees	
Efficiency & effectiveness	Productivity Budgets acc. to results	Performance measure Results measure	Efficiency Evaluation of results
Service to clientele	Putting customers first	Service	Putting people first
Accountability		Transparence	Transparence
			Accountability
People, number one resource	Empowering employees	Team performance pay	

Government Reforms in Australia, Britain, France and New Zealand (Ottawa: Consulting and Audit Canada, 1993); Al Gore, *Creating a Government That Works Better and Costs Less, Report of the National Performance Review* (Washington: USGPO, 1993); *Commisariat général du plan* (François de Closets), *Le pari de la responsabilité: rapport de la Commission Efficacité de l'Etat* (Paris: La documentation française, 1989; Administrative Reform Committee (Gyosei Kaikaku Inkai), *Gsosei no Yakowari Wo Tomasu* (Tokyo: Okurasho Shuppankyo, 1997) (Translated by François Simard).

• accent on results, both in planning and in evaluation of programmes and people;

• service to the public, with a special concern for quality, citizen as client;

• delegation of authority as close as possible to the level of action, and empowerment of employees;

• greater attention to cost through comprehensive auditing, contracting out, and introduction of competition;

• private sector techniques for motivating employees, such as merit pay, mission statements, and quality circles.[23]

Why was New Public Management attractive to governments in so many countries? Some of its ideas are as old as management itself. They spring from the desire to improve. Another powerful motivator came from the financial problems that beset governments from the beginning of the 1980s. The various versions of welfare state seemed to be too expensive, and the Keynesian economics on which they were based were discredited because politicians had taken to running systematic deficits in order to finance government programmes. There were also reactions to public sector unions, strikes, and the rigid bureaucracy that came from combining big government with collective agreements. Finally, the 1980s were a time when conservative ideologies experienced a revival. The election of Margaret Thatcher in Britain and Ronald Reagan in the United States gave powerful support to the New Public Management. As Wilson and Dwivedi have put it in the Canadian case:

> The New Public Management reform agenda really became manifest in 1984 when a Progressive Conservative government swept to power in Canada. The public agenda of the new government was clear: attention to federal deficit reduction, less generous social programmes, cutbacks in spending, tax simplification, deregulation and the privatization of many Crown corporations — all were components of a distinct philosophy to reduce the role of government in Canadian society.[24]

However, there are adherents to public management who do not believe in reducing the state for its own sake, such as Osborne and Gaebler in the United States, and Sandford Borins in Canada.

We turn now to examine the way in which the public management movement appeared in Canada, and how these ideas and practices were grafted onto the previous political and administrative culture.

2 · The New Public Management Movement Comes to Canada

While it might be possible to find earlier manifestations of the management movement, the first important occasion — and it was recognized as such at the time — was the introduction of the new position classification scheme in 1919. As we saw in Chapter 3, this event was the occasion for a dramatic switch from the British tradition of a small number of broadly defined classes of clerks and special officers to an extremely detailed and specific identification of different jobs within the Canadian administration.

Although the new classification and the system of competitive examinations that accompanied it represented a major change in the way the civil service conducted business, it was nonetheless a limited innovation in light of what followed. It was an efficiency-driven and static approach. While it may have helped facilitate the hiring of the best qualified person for a narrowly defined job, it complicated the orderly promotion of experienced public servants as it produced a large number of very short career promotion ladders. It also impeded flexible use of existing personnel, since people were hired to fill narrowly defined positions.

THE GLASSCO REPORT

While there were several reports of importance in the interval, the next step in the advent of modern management was the Glassco Royal Commission on Government Organization, whose five reports were published from 1962 to 1964.[25] The commission, established by Prime Minister Diefenbaker, appears to be the Canadian counterpart to the two commissions chaired by former president Herbert Hoover in the United States.[26] Volume 1 of the Glassco Commission's report is entitled *Management of the Public Service,* and its four subsequent volumes all have the word management in their subtitles.

The main thrust of the Glassco Report was that the government and its administration were not structured to do their jobs properly. In general, central agencies were neither empowered nor competent to develop and implement overall policies, while the Treasury Board and the Civil Service Commission intervened excessively in day-to-day operations of departments, thus depriving the latter of the chance to manage their own affairs and the responsibility to answer for this management. Consequently, the Glassco Report's main recommendations were structural. Two of the most important were acted upon before the end of the 1960s. In 1967, the job of president of the Treasury Board became a separate cabinet post from that of Minister of Finance, the staff was transferred from the Department of Finance to the new department, and the Treasury Board became responsible for overall administrative policies and collective bargaining as well as for expenditure management.[27] Then, in 1969, the post of Comptroller of the Treasury was eliminated, and the responsibility of controlling commitments and authorized expenditures transferred to departments and agencies.[28]

In many ways, the Glassco Report was anchored in the traditional conception of management. One critic wrote that there was nothing in its principles that one could not find in the writings of the French management engineer Henri Fayol.[29] However, looking back, one finds many precursors of contemporary themes in the report. To begin with, the report said that government "will seldom be viewed as better than a necessary evil," thus reflecting the business views of its chairman, and anticipating the dominant philosophy of the 1980s.[30] Its overall theme of "Let the managers manage" was also a precursor of the New Public Management movement.[31]

The report also favoured cost recovery wherever possible in order to encourage awareness of and responsibility for the real cost of government services. Even so, the commission went beyond the main thrust of its mandate to say that "even greater is the importance of a service responsive to public wants and expectations," and it cautioned that "excellence (in the management of public affairs) cannot be sustained indefinitely without public recognition."[32]

Thus the Glassco Report paved the way for structural changes that allowed the government to have an overall administrative policy, while departments assumed more responsibility for the management of their affairs. While it also contained some themes that were to be increasingly popular, the report did not really deal with the next wave, which was to be that of programme budgets.

PPBS

While the Glassco Commission was at work, officials in the Treasury Board had already begun studying programme budgeting as it had been introduced in the Department of Defence in Washington, D.C.[33] In 1963, pilot studies were conducted in four departments, followed by two policy orientation documents issued by the Treasury Board: *Financial Management in the Departments of the Government of Canada* (1966) and *Guide to PPBS* (1969). The system was introduced throughout the federal government in 1970.

If one had to choose a single intellectual step that made possible the New Public Management movement, it was surely the introduction of PPBS. For the first time, instead of presenting budgets by showing the costs related to each administrative unit, managers were asked to define the objectives of each principal task, to identify standards by which the successful attainment of these objectives could be measured, and to link the achievement of desired results with costs. Here was a revolution![34] Since parliamentary democracy had been introduced, in Canada (as elsewhere) budgets had been primarily concerned with obtaining legislative authorization for kinds of expenditures: for example, salaries, benefits, construction, equipment, supplies, travel. These were what the new system called "inputs"; never before had there been systematic examination of what was done with these funds (the outputs) and their link with the stated objectives. Henceforth it would be possible to examine budgets for their coherence and logic: if there were a programme to increase air traffic safety, what were the means proposed to do it, and how would success be measured?

An integral part of this reform was the introduction of cost-benefit analysis for public investment projects.[35] The objective was to include in the analysis every imaginable cost and advantage of each project and to put a price on each one.

PROGRAMME EVALUATION AND COMPREHENSIVE AUDITING

Although the Treasury Board was interested in the evaluation part of the PPB system, it took longer to implement than it did to introduce new planning. In 1974, it introduced a system for measuring output and unit cost called the Operational Performance Measurement System (OPMS). This amounted to measuring efficiency, since cost and production were linked, although impact or effectiveness could not be measured this way.

1976-77 saw the denunciation of runaway spending by the Auditor General and the creation of the Lambert Commission. Even before the Lambert Commission submitted its final report, two important new steps were taken which were only possible because programme budgets existed. First, in 1977, the new position of Comptroller General was created in the Treasury Board to develop policies and guidelines for financial management and internal audit. A direct consequence was the issuing of a Treasury Board policy circular requiring all departments and agencies to introduce programme evaluation. This was followed in 1981 by another Treasury board circular, *Guide on the Program Evaluation Function*, and a companion document, *Principles for the Evaluation of Programs by Federal Departments*.

Following these initiatives, in a manner typical of modern public administration, the programme evaluation function developed rapidly, both as an activity and as a career. The Canadian Evaluation Society was founded in 1981 and created its own professional journal in 1986. By 1989, it had approximately 1000 members, drawn from all levels of government.[36]

Evaluation is the ultimate stage of the rational planning process that was introduced with PPBS in 1970. Just as programme budgets did not live up to all their promise, so evaluation has frequently been criticized as inadequate or ineffectual.[37]

CREATION OF A MANAGEMENT CULTURE: THE MANAGEMENT CATEGORY AND COSO

In 1979, two important reports were submitted to the federal government. The Lambert Report was concerned with financial management and accountability,[38] while the D'Avignon Committee's Report dealt with personnel management and the merit principle.[39] Both reported that changes were needed in the highest levels of management within the administration.

For our concerns, the most important finding of these two bodies was the insufficient attention given to management at senior levels of the administration. The Lambert Commission had surveyed incumbent deputy ministers and found that while they considered themselves — but not their ministers nor central agencies — to be in charge of their departments, they were chosen more for their competency in policy matters than for their management abilities.[40] This preference for policy questions would seem to be a key component of the culture of higher officials in Canada.[41] Until the late 1970s, the government had given very little attention to management training.[42]

The D'Avignon Committee argued that senor officials were ready to implement a "philosophy of management," but that one had never been formulated for them on a government-wide scale.[43] Both reports found that clear statements of objectives, greater delegations of powers and responsibilities, and a requirement to account for their management in terms of results achieved were lacking.

The government seems to have had these two reports in mind when it created the new Management Category in July 1980.[44] The purpose in creating the new category was to unite in one group the top managers of the federal government. It included the members of the former Senior Executive Group and the top grades of 55 occupational and professional groups, thus uniting in one category those who were not unionized because of their management responsibilities.[45] Members of this new group could then be selected and trained with a view to strengthening their management capabilities. Members of the new category were to be appointed to a level rather than to a position. This meant that they could be assigned ("deployed") by deputy ministers as the need arose, without the impediment of having to respect detailed job descriptions.[46] It was expected that members of the new category would identify with central management;[47] they would be evaluated and paid according to their performance. Clearly the recommendations of Lambert and D'Avignon are reflected in this new policy. Moreover, it was prepared with the assistance of the Hay Associates consulting firm; one of its objects was said to be to facilitate comparisons with the private sector.

These intentions were followed up during the 1980s. The practice of frequent rotation of deputy ministers, which dates from the 1960s, was continued during these years. Bourgault, Dion and Lemay have shown that between the mid-1960s and 1988, federal deputy ministers had much less experience of their departments upon nomination (down from eight years to three), were likely to remain there much less time (2.7 years as opposed to an average of six years in the 1960s), but were more likely to have been deputy minister in another department (41 per cent between 1967 and 1988, up from only 24 per cent from 1947 to 1967).[48] Their attachment to their departments was thus weakened. In fact, such short terms were coming under criticism, since it seemed unlikely that projects requiring sustained long-term attention could be carried through under such conditions.[49]

During these years, changes in selection practices altered the profiles of deputy and assistant deputy ministers. From 1967 to 1987 the presence of those with law degrees in this group fell from 22 to 13 per cent, while management and accounting graduates rose in numbers from 9 to 16 per cent and humanities and social sciences graduates rose from 4 to 11 per cent. There was also a decline in the level of academic achievement in this group: from 30 per cent possessing a PhD in 1967, the number fell to 16 per cent twenty years later, while those with no more than a bachelor's degree rose from 18 to 31 per cent. These two trends lead Barbara Carroll to speculate that in the wake of the stress on management in the Glassco, Lambert, and D'Avignon Reports, substantive technical expertise has been neglected in favour of a preference for generalists with managerial credentials. As she put it,

> The culture of the Canadian federal bureaucracy may have become: if
> you wish to get ahead in the Department of Agriculture it would seem
> advisable to forget your skills as an agronomist and obtain an MBA.[50]

Following his appointment as Clerk of the Privy Council in 1986, Paul Tellier took steps to increase the management component of the annual rating of deputy ministers. Since the early 1970s, deputy ministers have been evaluated by the Committee of Senior Officials (COSO), chaired by the Clerk of the Privy Council. In a period of budgetary restraint, the need for deputy ministers to respond to the policies of the central administration, in addition to being good managers of their departments, had become more pressing. Under Tellier, these ratings and the bonuses that they controlled were increasingly dependent upon conformity to the needs of central management. A typical statement was that of one member: "We want the members of COSO to think corporate, think government-wide instead of just the department."[51] The result is that deputies are evaluated on their "solidarity with the corporate authority" and then on their management of their department. According to Bourgault, Dion and Lemay this evaluation system has encouraged a common outlook, a "solidarity stamped with managerialism."[52]

Completing the measures to introduce a management philosophy in the federal administration was the creation in 1989 of the Canadian Centre for Management Development (CCMD), an innovation to which we return below.

OPERATIONAL DECENTRALIZATION: IMAA AND SOA'S

As we saw above, the Glassco Commission had recommended loosening the control of central agencies over operating departments and agencies. As a result, the post of Comptroller of the Treasury was abolished in 1969, and when a new post with the same name was created in 1977, it no longer had the function of prior approval of commitments and expenditures. In the field of recruitment and selection, the Public Service Commission used the powers given it in the Public Service Employment Act to delegate staffing powers to government departments. By 1981, almost all appointments (98 per cent) were made within departments, subject to audit by the commission.[53]

While the Lambert Commission recommended clarifying the powers and responsibilities of deputy ministers, the next step in this direction went beyond anything recommended by Lambert. This was the regime called Increased Ministerial Authority and Accountability (IMAA), introduced in 1986. The immediate source of inspiration was the chapter of the 1983 report of the Auditor General on the constraints to effective management in the federal public service.[54] Based on extensive interviews of senior public servants, the report identified excessive controls and procedural requirements as major impediments to better management. As a result, IMAA introduced an entirely new contractual basis of relations between the Treasury Board and departments of government.

There were two prongs to the new policy. First, the Treasury Board screened its policies and procedures in order to reduce the requirement for departments to seek authorization from the board. This has had dramatic effects, reducing the number of submissions from 5100 in 1983-84 to 2740 in 1988-1989. A decline has also occurred in the requests made by departments to the secretariat of the Treasury Board.

Second, contractual changes came through the negotiation and signing of Memoranda of Understanding (MOU's) between the Board and individual ministers and deputy ministers. These were package arrangements which delegated powers and responsibilities and established means of accounting for the use of them. Targets were set for departmental performance and operation for a three-year period. Deputy ministers made annual Management Reports that noted progress and problems encountered. The arrangement was given a major review at the end of the three-year period, when a new MOU was negotiated.

Before this programme was replaced by a business planning initiative in the mid-1990s, ten departments and agencies had signed MOUs. Donald Savoie gave a favourable evaluation of this regime, which sought to give managers more autonomy, while retaining final responsibility for financial management with the Treasury Board, but in the end, Aucoin argues that it failed for lack of government leadership.[55]

A further step toward decentralization was the introduction in the late 1980s of the concept of Special Operating Agencies (SOA's). This idea involved identifying activities with "low policy implications" that could be granted autonomous status within government departments.[56] In return for freedom from a number of central controls, these agencies were required to operate as businesses. To be chosen, units had to be wholly responsible for the delivery of a service to the public or to other government agencies, had to be able to have separate accounting from the parent department, to have a stable policy framework and a clear mandate.[57] The first units to be so designated were the Passport Office, Public Service Staff Training at the Public Service Commission, the Government Telecommunications Agency and Communications Services, and Consulting and Audit Canada, both in the Department of Supply and Services. As of April 1996, there were 16 SOA's, a very modest figure compared to the 91 Executive Agencies (covering about 60 per cent of the public service) in existence in Britain in 1993, and the 123 Centres de responsabilité in France in 1992.[58]

This idea, borrowed from the Swedish and British examples, carries the managerialist philosophy to a logical conclusion. While these units are not separate employers (the pay and classification systems still apply to them), they are close to mini public corporations within departments. They have a stronger contractual link to the Treasury Board and to their host department than most public corporations do, and their independence and performance are regularly reviewed. They represent a challenge to established ways of thinking, for they require that central agencies and ministers abstain from interfering in their internal operations. Moreover, they raise the spectre of privatization, since their very creation facilitates such a change. While this experiment has been met with enthusiasm by the interested parties, in a joint evaluation published in 1994 the Auditor General and the Treasury Board said that a condition of its extension would be "widespread acceptance of the very idea of SOA's" by all actors in the administrative system. According to Peter Aucoin, such acceptance requires the end of the resistance to separating control of policy and operations which has made innovations of this kind possible in Sweden, Britain, and New Zealand.[59]

THE CANADIAN CENTRE FOR MANAGEMENT DEVELOPMENT

The various themes developed in the previous sections reached their peak in the creation of the Canadian Centre for Management Development (CCMD) and Public Service 2000. Like every innovation, CCMD represented a judgement about the needs of the day and the inability of existing arrangements to completely satisfy them. To begin with, the D'Avignon Committee found that the higher levels of the federal administration only tolerated training and development without any profound understanding or commitment. It said the approach of the responsible agency, the Public Service Commission, was very limited and deplored that the Treasury Board had not taken a leading role in defining the employer's needs, goals and policy. It recommended that "training in personnel administration and human resource management be a prerequisite to appointment to a management position."[60]

The creation of the Management Category in 1980 provided the pool of candidates for management training. The experience of the PSC's Centre for Executive Development (CED) was considered invaluable in preparing the way for CCMD, but it was thought to be insufficient. In testimony before a Senate Committee, Jack Manion, the Deputy Clerk of the Privy Council and future principal of CCMD, said that the CED was too inward-looking and not professional enough. It had few experts in pedagogy and very few of its teaching personnel came from outside the public service. In its nine-year existence, the CED had produced little in the way of pedagogical material or research studies, for which there was an unmet need. Moreover, the government had looked at the methods for executive development in the United States, France and Britain, and it wanted a national school of administration of comparable rank.[61] Finally, the context of the 1980s gave a new urgency to management training and development. Cuts in budgets and personnel and the delegation of responsibilities under the IMAA regime increased the need for managers capable of increasing productivity and being held accountable for the results achieved.[62]

All of these considerations are present in the statement by Treasury Board President Don Mazankowski announcing the creation of CCMD:

> The Centre's principal purpose will be to enhance public sector management capacities and develop and promote a strong corporate culture in the Federal Public Service. Our vision is a credible, national, world-class centre of excellence in teaching and research into public sector management.[63]

Since its creation, CCMD fulfilled many of these ambitions: it has appointed outside staff, senior fellows such as Donald Savoie (University of New Brunswick) and Guy Peters (University of Pittsburgh), held annual seminars for university professors of public administration and management, funded academic research of immediate interest to the federal government, and overseen the preparation of a number of case studies.

Even so, CCMD believed that public servants learn best from each other. Its first "management model" was based on interviews with deputy ministers and the characteristics of successful federal agencies which had been published by the Auditor General of Canada in 1988.[64] As the Clerk of the Privy Council said in his preface to the document presenting the model:

> The centre's philosophy is to share the knowledge and skills of all members of the management category. In short CCMD's approach to learning is peer driven ...[65]

Such an attitude seems at once to reveal the centre's strategy and a major fact of the Canadian administrative culture. The strategy was based on principles of adult learning.[66] Knowing its clientele, the direction of the Centre presumably realized that experienced public servants are suspicious of academics and theories and much prefer to learn from each other and their peers elsewhere.[67] Extensive reliance on case studies was designed to draw on those resources already present in the senior ranks of the public service.

While CCMD was a key instrument in the policies generated in the 1980s to improve management skills of senior public servants and to increase their sense of belonging to a common culture, it fell victim to the downsizing movement of the 1990s. Its research programme has been judged to be too academic, and its courses have not always succeeded in attracting the best candidates. In 1997, it closed one of its two campuses, reducing its staff from 150 to about 70 and contracting out for most of its programmes to the private sector.[68] Whether the Centre will be able to do better under these conditions remains to be seen.

3 · Public Service 2000: Apotheosis of the Canadian Public Management Movement

Very shortly following the creation of CCMD, Prime Minister Mulroney announced the creation of the Public Service 2000 studies to prepare the necessary changes to allow the public service to meet the challenges of the end of the century. The operation was very condensed: announced in December 1989, its ten working groups had reported by the summer of 1990, and the subsequent White Paper was published in December, 1990.[69]

While the report seems to have been commissioned in order to restore or repair relations between the government and the public service,[70] what concerns us is what it reveals about the culture of the senior levels of that service. This was an in-house operation. In contrast with the Glassco and Lambert Royal Commissions, and the D'Avignon and Nielsen Reports, the study teams and the overall operation were entirely staffed by public servants. As the manager of PS 2000, career administrator John Edwards put it, the operation was "unabashedly management driven." It mobilized approximately 80 deputy ministers and assistant deputy ministers, plus another 40 senior officials.[71]

The White Paper indicated clearly that the intention of the government and the senior officials who produced the report was to effect a change of organizational culture. It began with a statement of the "simple and unchanging" values of the public service which we reproduced in Table 3.1. However, changes in the world economy, Canadian society, technology, and public attitudes and expectations, combined with the now chronic problem of increasing public debt and the impact of the Charter of Rights and Freedoms, imposed changes in the priority of different values and in their achievement.

These new values, as we saw in Table 5.1 were: 1) improved service to the public; 2) innovation; 3) empowerment of employees; 4) improved management of people; and 5) increased accountability. All of these were to be achieved within an environment of severe restraint, rising expectations and rapid change.

The government was conscious that it wanted a true shift in priorities:

The Government wants to create a client-oriented Public Service, a major change since the Public Service has not been used to regarding Canadians as clients. Rather, it has seen itself principally as an institution of government performing necessary tasks as specified from time to time by the Government of the day.[72]

A first step in this process was to require that each department develop a mission statement.

In the renewal process, the overall change of culture had to begin with top management. It was the intention to "shift the balance away from centralized control that is motivated by the desire to be 'error free,' towards risk-taking and innovation aimed at doing a better job."[73] A year later, the Clerk of the Privy Council (under the Public Service Reform Act of 1992 designated as head of the Public Service of Canada) wrote that the old "command and control" model was not dead, but that it was being rapidly replaced by a new culture that put people first and which operated more by consultation than by unilateral command.[74]

As in the case of many reforms, the idea was to innovate while claiming not to abandon any traditional values. However, if we look at the ten reports prepared by PS 2000 task forces, a different picture emerges. In Table 5.2, we present a rough count of the values present in the reports. In the upper part of the table, a number of traditional values receive scant support: merit, pride, loyalty, neutrality, honesty, and integrity. Some are viewed in a negative light: tradition and prudence give way to leadership and innovation. Values that are given heavy emphasis in virtually all reports are justice and equity, efficiency, effectiveness, and service. Almost as important are accountability, communication, and participation.

Thus the government White Paper gives more weight, in its introduction, to traditional values than do the task force reports. These latter, however, show keen awareness of potential conflicts. Two reports in particular draw attention to them. The report on Administrative Policy and the Role of Common Service Agencies notes a conflict between the values of prudence, economy and probity and that of giving priority of service to the clientele.[75] The report on Staffing found many possible conflicts, for example, between the values of equity and service, between managerial discretion and the values of openness and justice.[76] In both cases, the recommendation was to find the optimum equilibrium among these competing values. For its part, the report on Workforce Adaptiveness recommended abandoning the standards of objectivity and neutrality. Its authors argued that adaptive public organizations respect traditions and rules, but know when and how to adapt them.[77]

TABLE 5.2: PRESENCE OF TRADITIONAL AND NEW PUBLIC MANAGEMENT VALUES IN THE TEN PS 2000 REPORTS

Value	Merit	Service to the public	Common Services	Budgetary Control	Labour Relations	Workforce Adaptation	Pay and Benefits	Classification of prof. groups	Staffing	Management Category	Training & Development
Competence		■■	■■			■	■■		■■	■	■
Professionalism		■		■		■■	■		■■	■	■
Tradition		(-)				(-)				■	
Pride, honour		■				■■					
Neutrality		■■	■	■		(-)		■	■■		
Uniformity/ national objectives		■■	■				(-)				
Loyalty, fidelity		■	■			■			■		
Honesty/integrity		■	■■			■			■		
Prudence		■ (-)	■ (-)								
Justice/equity		■■■	■■		■	■	■■	■■	■■■	■■	■■
Accountab/responsab.		■■■	■■	■■	■			■■	■■	■■	■■
Efficiency, productivity		■■	■■	■■	■	■	■	■■	■■	■■	
Economy		■	■■				■			■	

Key: ■ = one mention; ■■ = two to four mentions; ■■■ = five or more mentions

Effectiveness

Service

Quality

Representativity

Excellence

Communication

Participation/
consultation

Openness

Transparence

Trust, confidence

Appreciation,
recognition

Creativity, innovation

Team-building

Leadership

Commitment, passion

Persistence, determination

(-) = negative mention

Two major conclusions may be drawn about the kind of administrative culture proposed by the authors of the PS 2000 reports. First, while new managerial values are put forward to challenge traditional values, the new values include some that are found chiefly in the public sector: justice and equity, accountability, and representativeness.

Second, this is a humanistic version of public management. Of the four management principles outlined in the PS 2000 White Paper, the one concerning people begins with the affirmation that "The members of the Public Service will be treated as its most important resource."[78] In the same vein, the Auditor General's report on "Well-performing Organizations" attests that public servants should be encouraged and supported, motivated by managers and by a clear understanding of their mission, and evaluated on the results they achieved. Perhaps it is understandable that senior managers would place high importance on their personnel, but not all public management thinking follows this humanistic trend. Pollitt has shown that the Thatcher and Reagan approaches to public management were mainly concerned with downsizing, cutting budgets, and holding public servants to account.[79] As a general rule, the version of the new public management that draws from Public Choice Theory has little regard for employee motivations other than personal gain and advancement.[80] As we saw in Table 5.1, the need to reduce costs, while acknowledged in PS 2000, was not a major theme as it was in Britain and the US. Table 5.2 indicates also that although efficiency was one of the most consistently important values present in the Task Force reports, economy is only mentioned in four reports, and not often.

What does the PS 2000 exercise reveal about the existing administrative culture? The senior cadres of the public service appear to have evolved a long way from the attitudes of the 1970s, when policy development was the main concern. They have embraced the ideas of service, innovation, and accountability. They profess to have adopted a new "guide and encourage" rather than "direct and control" approach to management. In some cases this idealism became very strong indeed:

> Once alignment (of values) is achieved, managers are freed from command-and-control type responsibilities. Employees know precisely what they are working toward…and understand generally what will help the organization achieve its goals and what is tangential and counterproductive.[81]

In periods of fiscal restraint, it seems unlikely that this kind of atmosphere is attainable, but we will return to this point in our conclusion.

The PS 2000 operation reveals a managerial culture that, for all its intentions to include employees in every kind of decision respecting their work, began by excluding them from the process. While the head of the operation, John Edwards, later said that "ideally all stakeholders" should participate in such an operation, those responsible for PS 2000 appear to have felt that employee associations would treat the occasion to try to improve the lot of their members, so that it would be another arena for collective bargaining.[82] If, as he says, the Professional Institute of the Public Service demanded the withdrawal of the report on staffing after it had been made public as a condition of participation in consultations, then the perception of Mr. Edwards and his colleagues was probably right.

The follow-up to PS 2000 gave institutional support to the ideas of a more flexible and decentralized management. Although it represented only about 10 per cent of the reforms undertaken, the *Public Service Reform Act* of 1992 is important because changes to the legislative framework are infrequent and of service-wide impact. While reaffirming the role of the Public Service Commission in recruitment, promotions, appeals, auditing, and training, the act introduced three major changes in the staffing of the public service.[83] First, the Commission may now determine cases where merit is measured against a standard of competence rather than competitively against the competence of other candidates. Second, standards of selection are to consider "the nature of the duties to be performed and the present and future needs of the Public Service" (such an extension to future needs had been recommended by the D'Avignon Report in 1979). Third, within the limits of the classification of professional groups, deputy ministers now have the authority to deploy new or existing personnel as they see fit. All of these measures increase the flexibility of personnel management. In return, employees obtain the right to appeal a deployment that they consider illegal or an abuse of power. Henceforth, the probationary period will apply to the initial appointment only, a move that increases security in a classification system which requires people to change jobs often.

Other non-legislative changes will alter the culture of the public service. Operating budgets have integrated the budgets for personnel, operations, and capital of each programme, thus increasing the authority of deputy ministers to use financial resources where needed. The number of layers of managers below the deputy level was reduced in most departments, with the aim of shortening the communications distance from the front-line to the top. Almost all departments have adopted mission statements and service standards that measure how well an organization's primary mission is being fulfilled. Departments are being actively encouraged to consult their organized client groups and to survey the others. A number of these surveys show high degrees of client satisfaction with the service received.[84] This finding raises a curious fact of Canadian and other political cultures: high satisfaction of citizens with services received or contacts with the bureaucracy does not seem to affect the generally negative impression that people have of the state and its administration.[85]

4 · Restructuring and Programme Review

The lack of emphasis on savings and the prominent place given to accountability in Public Service 2000 seem to reflect particularly Canadian characteristics within the New Public Management movement. It was not that the government was indifferent to cost cutting; quite the contrary. The Progressive Conservative government of Brian Mulroney (1984-1993) had given a high priority to deficit reduction and had some modest success, due as much to increases in revenues as to cuts in spending.[86]

Although the Mulroney government announced that it would review all programmes to test their merits, in the end the reports of the 1985-86 Task Force under the direction of Deputy Prime Minister Eric Nielsen were not applied in a vigorous manner. The government chose, instead, to cut generally across the board.[87]

When the Liberal Government of Jean Chrétien took power in the autumn of 1993, it decided to launch a review of all existing programmes in order to arrive at an analysis of needs and possibilities. While this operation was very much in tune with the doctrines of public management, it had none of the rhetorical development of PS 2000. Instead, it was largely carried out between departments and agencies on the one hand and central agencies and ministers on the other.[88] For each programme, officials were to answer six questions: 1) Do the programme areas continue to serve a public interest? 2) Is a government role still necessary? 3) Could it be delivered better? 4) Could the program be better administered by the provinces? 5) Could it be privatized? And 6) can the government still afford it?

Part of this operation was concerned with the government's announced intention to cut the public service by 45,000 persons from its size of about 220,000. Following Brian Mulroney as Prime Minister in 1993, Kim Campbell had carried out a dramatic reduction in the number of departments, from 32 to 23, and cut cabinet committees from 11 to 5.[89] The same restructuring cut 9 deputies' positions and 53 assistant deputy ministers (from 319 to 266), and reduced both policy and evaluation staffs in departments. After his election in 1993, Jean Chrétien's government continued this trend, cutting the size of cabinet by one portfolio, further reducing the number of cabinet committees to four, and abolishing the position of Chief of Staff in ministers' personal office staffs.[90] As a companion exercise to programme review, the Minister responsible for the renewal of the public service, Marcel Massé, undertook a review of autonomous boards and agencies and proceeded to recommend the elimination of many of them.[91]

5 · Canadian Administrative Culture in the Wake of New Public Management Reforms

Some aspects of contemporary Canadian administrative culture were discussed in the previous chapter. Here we wish to look at its various elements in light of roughly fifteen years of intensified management reform. If administrative reforms have any merit, there ought to be changes consequent upon new rules and practices[92] concerning the appointment and evaluation of deputy ministers, increased delegation of power to departments, increased autonomy for Special Operating Agencies, larger departments and delayering, the suspension of collective bargaining, and the attempt to shift to a client-centred culture.

In all of these matters, we have only partial answers, in which hard fact must be evaluated and extrapolated with care. Based on the figures presented in the previous section on "Creation of a management culture," it is clear that deputy ministers do not spend enough time in their departments to become established. Moreover, the emphasis on respecting the corporate culture during their evaluation by the coso has changed the dynamics of being a deputy. Apparently deputies have accepted the system, although they are more satisfied with their own evaluations than they are with the coso.[93]

While they are not so homogeneous a group as they were in the heyday of the Ottawa mandarins, the deputy ministers still demonstrate a common culture based on their education (all had bachelor's degrees, three-quarters had master's degrees in 1993, and three-quarters had studied in the social sciences and the humanities), their sense of belonging to the top administrative elite in Ottawa, a set of common tasks and constraints, and the determined efforts of Paul Tellier during his tenure as Clerk of the Privy Council Office from 1985 to 1992, to create a corporate culture.[94]

Interviews of the deputy ministers in office in the fall of 1993 showed that they had all made the shift from being mainly policy-oriented to being also management-oriented. While they approved of Paul Tellier's use of meetings and evaluations in the name of a common culture, they all had to live with a conflict between the need to cooperate with the centre and the need to protect their departments' interests (their "turf"). Some of them felt that there was too much stress on consensus. They were ambivalent about the many interdepartmental meetings they were required to attend. On the one hand they did not want to miss anything of importance, but on the other, they found many of them too long and unnecessary. Some made their resistance known by sending an assistant deputy minister or some other representative to meetings, but the others resented this because these delegates could not commit their departments without consulting the deputy.

The restructuring of 25 June 1993 undermined their cohesion. The firing of 9 deputies and 53 assistant deputy ministers came as a shock; the sudden nature of the reorganization shook their faith in the collegial system. The natural reaction was to concentrate on themselves and on their own departments.[95]

Almost everything separates the deputy ministers from the rank and file: manner of appointment, power, prestige, hours, and kind of work. Above all, whereas the middle and lower ranks have long been observed to accommodate well to working to rule, the deputies have a high tolerance for ambiguity.[96] As the first appointee to the post of Comptroller General, Harry Rogers, himself a transplant from the business world (Xerox Corporation), stated, "Government is infinitely complex"—much more so than business.[97] The Tait Task Force on Public Service values and Ethics referred to a "fault line" running through the public service, separating those at the highest levels from the others. The causes of this rupture are multiple: the feeling that senior managers do not practice what they preach, the sense of not participating in the decision-making process, and a tension between accountability to customers and to ministers and members of Parliament.[98]

Donald Savoie has commented on the two levels of culture observed by Zussman and Jabes at the highest level of the federal administration. As he points out, deputy ministers work very hard for much less than they could earn in the private sector; they see their immediate colleagues working hard also, and they have difficulty understanding why the public service has such low esteem with the public. Lower down the ladder, executives had less access to ministers, less faith that their deputies were "committed to the future of the organization."[99]

If Savoie's respondents are right, delayering should alleviate the problem of being too far from decision-making levels and the front line of operations, but nothing is being done about the short duration of deputies' appointments. As we saw above, the government has been acting as if it believed it is possible to have successful departmental management with a corps of managers trained in how the government operates and in management ideas, but scarcely familiar with the workings of their own departments.

In the wake of the restructuring of 1993 and the programme review introduced in 1994, the Association of Professional Executives of the Public Service of Canada (APEX) carried out extensive consultations with its 3600 members. 135 executives were consulted in the fall of 1994. Focus groups were held across the country, involving 228 participants with an additional 160 written contributions. The following points emerged as a consensus: the senior executives agreed that spending had to be cut, and they preferred an in-depth programme review to further across-the-board cuts. At the same time, they felt that they needed new skills to cope with the new demands on them. They wondered how to rebuild *esprit de corps* and to regenerate commitment. They noted that increased tension over loss of jobs had led to a dramatic increase in the number of harassment grievances, believing that some employees thought they would not be cut if their complaint was in process. They worried about the effects of programme review on service delivery and on morale.

The members of APEX consulted thought that their participation in the programme review had been minimal. They preferred a PS 2000 type of management and considered that programme review would be less stressful if they knew what the desired end product was. Above all:

> Executives wonder what will replace the "moral contract" that was deemed to exist in the past between the government and senior public servants, an understanding based on the concept of an exchange whereby executives provided loyalty, hard work and accepted somewhat uncompetitive salaries and benefits, in return for secure employment with reasonable career progression.[100]

The Tait Task Force on Public Service Values and Ethics found a widespread sense of betrayal both over the fact of downsizing and the way it was done. Many felt that they had been made scapegoats, their union rights were over-ruled by legislation, and the process was sometimes "punitive, secretive and capricious." There was irony in the fact that this occurred so soon after PS2000 had declared that people were the most important resources of the public service.[101]

Disenchantment appears to increase as one moves down the hierarchy. The leadership of the Professional Institute of the Public Services (PIPS) and the Public Service Alliance of Canada (PSAC) have responded to wage freezes with anger and criticism of the government. The PSAC went on strike against wage restraint in the autumn of 1991, the first national public service strike in ten years.[102] It refused to cooperate with the programme review. On the other hand, Arthur Kroeger reported that many middle managers had contributed to the review beyond the hopes of Treasury Board. This was not surprising, he said, because middle managers know where the design defects are.[103] Both PIPS and PSAC challenged what they considered the abusive recourse to contracting out in the federal government when the Government Operations Committee of the House of

Commons held hearings on this subject in the fall of 1994.[104] PSAC worries about the "deskilling" of the public service that it fears will follow increasing recourse to contractual employees.[105]

Insecurity continues to affect the morale of the public service. Both the testimony of researchers and the attitude of the PS 2000 team indicate that the avoidance of risk-taking is a deep-seated trait.[106]

Departments continue to have strong cultures of their own, in which the rules may be seen as means to avoid central control and to satisfy some particular need. In their research on front-line employees (of all three levels of government in Canada), Carroll and Siegel found that the departments with the strongest cultures and sense of professionalism were those with a dominant technology and a shared education.[107] The will to defend existing departmental powers against their transfer or abolition would seem to be stronger than another long-standing element of the federal public service culture, elite accommodation. When the government created the Space Agency with the aim of having one coordinating agency to enter into a partnership with industry, the relevant departments (Communications, National Research Council, and Energy Mines and Resources) succeeded in keeping many powers that had been planned for transfer.[108]

All of this may be changing. In her survey of the EX group, Frances Taylor found survey respondents and focus group members reluctant to endorse advocacy actions such as "turf wars" and budget-maximizing. On the other hand, she found that loyalty to the other members of one's unit is strong. She also found a number of members of the EX group open to the idea of appointment-to-level and frequent rotation as ways of reducing departmental loyalty and of broadening horizons.[109]

The capacity for departmental resistance to central controls is one problem raised by the delegation of extensive powers in personnel administration. Among them are inflated job descriptions, restricted competitions, promotions disguised as reclassification, and rigged competitions.[110] In his report for 1984, the Auditor General worried about the gradual increase of promotions without competitions as a result of reclassification: in 1983, they were 22.6 per cent of all promotions. In 1993-1994, this had risen to 46.5 per cent.[111]

Worst of all was the high degree of scepticism about internal recruitment competitions. In the mid 1980s, when Nicole Morgan asked fifty employees at random, three-quarters of them said that competitions were slanted. One employee claimed, just from reading a job description, to know the person for whom the competition had been prepared.[112] At the beginning of the 1990s, a survey of roughly 10 per cent of the public service found almost identical figures: 79 per cent of women and 75 per cent of men surveyed believed that a job offer was only posted after the future jobholder

THE NEW PUBLIC MANAGEMENT MOVEMENT COMES TO CANADA

had already been chosen.[113] This reaction lends support to the contention of former mandarin Al Johnson that one power that should not be delegated to departments is control over the merit system.[114] The Tait Task Force on Public Service Values and Ethics also stressed the dangers to the merit system, and thus to the non-partisan and impractical character of the public service if too much managerial discretion were allowed in this area.[115]

A combination of formal rules and actual practice occurred in the extension of closed competitions (those reserved to members of the public service) to include members of the military, the RCMP, and the Canadian Security and Intelligence Service. This "khaki parachute" was criticized by both the D'Avignon Committee and by the Task Force on Barriers to Women in the Public Service. It was only abolished by the Public Service Reform Act of 1992.[116]

All of this suggests a public service where the protection of those already in the system is a paramount value. Further evidence is given by the relatively few people fired for incompetency. In 1984, Nicole Morgan found that 0.7 per cent of the entire population of the public service had been fired. By 1991-92, only 0.17 per cent (less than 400 people) were let go in a public service of 223,598; it seems that either the public service has improved or managers are more indulgent.[117] At the same time, many observers have commented on the aging of the public service. The combined effects of massive recruiting in the 1970s and retrenchment (together with seniority) in the late 1980s has meant that the numbers of public servants under the age of thirty has declined from 26 per cent in 1980 to 8.1 per cent in 1997.[118]

Change has come to the public service however, even in these years of reduced hiring. As we saw previously, francophones have gone from 22.0 per cent of the public service in 1967 to 29.2 per cent in 1997, which is more than their presence in the population of Canada (23.3 per cent in 1991). More importantly, they have gone from 11.5 per cent of the executive category in 1967 to 25.4 per cent in 1997. While there has been a levelling out recently, these figures are widely regarded as having met the major goals of the Official Languages Act. What remains more problematic are the atmosphere of work and the real use of both languages.[119] The new act, adopted in 1988, specified that superiors must be able to communicate with subordinates in their language and that senior managers must be bilingual, goals that were approved by the Official Languages Commissioner.[120]

The presence of women in the public service has followed a somewhat similar path, but the efforts required and the stakes are greater. In the public service overall, women have passed from 21.5 per cent in 1967 to 50.0 per cent in 1997. Their progress has been more rapid at the level of the executive category: in 1967, there were 1.0 per cent of this group who were women; in 1997 the figure was 23.0 per cent. However, the results are still a very long way from proportional representation. Finally, an appropriate representation of visible minorities and native people is still a challenge before the government.

There is a cultural division between men and women in the public service at least as deep as there is between francophones and anglophones, and probably greater. In the survey done for the Working Group on the Obstacles Encountered by Women in the Public Service, two-thirds of the women respondents believed that a "glass ceiling" exists, which prevents women from reaching the highest levels. Men disagreed. The largest disagreement came at managerial levels: 79 per cent of women managers held this belief, while 62 per cent of the men at the same level did not believe in the glass ceiling. Women tended to believe that they had to be more competent than men to be promoted: 67 per cent overall, 79 per cent of women managers and 77 per cent of women in senior positions. Three-quarters of the men who responded disagreed with this idea, and 54 per cent strongly disagreed.

Also, 54 per cent of the men thought that women's positive action programs gave women an unfair advantage, with the proportions rising along with rank until 66 per cent of senior managers thought this way. A large majority of this latter group (59 per cent) thought that for the same reason women got promoted beyond the level of their competence, whereas 53 per cent of women did not think so. It seems to be a case of another kind of two solitudes. One brighter note was that approximately one-half of both women and men thought that men and women were treated equally in their own department. Apparently, it is elsewhere that unequal treatment is more prevalent.[121] Once again, departmental loyalty attenuates other judgements.

We should also consider the impression held by some politicians and journalists that the public service lives in tranquil comfort, little affected by recessions and financial crises.[122] If this is so, it is a good example of "goal displacement" as defined by Robert Merton: the rules and the advantages they bring become ends in themselves rather than the goals for which the bureaucracy was created.[123]

These are among the reasons for introducing the New Public Management philosophy into the Canadian government. The question remains as to how compatible this philosophy is with traditional public service values. It is to this subject that we turn in the last chapter.

Notes

1 Alfred D. Chandler Jr., *The Visible Hand: The Managerial Revolution in American Business* (Cambridge Mass.: Harvard University Press, 1977).

2 A.A. Berle and Gardner Means, *The Modern Corporation and Private Property* (New York: Macmillan, 1934); and John Kenneth Galbraith, *The New Industrial State* (Boston: Houghton-Mifflin, 1967).

3 Wilson 201.

4 Robert B. Denhardt, *The Pursuit of Significance* (Belmont CA: Wadsworth, 1993) 8.

5 Wilson 493.

6 Hood, "A Public Management for All Seasons," *Public Administration* 69 (1991): 3, calls it a doctrine, while it is mentioned as an ideology by Christopher Pollitt, *Managerialism and the Public Service: the Anglo-American Experience* (Cambridge Mass.: Basil Blackwell, 1990) 6-10, and Gow, *Learning From Others* 133.

7 Timothy W, Plumptre, *Beyond the Bottom Line, Management in Government* (Halifax: Institute for Research on Public Policy, 1988) 37. POSDCORB stood for planning, organizing staffing, coordinating, reporting, and budgeting. See Luther Gulick, "Notes on the Theory of Organization," *Papers on the Science of Administration*, ed. L. Gulick and L. Urwick (New York: Institute of Public Administration, 1937); repr. Hodgetts and Corbett 38-66.

8 Hood 3-4.

9 Peter Drucker, *The Practice of Management* (New York: Harper Bros, 1954) 12.

10 H.A. Simon, D.W. Smithburg and V.A. Thompson, *Public Administration* (New York: Knopf, 1961) 3.

11 E. Sam Overman, "Public Management, What's New and Different?," *Public Administration Review* 44:3 (1984): 285.

12 J. Chevallier and D. Loschak, "Rationalité juridique et rationalité managériale dans l'administration française," *Revue française d'administration publique* 24 (1982): 679-680 (trans. Dwivedi and Gow). This definition is taken up with approval by Adrien Payette, "Eléments pour une conception du management public," *Management public: Comprendre et gérer les institutions de l'Etat*, ed. R. Parenteau (Sillery: Les Presses de l'Université du Québec, 1992) 6. It is also close to that given by André Gagné in *Le management des affaires publiques*, ed. Alphonse Riverin (Chicoutimi: Gaëtan Morin, 1984) 7: "By management we mean the search for the best possible use of resources, taking into account constraints, risks and uncertainties, to attain goals and objectives" (trans. Dwivedi and Gow).

13 The mandate of the Royal Commission on Financial Management and Accountability is given in Order-in-Council PC 1976-2284, of 24 December 1976, and published on page v of the commission's final report.

14 Paul M. Tellier, "The renewal of the Public Service," J.J. Carson Lecture, Faculty of Administration, University of Ottawa, 8 March 1990: 7.

15 Denhardt 6-9.

16 Hood 11.

17 Hood 15.

18 Jeanne Siwek-Pouydesseau, "La critique idéologique du management en France," *Revue française de science politique* 19:5 (1974): 966-93; and Reginald Whitaker, "Scientific Management Theory as Political Ideology," *Studies in Political Economy* 2 (1979): 75-108.

19 Virginia H. Ingersoll and Guy B. Adams, "Beyond Organization Boundaries: Exploring the Managerial Myth," *Administration and Society* 18 (1986): 365.

20 Hodgetts, "Implicit values" 35-36; Gilbert Larochelle, *L'imaginaire technocratique* (Montréal: Boréal, 1990) 164-70, 215; Dwight Waldo, *The Enterprise of Public Administration* (Novato CA: Chandler and Sharp, 1980) ch.5; and Kernaghan and Siegel 294-302.

21 Douglas Hartle, "The Report of the Royal Commission on Financial Management and Accountability (the Lambert Report): A Review," *Canadian Public Policy* 3 (1979): 366-81; and Stephen Elkin, "Toward a Contextual Theory of Innovation," *Policy Sciences* 16 (1983): 367-87.

22 Hood 4, 9; Chevallier and Loschak 715-16; Peter Aucoin, "Administrative Reform in Public Management: Paradigms, Paradoxes and Pendulums," *Governance* 3:2 (1990): 115-37.

23 For another summary, see Sandford Borins, *Government in Transition: A New Paradigm in Public Administration*, Report on the Inaugural Conference of the Commonwealth Association for Public Administration and Management (Toronto: CAPAM, 1994).

24 V. Seymour Wilson and O.P. Dwivedi, "Plus Ça Change, Plus C'est La Même Chose," *Public Administration in Canada: State of the Discipline and Profession*, ed. Morton R. Davies, John Greenwood, Lynton Robins and Nick Walkley (Aldershot, UK: Ashgate Publishing, 1998) 94.

25 Plumptre 409-27.

26 D.C. Rowat, "Canada's Royal Commission on Government Organization," *Public Administration* 41 (1963): 197.

27 Canada, *Act Amending the Financial Administration Act*, 14-15-67 Eliz. II (1967) ch. 74. As A.W. Johnson put it, as a result of this law, the Treasury Board had become "the Cabinet's Committee on the Expenditure Budget and the Cabinet's Committee on Management." A.W. Johnson, "The Treasury Board of Canada and the Machinery of Government of the 1970s," *Canadian Journal of Political Science* IV:3 (1971): 347.

28 17-18 Eliz. II (1968/69) ch.28.

29 T. H. McLeod, "The Glassco Commission Report," *Canadian Public Administration* 6:4 (1963): 400-03.

30 *Glassco Report*, vol.1: 25. For a critical appraisal of this point of view, see M.G. Taylor, "The Glassco Report: a Panel Discussion," *Canadian Public Administration* 4 (1962): 395-98. The same point is made by McLeod.

31 The phrase was not in the report, but became a slogan drawn from its conclusions. See O.P. Dwivedi, "On Holding Public Servants Accountable" 152.

32 *Glassco Report*, vol.1: 63, 25.

33 Donald Gow, *The Process of Budgetary Reform in the Government of Canada* (Ottawa: Economic Council of Canada, 1974); Gow, *Learning From Others* (case no.1) 145-148.

34 Ivo Krupka has commented, on an earlier version of this study, that none of the senior mandarins introducing PPBS into Canada thought that they were enacting a revolution. It is not necessary for them to have been aware of it for our point of view to be valid.

35 Treasury Board of Canada, *Benefit-Cost Analysis Guide* (Ottawa: Supply and Services, 1976) 3.

36 Gow, *Learning From Others* 194-99.

37 R.V. Segsworth, "Downsizing and Program Evaluation: An Assessment of the Experience in the Government of Canada," Bernier and Gow 249-59; and Senate of Canada, *The Program Evaluation System in the Government of Canada* (Ottawa: Report of the Standing Committee on National Finance, 1991).

38 *Lambert Report.*

39 Canada, *Report of the Special Committee on the Review of Personnel Management and the Merit Principle* (D'Avignon Committee), (Ottawa, Supply and Services, 1979). Hereafter cited as the *D'Avignon Report.*

40 *Lambert Report*, Appendix B, questions B-19 and B-20.

41 Plumptre 82-84; and Gow, *Learning From Others* 36. However, Seymour Isenberg found that senior federal executives gave almost as much importance to general management experience as to intellectual qualifications for their jobs; see his, "Profile of the Management Environment in the Federal Public Service," *Optimum* 10:1 (1979): 13.

42 The Glassco Commission's *Report* on the Organization of the Government of Canada, vol.1 (Ottawa, 1962) 278, noted that training and development had been too long neglected in the federal public service. In a memo prepared for the Glassco Commission, it was written that "Government has neither sought, developed nor paid for good administrators." Cited by Sylvia Nadon, *Emergence de l'administration publique comme spécialité: l'apport des universités canadiennes*, diss., Université de Montréal, 1996; and D.A. Worton, *The Dominion Bureau of Statistics* (Montreal: McGill-Queen's University Press and Institute of Public Administration of Canada, 1988) 270.

43 *D'Avignon Report* 42-54.

44 Treasury Board News Release 80/34 of 10 July 1980 cites the two reports as well as the previous report on collective bargaining in the public service by Jacob Finkelman (1974), a recommendation of the Public Service Commission to the D'Avignon Committee and the position of the Auditor General of Canada.

45 Treasury Board News Release 80/34; H.L. Laframboise, "Overview of the New Management Category," *IPAC Bulletin*, 5:2 (1981) 8; and Treasury Board of Canada and Public Service Commission, *The New Management Category: Its Meaning for You* (Ottawa, 1980).

46 Public Service Commission, "The New Management Category," *Annual Report* (1980) 9. The report recalled that a survey done for the Lambert Commission had found "wide support" among deputy ministers for appointment-to-level.

47 Former career diplomat D'Iberville Fortier told a group of students at the Université de Montréal, in March 1993, that belonging to the Management Category had dramatically changed the perspective of senior members of the Department of External Affairs. Where they had previously identified with the diplomatic corps, they were now drawn into a broader relationship, which placed some of their loyalty outside the department.

48 Jacques Bourgault, Stéphane Dion and Jacques Lemay, "Creating a Corporate Culture: Lessons from the Canadian Federal Government," *Public Administration Review* 53:1 (1993):75.

49 For such criticism, see Jacques Bourgault and Stéphane Dion, "Governments Come and Go, But What of Senior Civil Servants?," *Governance* 2:2 (1989): 29-30; Osbaldeston 146-47: *Lambert Report* ch. 10 and recommendation 10.1; and B. Carroll, "The Structure of the Canadian Bureaucratic Elite: Some Evidence of Change," *Canadian Public Administration* 34:2 (1991): 369.

50 Carroll 371.

51 Bourgault, Dion and Lemay 75.

52 Bourgault, Dion and Lemay 79.

53 Public Service Commission of Canada, "The Story of Staffing Delegation 1967/1981," *Annual Report* (1981) 1-2.

54 Auditor General of Canada, *Report for the Year Ending 31 March 1983* (Ottawa: Supply and Services, 1983) ch.2. The debt to this report is recognized in Treasury Board of Canada, *Increased Ministerial Authority and Accountability* (January, 1988) 3.

55 Savoie, *The Politics of Public Spending* 117-120; and Peter Aucoin, *the New Public Management: Canada in Comparative Perspective* (Montreal: Institute for Research on Public Policy, 1995) 128.

56 Ian D. Clark, "Treasury Board Today and Tomorrow," Annual Seminar for University Faculty, Canadian Centre for Management Development, Touraine, Quebec 22 February 1990.

57 David Roth, "Special Operating Agencies in the Canadian Government," Annual Conference of the Institute of Public Administration of Canada, Halifax, 26 August 1991.

58 Denis St-Martin, *Institutional Analysis of Recent Machinery-of-Government Reforms in Australia, Britain, France, and New Zealand* (Ottawa: Consulting and Audit Canada, 1993) 13 and 16. St-Martin notes that the French centres are not as business oriented as Canadian and British agencies.

59 Aucoin, *The New Public Management* 146-47. The study cited by Aucoin is by the Steering Group on Special Operating Agencies, *Special Operating Agencies: Taking Stock. Final Report* (Ottawa, 1994).

60 *Report of the Special Committee* 210-211, 220.

61 Comité sénatorial permanent des finances nationales, procès-verbal, 29 septembre 28, 1988: 19, 8.

62 Public Service Commission, "The Canadian Centre for Management Development," *Dialogue* 13:3 (1988): 3-4.

63 Don Mazankowski, "A new commitment to public sector management," Public Policy Forum, Toronto, 14 April 1988: 6.

64 "Attributes of Well-Performing Organizations," *Report of the Auditor General of Canada for the Fiscal Year Ending 31 March 1988* (Ottawa: Supply and Services, 1989).

65 Paul M. Tellier, "Preface," *A Management Model*, ed. John L. Manion (Ottawa: CCMD, Supply and Services, 1989).

66 Sandford Borins, "The Advanced Management Program: a Design Framework" (Ottawa: CCMD, 1989) 8-9.

67 This is a major finding of Gow, *Learning From Others*, especially in chapter 2.

68 "Federal School For Executives Faces Major Cuts," *The Ottawa Citizen 19* December 1996: A4.

69 Government of Canada, *Public Service 2000: The Renewal of the Public Service of Canada* (Ottawa: Supply and Services, 1990).

70 John Manion attributes the creation of PS 2000 to three sources: the work undertaken by the Committee of Senior Officials after the first studies by David Zussman and Jak Jabes showed how low morale was in the public service; further studies by CCMD and by the Public Policy Forum, a private sector group aimed at promoting a quality public service; and pressure from the Auditor General to offer a better service to the public and to the government. See Manion, "Career Public Service in Canada: Reflections and Predictions," *International Review of Administrative Sciences* 57:3 (1991): 361-71.

71 The quote from John Edwards is from a speech to the 1990 Apex symposium, cited in Robert J. McIntosh, "Public Service 2000: the Employee Perspective," *Canadian Public Administration* 34:3 (1991): 505. Also, John Edwards, "Public Service 2000: A Retrospective and a Look Ahead," Annual Conference of the Institute of Public Administration of Canada, Halifax, 27 August 1991.

72 *Public Service 2000* (emphasis in original).

73 *Public Service 2000* 103.

74 Paul M. Tellier, *First Annual Report to the Prime Minister on the Public Service of Canada* (Ottawa: Supply and Services, 1992) 11.

75 *Rapport du Groupe de travail sur les politiques administratives et le rôle des organismes de services communs* (Ottawa, 1990) 13, 17, 23.

76 *Rapport du groupe de travail sur la dotation* (Ottawa, 1990) 10, 14-15.

77 *Rapport du groupe de travail sur l'adaptation de la main-d'oeuvre* (Ottawa, 1990) 5, 8.

78 *The Renewal of the Public Service of Canada* 47. The other principles are service, innovation, and accountability.

79 Pollitt 134, calls their approach "neo-Taylorism."

80 For a survey of this literature, see André Blais and Stéphane Dion, eds, *The Budget-Maximising Bureaucrat: Appraisal and Evidence* (Pittsburgh: University of Pittsburgh Press, 1991).

81 Donald Hall and Timothy Plumptre, *New Perspectives on Training*, Report Prepared for the Training and Development Task Force, PS 2000 (Ottawa, 1991) 13.

82 J. Edwards, "A Retrospective and a Look Ahead" and "Response to the McIntosh critique of PS 2000," *Canadian Public Administration* 35:2 (1992): 258-59.

83. Statutes of Canada (1992) c. 54, sections 10, 11, 34.

84 Tellier, *Public Service 2000: A Report on Progress* 23.

85 For a previous Canadian study, see David Zussman, "The Image of the Public Service of Canada," *Canadian Public Administration* 25:1 (1982): 63-80. Also Charles T. Goodsell, *The Case for Bureaucracy*, 2nd ed. (Chatham NJ: Chatham House, 1985).

86 Michael J. Prince, "Canada's Public Finances Under Restraint: Has Ottawa Shrunk?," Bernier and Gow 25-32.

87 V.S. Wilson, "What Legacy? The Nielsen Task Force Review," *How Ottawa Spends 1988-89*, ed. Katherine A. Graham (Ottawa: Carleton University Press, 1988) 23-47; and Savoie, *The Politics of Public Spending* 136-38.

88 Amelita Armit and Jacques Bourgault, eds., *Hard Choices or No Choices: Assessing Program Review* (Toronto: Institute of Public Administration of Canada and Canadian Plains Research Centre, 1996), especially the chapters by Arthur Kroeger, "Changing Course, the Federal Government's Program Review of 1994-95" 21-28; and Mohammed Charih, "La révision des programmes fédéraux, un examen du processus" 29-37.

89 Aucoin, *The New Public Management* 120.

90 Aucoin, *The New Public Management* 53, 120.

91 A press communiqué of 16 February 1995 from the Minister Responsible for Public Service Renewal gave the result of this review as the elimination of 73 agencies, boards, and councils, and the restructuring and rationalization of 47 others.

92 Neo-institutionalist theory is based on just such an assumption. See James G. March and Johan P. Olsen, *Rediscovering Institutions: The Organizational Basis of Politics* (New York: Free Press, 1989); and Lynne G. Zucker, "Institutional theories of Organization," *American Sociological Review* 13 (1987): 443-64.

93 Jacques Bourgault and Stéphane Dion, *How Should the Performance of Senior Officials be Appraised? The Response from Federal Deputy Ministers* (Ottawa: CCMD, 1993). Sixteen out of 21 deputies were consistently satisfied with their appraisals, but only 12 were satisfied with the COSO.

94 Johann Gauthier, *La culture organisationnelle des sous-ministres canadiens*, MSc thesis, Université de Montréal, 1996; and Bourgault, Dion and Lemay 73-80.

95 Gauthier 88-89.

96 Osbaldeston 50, 106; and J. Bourgault and S. Dion, "Canadian Senior Civil Servants and Transitions of Government: the Whitehall Model as Seen From Ottawa," *International Review of Administrative Sciences* 56 (1990): 163-164.

97 Joan Cohen, "Ottawa's Managerial Revolution," *Report* magazine (June 1979): 12-13.

98 Government of Canada, *A Strong Foundation: Report of the Task Force on Public Service Values and Ethics: A Summary* (Ottawa: Privy Council Office, February 1997): 13-14.

99 Savoie, *The Politics of Public Spending* 234.

100 Association of Professional Executives in the Public Service, *APEX National Consultations* (Ottawa: APEX, 1 February 1995).

101 Tait Task Force, *Discussion Paper* 21-22. This opinion was confirmed by Ruth Hubbard, President of the Public Service Commission of Canada, "People: Hearts and Minds — Towards a Rebirth of the Public Service Ethic," *Public Administration and Development* 17:1 (1997): 110.

102 Tellier, *First Annual Report* 10.

103 Kroeger, "Changing Course" 23. Frances Taylor also found openness to change in her study of APEX members (see note 109).

104 J.I. Gow, "Managing All Those Contracts: Beyond Current Capacity?," *New Public Management and New Public Administration in Canada*, ed. M. Charih and A. Daniels (Toronto: IPAC and L'Ecole nationale d'administration publique, 1997) 235-61.

105 John Bagelow of PSAC in a panel on "The End of Staffing As We Know It," APEX Annual Conference, Ottawa, 5 June 1996.

106 Savoie, *The Politics of Public Spending* 240; and *Public Service 2000* 20: "Conformity tends to ... become an end in itself."

107 Barbara W. Carroll and David Siegel, *Service in the Field: The World of Front-Line Public Servants* (Montreal and Kingston: McGill-Queen's University Press and IPAC, 1999) 206.

108 William Coleman and Michael Atkinson, "Obstacles to Organization Change: the Creation of the Canadian Space Agency," *Canadian Public Administration* 36:2 (1993): 139-42.

109 Frances Taylor, *Behaviourial Traits of Federal Public Executives*, Summer project, Faculty of Business Administration, University of Ottawa, 1995: 8, 20. This study was done with the collaboration of the Association of Professional Executives in the Public Service (APEX). It seems useful as a

general indication of EX attitudes, but a disappointing return rate and turnout for the focus groups mean that it is not a reliable statistical survey.

110 Nicole Morgan, *Implosion: analyse de la croissance de la fonction publique fédérale canadienne, 1945-1985* (Montreal: Institute for Research on Public Policy, 1986) 128-30. On page 129, Morgan cites the report of the Auditor General for 1982 to the effect that 60 per cent of public servants were sceptical about their job description.

111 *Rapport du vérificateur général du Canada pour l'année se terminant le 31 mars 1984* (Ottawa: Approvisionnements et Services, 1984) 8-10; Public Service Commission of Canada, *Annual Report 1993-94* (Ottawa: Supply and Services, 1994) 41.

112 *Annual Report 1993-94* 131. One of the authors was told the same thing by a division head thirty years earlier.

113 *Au-delà des apparences*, Rapport du groupe de travail sur les obstacles rencontrés par les femmes dans la fonction publique, vol. 1 (Ottawa: Approvisionnements et Services, 1990) 134-35.

114 A.W. Johnson, *Reflections on the Reform of the Federal Administration of Canada, 1962-1991* (Ottawa: Office of the Auditor General, 1992) 39.

115 Tait Task Force 30-31.

116 Kenneth Kernaghan, "Career Public Service 2000: Road to Renewal or Impractical Vision?," *Canadian Public Administration* 34:4 (1991): 566.

117 Morgan, *Implosion* 131; Public Service of Canada, *Annual Report Statistics*, 1992 (Ottawa: Supply and Services, 1993) 58. Actual figures were: for breach of conduct or misconduct, 61; for incompetence or incapacity, 53; for abandonment of position, 54; and rejected on probation, 221.

118 Nicole Morgan, *Nowhere To Go* (Montreal: Institute for Research on Public Policy, 1981) ch.1; Savoie, *The Politics of Public Spending* 239-40; Public Service Commission reports for 1980 (Table 9) and 1992 (Table 9).

119 The Official Language Commissioner has drawn attention to this problem in recent annual reports: for 1993: 52-6; for 1994: 32-5; and for 1996: 59. In this last case, preliminary results of a survey carried out by the Treasury Board found that 93 per cent of anglophones were satisfied with opportunities to work in the language of their choice, but only 79 per cent of francophones were similarly satisfied. Also Philippe Dubuisson, "Fonction publique fédérale: le français piétine," *La Presse* 25 March 1991: A1.

120 *Official Languages Act*, s.c. 1988, c. c-72, art. 36.c. See the synopsis of the new act in the Official Languages Commissioner's *Report* for 1988 (Ottawa: Supply and Services, 1989) 287-93.

121 *Au-delà des apparences* 58-59.

122 Catherine Leconte, "Le bilan désabusé de Claude Castonguay: Le monde douillet d'Ottawa est détaché de la vie réelle," *Le Devoir*, 14 December 1992; Patrick Doyle, "A lesson in belt-tightening," *Toronto Star*, 11 February 1990; Savoie, *The Politics of Public Spending* 211-16, 351-52.

123 Robert King Merton, "Bureaucratic Structure and Personality" 560-68; repr. Merton *et al.* 365. The counterpart of this immobility may be the longstanding lack of interest in the management of the public service shown by both ministers and parliament. See Kroeger, "Changing Course" 24 and Aucoin, *The New Public Management* 79.

SIX

Canadian Administrative Culture Between Past and Present

After summing up our findings on the culture of the federal administration of Canada, we will return to the evaluation of emerging public management culture in terms of both deontology and teleology. That is to say, having clarified what we think about the evolution of the culture of the Canadian administration, we will express a normative and ethical opinion on the emerging culture, and we will try to analyze the likely consequences of current values, symbols, and practices.

1 · The Findings of Our Study

In Chapter 1 we adopted a broad definition of administrative culture, drawn from the tradition of anthropology. Culture in this sense refers to the shared values and representations of the members of an organization, and not simply what top management believes or wants it to be. Beyond organization, we kept the idea of administrative culture to remind us that the federal administration is composed of many organizations, each with its own culture, even while they are part of the broader culture of the entire administration.

Canadian administrative culture was seen in Chapter 2 to have its sources in geography and climate, in religion, in the political culture, in economic values and practices, in the workplace, and in foreign examples. Its origins were found to be the British parliamentary system and federalism, but also, since World War I, the American science and practice of public administration. We saw in Chapter 3 that the foundations of the desired Canadian administrative culture lay in the great constitutional doctrines inherited from the United Kingdom: the rule of law, ministerial responsibility, civil service anonymity and neutrality, appointment by merit, and the employees' right to association and, eventually, to collective bargaining. The challenge to these values by the growth of the administrative state was seen in Chapter 4, and the introduction of practices drawn from the New Public Management movement as solutions to this challenge was considered in Chapter 5.

We recognized that the overall Canadian administrative culture included many sub-cultures. We found the locus of these to be that of the department or agency to which an employee belonged, their gender, and their language. In Table 6.1, we have summed up the common administrative culture of the federal government with reference to a fourth kind of division, that of rank. It seemed clear that distinctions should be made between the values, perceptions, and symbols which are important to deputy ministers, other senior officials, and the other public servants, who are for the most part unionized employees. There are further distinctions to be made among scientific and technical public servants, diplomats, administrative staff, clerical, and manual groups and region, but these are beyond the scope of this study.

In Table 6.1 we have summarized the principal values as the system desired them to be — how political and administrative actors were supposed to behave, according to the dominant ideas of the time. For roughly fifty years after the adoption of the Civil Service Act of 1918, Canada espoused a version of the Westminster Model which corresponded closely with the version of bureaucracy put forward by Max Weber. In this model, parliament was responsible for adopting the rules binding society, ministers were responsible for policy decisions of the government and overall supervision of their departments, and civil servants were responsible for the impartial and objective administration of public services, according to the rules laid down by the law and the Cabinet. The qualities of good public servants were first of all loyalty to the government and particularly to their minister, followed by efficient, discreet, and disciplined service.

During this fifty-year period — and beyond it — new values were added to the list without the basic model being challenged. The rise of discretionary powers and recourse to administrative regulation led to attempts to ensure the accountability of public servants. Administrative tribunals and procedural requirements came first, then employee appeals, access to information, and the Charter of Rights and Freedoms. These rules and institutions increased the rights of citizens and public servants against arbitrary, unjust, or illegal decisions taken by ministers and public servants. Recognition of the right to collective bargaining increased this trend with respect to employees, while programmes of employment equity introduced new values into the merit system.

When we looked at the values members of the three groups manifested over these years, we found that deputy ministers had evolved a set of values that allowed them to be both active and passive: active because they were

TABLE 6.1: RECAPITULATION OF THE EVOLUTION OF KEY VALUES IN ADMINISTRATIVE CULTURE OF CANADA

KEY VALUES AS DESIRED

Canadian Version of Whitehall Model (1918 – 1967)	Values Added by Amendment (1967 – 199—)	Public Management Model (1967 – 199—)
Ministerial responsibility	Public service accountability	Public service accountability
Supremacy of Parliament	Increase of administrative regulation	Public service entrepreneurship, innovation
Rule of Law	Charter of Rights and Freedoms (1982)	Results oriented
Obedience	Collective bargaining (1967)	Client oriented
Discipline	Rights of appeal	
Merit	Employment equity	Personnel oriented Flexible merit
Secrecy	Access to information	Partnerships
Political neutrality	Ban on political activity unconstitutional	
Seniority	Job security	Excellence

KEY VALUES AS OBSERVED

Deputy Ministers

Active-passive personality	Greater autonomy, but still active-passive
Tolerance for ambiguity	Increasing list of values to respect
Policy orientation	Management orientation
Specialists of sector or department	Corporate culture
Elite accommodation	Elite accommodation/partnerships

Deputies and Senior Officals

Moderation and caution	Risk-taking encouraged
Pro-department	Departmental autonomy reinforced
Public interest	Market testing
Intrinsic rewards (appreciation and power)	Demoralization
Emulation of colleagues in other Canadian and US governments	Emulation widened to OECD governments

Others

Security	Security
Moderation	Moderation
Seniority, defense of acquired rights	Defense of status quo
Little concern for outsiders	Women and minority groups progress
	Little concern for youth

expected to anticipate ministers' needs, to bring forward policy proposals for ministers' consideration and run their departments efficiently; passive because they had ultimately to defer to their political masters. There was no sense that deputies were more than "servants of the Crown." As a result, deputy ministers were seen to favour policy development over management and to have a high tolerance for ambiguity, since the multiple values that they were to respect were frequently contradictory. Deputies and other senior public servants evidently believed in consensual arrangements with elite groups in society rather than relations of strict regulation.

At the level of senior officials, a similar mixture of moderation and caution was observed. While public servants believed in serving the public interest, they tended to put departmental interest first. High flyers understood that it was useful to get into the circuit of central agencies, that is the Privy Council Office, the Treasury Board, the Department of Finance, the Public Service Commission, and possibly the Bank of Canada and the Department of External Affairs, but while on the staff of a department, they saw it as their duty to protect its interests against incursions from ministers, members of Parliament, central agencies, pressure groups, or other departments and agencies.

These senior officials were hard-working and competent. Several surveys, chief among them that of Zussman and Jabes, found that they were more likely than their counterparts in private industry to value such intrinsic rewards as participation in key decisions and public appreciation of their service. They were much more likely to be influenced by their colleagues in other governments than by theoreticians. Intensely practical people, they preferred evidence of feasibility to claims of new wonder cures. They have been demoralized by financial cutbacks and institutional restructuring to the point that they worry about both the capacity of their organizations to deliver necessary public services and the "moral contract" upon which their careers were based. Asked to be faithful servants of the government of the day while earning less than they would in the private sector, they wonder what reward system will be found to replace the job and career security that had been part of this contract.

At the level of professional and other public servants, we found that the goal of security was paramount. This long-standing value had at its source in part the fear of losing one's position after a change of government, but there is evidence that many candidates for the public service were already seeking security before their entry into it, and that they were attracted by regular hours and social benefits, most notably, pensions. As we said in Chapter 3, it was also alleged that the presence of large numbers of veterans in the public service contributed to a passive attitude towards the hierarchy and a reluctance to support full-scale unionism. Over time, the preference for security led to stress being laid on seniority and the defense of acquired rights, but it did not lead to any special sympathy for those who thought themselves excluded by the system and who wanted employment equity programmes. Those public servants who had input into the policy system seemed to be moderate in their opinions. They were not all timid bureaucrats, however. A study done for the Royal Commission on Bilingualism and Biculturalism found that, compared to the American government, the Canadian public service had a higher rate of people entering the public service at every level, and of "in-and-outers," people who had successive employment in the public and private sectors.[1]

While the key values espoused by the Canadian administration evolved on a piecemeal basis without affecting the basic pattern, in the early 1960s the challenging paradigm of Public Management began to emerge. While reforms have been undertaken in the name of better management at least since 1918, the kind of management they proposed was what has been called "administrative management."[2] As we saw in Chapter 5, the New Public Management model is a coherent alternative to the traditional model of modern times.

With the introduction of methods and concepts borrowed from the management of private corporations, Public Management has succeeded in overcoming the long-standing predominance of political science and law in theorizing about public administration. From a system closely resembling the Weberian model of bureaucracy, the New Public Management movement has in a sense taken Canada back to the position of Woodrow Wilson in his famous article of 1887, in which he declared that administration was essentially the same whether carried out in business or in government, and should be left to specialists.

We saw the introduction of these new management values into the Canadian system in the 1960s with the Planning Programming and Budgeting System (PPBS). Budgets for the first time were to be prepared in terms of the objectives of each programme, and measurements of success were to include not only unit cost of production, but also results obtained and their impact, thus opening the door to the evaluations of a decade later. Senior public servants began to be spoken of as not only managers, but also as entrepreneurs. Conformity gave way to innovation as a commanding value. Citizens were to be thought of as clients, their wishes to be discovered by opinion polls and complaint mechanisms. Personnel were to be considered a priority resource, empowered to better serve their clients. A new flexible approach was proposed to hiring and promoting, which would be more dynamic than the traditional merit system with its exclusive concern for the requirements of the position to be filled. Excellence became a watchword and with it, the idea that the best should be paid more and the worst disciplined. As the financial pinch worsened, the idea of partnerships was launched, replacing the old authoritarian state by a new frugal cooperative one. Even so, an increasing emphasis was put on accountability. In the 1970s, this came from the recognition by members of parliament that public servants wielded many powers for which they were not accountable to parliament. As the New Public Management movement took hold, the rationale for accountability changed. The management theory proposed that decision-making should be decentralized as close to the client as possible. This meant that deputy ministers in turn should delegate powers to those managing programmes. Accountability was to move back up the ladder on the basis of the results that each subordinate layer had contracted to produce.

Despite the serious contradictions within the New Public Management movement, notably between the need for increased control by political leaders and the need to delegate as much as possible,[3] NPM had a new and coherent philosophy, which was meant to galvanize senior public servants, eliminate the excesses of the bureaucratic model, save money, and deliver better services. It was optimistic about optimizing.

These were the new values that were desired to be promoted. What did we observe about the values actually in place in the Canadian public service in recent years?

Concerning deputy ministers, we saw that the system has accorded them greater autonomy, but that they are still locked into the active/passive posture. They still have to respect the pre-eminence of their minister and the limits to the initiatives which they may take. At the same time, the list of values that they are officially enjoined to respect has become ever longer, since no one ever admits to letting go an older value when a new one is added. It seems clear that deputy ministers have taken a new managerial approach as desired by the system, after years of giving priority to policy considerations. We saw evidence that they had become more attentive to "corporate culture" as promulgated by the Privy Council Office and the Treasury Board. The idea of partnerships only reinforces the long-standing preference for elite accommodation. In one sense the *Public Service 2000* reports represent the values of the deputies of the day, since the working groups were composed almost solely of them and their assistant deputy ministers. If so, they are humanists, embracing an employee-centred version of management and adopting solutions without much regard to budgetary restraints. On the other hand, this was a version of their *desirable* values, not a version of what they truly valued. They may have been trying to humanize their political masters after five years of purgatory during the Mulroney era.

If we add the other senior officials to the group, we know that serious demoralization had set in during these years.[4] Such surveys as were available suggested that senior officials were willing to be held accountable for their actions so long as they had enough control over their work to be considered responsible for it. Far from being locked into past patterns, they were found to be open to reform. Increasing recourse to contracting out suggests that public service managers accepted the virtues of letting others execute many tasks formerly performed by their own staffs. Finally, the emulation that had been previously limited for the most part to the example of our American neighbours now extended to all the countries of the OECD, with Commonwealth partners Britain, New Zealand, and Australia seen as examples of how strong managerial medicine could produce results.

The ordinary members of the public service were on the defensive in recent years. Their concern for security became a defense of the status quo. With very little aggressive industrial action, we may say that they continued to be moderates. While French Canadians and women had made considerable progress (with respect to their representation in the federal public service), and presumably were shaping new attitudes throughout it, the new excluded group seemed to be young people. Acquired rights took precedence over new generations.

One aspect of public servant behaviour that is rarely remarked upon is their honesty in money matters. Various publications on scandals, patronage or otherwise, almost always target politicians and their staffs, but almost never public servants.[5]

What do these trends suggest for the future? In trying to evaluate the possible consequences of the New Public Management movement for the culture of Canada's public service, we will return to the two-fold approach we presented in the introduction. First, we will look at the new culture by comparing the new ideas with the classic version of the Westminster model which was predominant in Canada from 1918 to 1967. As befits an analysis of two paradigms of the desirable, we will examine them from a deontological point of view. Such an analysis is more in the realm of moral philosophy than of modern social science, but it is none the less necessary, because the New Public Management has above all proposed new models of the desirable. Since it proposes to be more realistic than the old paradigm it wishes to replace, we also examine it in teleological terms, in order to draw out the empirical bases for its claims, and to extrapolate some likely consequences from its introduction.

2 · A Deontological Appraisal of the New Public Management

The teleological approach, as we defined it in Chapter 1, concerns the causal relationship between means and desired ends. Teleology is the doctrine of final causes; and as an approach to the study of administrative culture, the doctrine would assert that processes and procedures in government administration ought to be determined by their ultimate purposes/ends. Thus the emphasis is on the effects observed, results achieved, and ends met. On the other hand, deontology is the study of duty and ethical/moral obligations of human beings as well as of the organizations they represent. By using this approach in the study of administrative culture, one focuses on the ethics and morality of the administrator. What sense of duty should the public servant have, towards whom, and how can this sense be operationalized? From a holistic viewpoint, a comprehensive study of administrative culture would not be complete unless both of these approaches were utilized. That is why we employ both of these approaches, although we realize that one treads a difficult ground by venturing into the realm of deontology.

Morality, which has been a guiding force in the history of human civilization, has been linked with religion; in this form, it seems to challenge the forces of secularism on which the modern government system is based. While the emphasis on secular government and democracy may have relegated the place of morality from the state to the individual's conduct and behaviour, it has, nevertheless, maintained a continuing tension between the ends of public policy and programmes and the moral standards by which they can be measured. But the tension is not always maintained: we witness unethical activities in the public sphere on the rise all over the world. If justice, equality, equity, and freedom are to be maintained, proximate political and administrative acts must draw on some ethical foundations such as public service as a vocation.[6] It is a concept based on the ideal of service to the community. That ideal draws upon the concept of sacrifice — a concept that rises above individualism and materialism in order to create a shared feeling or spirit of public duty among government officials. Of course, the concept of sacrifice, in the context of modern times, does not mean that public servants must take a vow of poverty. Rather it means adhering to the principle of serving others by setting a high standard of moral conduct and by considering a job as a vocation — a calling, with conviction and duty. By so considering public service, emphasis is placed on the *service* dimension: an ideal to be acknowledged by public servants as higher than other economic and material considerations. Public service then approaches the status of a profession, similar to medical practice or nursing, rather than a mere occupation. Public servants ought to have inner satisfaction from rendering service unto others rather than from material gains. For them the symbols and myths of public service are equally, if not more, valued than other employment-related benefits. For example, in its *Public Service 2000: The Renewal of the Public Service of Canada,* the federal government stated:

> the Government believes that public service is an ideal that should be fostered and that those who serve the public out of conviction and duty are making an important contribution to the maintenance of democracy.[7]

Canada, unlike its Southern neighbour, has pursued collectivist values when it came to economic and social development of the nation; these values are rooted in a belief that societies are formed for the benefit of all their members, not just some favoured ones. Government intervention was not only a necessity, but was also welcomed by the public. This philosophy of collective vision permeated our administration with the result that public servants were considered to be proactive when it came to pursuing such Canada-wide policies as universal medicare, unemployment insurance, old-age benefits, and related social welfare programmes. Sometimes, federal public servants may have been seen to pursue these policies zealously; but they were reflecting the belief that the public good ought to be pursued vigorously. They operated with a unified conception of the public interest or the national interest. This is the traditional or classical view of the role of public servants.

In this traditional or classical role, there are *correct* ways of doing things: standards and rules that should be adhered to. Public servants in this mould are also against any politicization of the administrative process. To them "[P]olitcs is to the professions as ambiguity to truth, expediency to rightness, heresy to true belief."[8] They also believe that administrative responsibility is primarily a moral question.[9] They are moved by a higher cause; and thus, believing that they, having been entrusted with the stewardship of the state, owe special obligations, have special expectations, and reside in a fiduciary world.[10] Examples abound of this kind of Canadian public servants such as R.B. Bryce, Gordon Robertson, Arnold Heeney, and A.W. Johnson, to name a few. This level of expectation is based on the doctrine of legitimate expectations, serving the larger interest of the community even-handedly.[11] Consequently, their world revolves around what Hennessy calls, a "genetic code of conduct" which includes the following values: probity, care for the evidence, respect for reason, willingness to speak truth to ministers, a readiness to carry out instructions to the contrary if overridden, an appreciation of the wider public interest, equity, and a constant concern for democratic ideals.[12] To them, any movement towards greater symbiosis with their political masters, as is the case in many countries, is to be avoided.

It is here where the deontological approach acquires a holistic tone; in the end, our public servants exist for the public they are employed to serve. It is this aspect that needs to be revitalized in our public services. Even with the current emphasis on down-sizing, the public service of Canada is not going to abdicate its belief in serving the collective interests of Canadians. Thus, it is safe to say that the public service in Canada expresses more concern for the collective than we observe in American society. This commitment to a collective vision is one of the cardinal virtues of our public servants; it is derived from the concept of public service as a vocation. If the profession of public service is not a calling, then it is merely a job; in that case, loyalty to a specific job will depend largely on what material benefits and satisfaction that job may provide. If this were so, how could one expect public servants to exhibit additional virtues such as service to Canada, prudence in the use of taxpayers' money, and commitment to the collective welfare of people in Canada? Abandonment of the commitment for public service as a vocation that would follow from the adoption of market-based practices would be highly undesirable. Any predisposition to reject duty and commitment to vocation among public servants is not going to serve Canadians well.

Complementing the above is the teleological approach that, while accentuating the positive elements of public service vocation, emphasizes the relationship between the desirable and the feasible.

3 · A Teleological Approach: Between the Desirable and the Desired

In this section, we examine the factual bases of the New Public Management model and the possible outcomes of its adoption by the public service in fact and not only in principle. This is the realm of the relations between means and ends.

Thinking about ends and means has always been at the heart of public administration as a discipline. It has long been recognized that there are two great paths to improving the performance of an administration: you can either try to improve the people by leadership, motivation, and training, or you can tinker with institutions and systems in order to produce the desired effect in them. In this sense, public administration specialists are all to some degree institutionalists.[13] Virtually all of the significant moments we noted in the modern history of the public service of Canada involved changes in the formal or informal rules which aimed at changing behaviour by clarifying roles, changing power relations, or introducing new constraints. Although administrative reformers keep hoping, or claim to know that their new institution, method or device can deliver what it promises, there are some truths that are so well established that we take them as postulates. The first is that the choice of objectives depends in part on the means available. That is, in public policy and administration, most choices are not moral absolutes, but depend on calculations of costs and benefits, not only to the public, but also to politicians and public servants. Second, administrative reforms have both intended and unintended consequences.

It thus behooves us here to try to understand the interaction between the means proposed by the New Public Management and agreed objectives of Canadian public life, as recognized in the constitution and in political and administrative institutions. Moreover, administrative reform proposals belong to the world of doctrine, of administrative rhetoric. Hood and Jackson have codified the characteristics of successful persuasion from a wide literature.[14] There are six: 1) symmetry, or showing that solutions fit problems; 2) metaphor, an image which appears appropriate; 3) ambiguity, or sending different messages to different participants; 4) suspension of disbelief, or getting around the audience's scepticism; 5) selectivity in argument; and 6) the concealment of private interest in the doctrine of the public good.

Applied to Public Management, this approach gives the following observations: 1) the symmetry seems to be there, for the managerial revolution is part of the world-wide triumph of democratic capitalist values. The image of the "hollow state," in which the state contracts out all but its planning and controlling functions, corresponds with that of the "hollow corporation."[15] 2) The metaphorical language of management seems easily adapted to the public sector, as in "corporate culture," "corporate management," "management by results," etc. 3) There is rich ambiguity in expressions like "value for money" or "excellence." 4) It requires the suspension of disbelief, corresponding to what Dunsire says of doctrine: "it makes plain, but in the manner of 'revealed truth' rather than the tentative hypothesizing of theory: it shows what must be done but as if it were *from necessity* rather than the mere instrumentalism of policy."[16] 5) Selectivity in argument is found in the recourse to examples, to "best practices," and to anecdotal evidence without considering contrary evidence. 6) As a doctrine based on private interest, it is said to meet the requirements of the public good. With these points in mind, let us turn to the main components of the Public Management movement, in order to weigh them against what we know of the Canadian administrative culture or public administration in general.

NEED FOR BUDGET RESTRAINT. Of the need to redress public finances there can be no doubt. This was not one of the major themes of PS 2000, but it has been a key to many reforms introduced since the late 1970s. This is not the place for a full-scale analysis of the budget, but there are a few considerations that need to be made about the factual basis of the claim that management can solve the problem. First, there is a good case to be made that the problem in Canada, starting in the mid-1970s, was one of a revenue shortfall rather than an excess of expenditure, at least in terms of the OECD countries. David Wolfe has shown that various fiscal expenditures (tax breaks, amortization, write-offs, etc.) were at the origin of the revenue shortfall.[17] As we saw, the Nielsen programme review of 1986 also reached the conclusion that the deficit of that era could have been eliminated if all tax expenditures were cut, pointing out that tax expenditures escaped all of the controls put in place by the federal government to restrain both statutory and discretionary expenditures.[18] The result is that in the 1990s, all these efforts to improve management concentrate on less than 20 per cent of overall spending.[19] At the macro level, the Lambert Commission's report showed the naivete of thinking that politicians would accept binding multi-year budget plans,[20] or even that there was an optimum to be sought when a decision resulted from a compromise.[21]

REDUCING BUREAUCRACY. There seems to us no doubt that the bureaucratic system built in Canada in the thirty years following World War II needed to be revised and reformed. We noted that the Glassco Commission sounded the call for such reform through better management. But the growth of the bureaucracy continued, and public sector bargaining only added to the ever longer list of rules. These created many entitlements within the public service which became restraints on government policy.

ACCENT ON RESULTS. The main solution to rule-bound administration has been to direct attention away from conformity and towards results produced. While it is surely helpful to evaluate what has been achieved by major programmes of public spending, this approach has been shown to be politically naive, both at the programme and at the macro-government levels. At the programme level, Donald Savoie found several of his public service respondents discouraged when politicians maintained what they considered to be useless programmes.[22] Every treatise on evaluation requires that the process begin with a clear statement of objectives, but many important public policies have more than one objective, and some objectives contradict others. In the case of military procurement, the requirement that major arms purchases contribute to national research and development policies and to regional development have slowed their completion tremendously and in some case jeopardized their capacity to meet technical requirements.[23]

SERVICE TO THE PUBLIC. No one can be against such an idea in principle, but it tends to reduce the relation of the administration with its environment to a mental picture of a business and its clients. It ignores two important considerations. First, our administrations have long tried, if not to delight, to achieve consensus with their powerful clients: mostly enterprises, but also pressure groups, unions, farmers' groups, and so on. The language of service to the client ignores the huge differences in power and influence that exist among government clients, thus sanitizing what are political relationships.[24] Second, the service rhetoric can easily produce a confusion of roles. As the Québec government recalled after publication of a parliamentary report saying that service to the public was the *raison d'être* of the Québec public service, it is the job and responsibility of the government in a democratic system to decide on the kinds and levels of services which will be offered to different categories of publics.[25] Front-line public servants are not responsible for overall policy, although they do have considerable discretion in the execution of such policy. On the other hand, the front-line public servants (federal and provincial) interviewed by Carroll and Siegel are bemused and discouraged to see headquarters "discover" the service approach after years of pleading on their part for more attention to it.[26]

DECENTRALIZATION AND DEVOLUTION. Part of the New Public Management doctrine holds that power should be delegated as far as possible to the front line public servants dealing with the public. This idea, combined with that of service to the public, leads naturally to the idea of distinct units such as Special Operating Agencies which have a clear mandate and a recognizable clientele. As the Swedish and British cases indicate, Canada could go much further along this path. However, by loosening the lines of political control, one creates the need for other forms of accountability. There is no indication whatever that parliament would be able to oversee a large number of autonomous government agencies; experience with crown corporations suggests the contrary. If Canada were to move strongly in this direction, it would seem necessary either to create much larger staffs for parliamentary committees and to accept that they play a much larger role in the manner of American Congressional committees, or else follow the Swedish model and create an Ombudsman with powers to investigate the behaviour of public servants and charge them with offenses if necessary. In addition, while it may be difficult to document, experience suggests that decentralization increases the risk of bureaucratic malpractice.

There are few reports of illegal use of funds in government departments under close scrutiny of the Auditor General, but many reports from decentralized institutions such as school boards, hospitals, and municipalities.

CONTRACTING OUT. It is widely believed that contracting out saves taxpayers a lot of money, while maintaining services,[27] but the officials in charge of contracting policy at the Treasury Board of Canada told us that they did not believe contracted services to be cheaper. In their view, contracting out was most useful to provide flexibility. Moreover, units within the public service are not allowed to compete when contracts are let; the argument of best price does not prevail in that respect. There is a link between decentralization of services and contracting out, because many employees fear that the creation of an SOA is but a prelude to contracting the service out.[28]

The limit of this movement towards contracting out would be the "hollow state," a state that would deliver nothing itself, but only plan, coordinate, and control, in the manner of the "hollow corporation."[29] But just as it may not be wise for a company to lose all of its manufacturing capacity, it may not be prudent for governments to push this trend too far. There is reason to believe that an organization must retain some competency in an area where it contracts out in order to evaluate the capacity and performance of its contractors and that the best combination occurs when public service units can compete with private companies.[30]

PERFORMANCE PAY. Public Management brings with it from business the idea that the best way to motivate managers is to reward successful performance financially and to punish poor results. We do not suggest that public servants are disinterested in their financial rewards, but we do hold that this attitude flies in the face of both political realities and what we know about senior public servants. It is unrealistic to think that the public sector could pay deputy ministers what chief executive officers of large corporations earn. With their top salary of $170,500 in 1994, deputy ministers earn about one-quarter of what the CEO's of the largest 300 companies in Canada earn.[31] Because this salary is already well above what ministers and MPs earn, it would be unfeasible for the government to try and close the gap between deputies' and private sector CEO salaries. For other senior public servants, the frequency of wage freezes since 1980 raises questions about the desirability of fixing their attention on monetary reward for top performance. As we saw in previous chapters, these senior public servants also have a strong motivation to participate in political decision-making, so once again the accent on money rewards seems misplaced. Moreover, this is another aspect of the New Public Management movement that is based on conviction rather than on proven fact.[32] Even if it were true that merit pay produced desired results, there seems to us to be a real danger that, combined with frequent rotations and insistence on "corporate" values, it could create a competitive individualistic mentality in senior public servants to the detriment to their commitment to serving the public interest.

ACCOUNTABILITY. We agree with Hood and Jackson that Public Management's concept of accountability is "impoverished and apolitical."[33] For his part, Ronald C. Moe has argued that Vice President Gore's National Performance Review of 1993 broke with a long tradition of reports that had stressed democratic accountability of all departments and agencies to both the President and Congress.[34] The emphasis on results is certainly of value, but there is a danger of neglecting political and legal dimensions.

According to Bruce Milne, public administration discourse with regard to organizational forms in this century has been presented as "choices between, or combinations of, markets, bureaucracies or democracies."[35] We note that the New Public Management mounts an essentially market-oriented rhetoric against the prevailing bureaucratic model. We shall be attentive to what place it leaves for political models. If we recall Table 5.2 from chapter 5, we can allocate most of the values found in the PS 2000 task force reports into one of these three categories: 1) bureaucratic values are present in such words as merit, competence, professionalism, tradition, honour, loyalty, honesty, integrity, neutrality, uniformity, and accountability. 2) Market values are represented by words like efficiency, productivity, economy, service, quality, effectiveness, excellence, creativity, innovation, team-building, and leadership. 3) Political values are found in such words as justice, equity, representativeness, participation, openness, and transparency.

These three sets of values have long been recognized by the three great themes of public administration literature: the managerial, the legal-bureaucratic, and the political. We find the present predominance of management thinking to sow confusion about political values and to neglect legal values.

If we look at what managers do, a lot of it is political. From Henry Mintzberg's list of managerial functions,[36] we note the following as having a particularly political dimension: the role of symbolic head, leader (involving choice of senior personnel and motivation of subordinates), the maintenance of a network of allies and informers, the monitoring of the external environment, the representative function (speaking for the organization), and the role of entrepreneur, resource allocator, and negotiator.

New Public Management has in part recognized the political nature of managerial work through its acceptance of a need for increased accountability. However, as we have seen, the notion of accountability tries to draw its main inspiration from the private sector and to reduce its scope to a question of results and costs. This flight from politics is painfully naive. If a decision is the result of bargaining, it cannot be judged in terms of a function to be maximized. A negotiated agreement must give something to all key players.[37] Moreover, politics may appear in the course of ordinary administrative activities for any of the following reasons: 1) because of the people involved. (For example, the client may be someone politically notorious, such as former Iraqi ambassador Al-Mashat, whose rapid admission to Canada as a landed immigrant created a scandal).[38] 2) Because of the source of information or pressure, as in the cabinet, the minister's staff, a central agency, a pressure group, or another government. 3) Because of the power relations involved, as when political pressure is applied, or the government's re-election is at stake, or public sector unions affected. 4) Because of the very nature of some kinds of work, such as major policy questions, representing a minister, conducting relations with another government, preparing a policy statement, and arbitrating among competing claims.[39]

Thus one side of the dilemma raised by the New Public Management's view of managerial work is its naivete. In this respect, the notion of entrepreneurship may be what Hood and Jackson call a "recipe for disasters by advocating measures that encourage information distortion and public risk taking, stifling voices of caution, experience and independence."[40] One of these disasters was forecast by J.E. Hodgetts when he wrote:

> if the inevitable drift of public management into the political realm of governance itself… is to be the path of the future, then we must be prepared to see senior managers assume the role of scapegoats for the failures of others who, in our system of responsible cabinet government, have hitherto been elected to bear that direct responsibility.[41]

It is because of considerations such as these that Nicole Morgan has expressed concern that in the new context senior public servants are learning for themselves that in politics appearances are more important than reality.[42]

Ministers are also managers. Under the existing Canadian system, and in spite of important delegations of powers to deputy ministers, ministers still retain overall responsibility for the management of their departments.[43] Since they are responsible for or partake in a number of the managerial functions outlined above, they have to be included in the group of managers, even though this idea seems almost unthinkable to most adherents to the NPM movement.[44] As we said above, poor political management is as much the origin of today's budgetary problems as is administrative mis-management.

The trouble with New Public Management, then, from the point of view of our study, is that it is all technique. If politics is about the art of the possible, or what is acceptable in a society, and if it is also about the major value choices of that society — the "authenticity" and "justice" values of R. Manzer[45] — then management has forgotten politics.[46]

Public Management also appears to neglect the importance of law in public administration. This can be seen at two levels. At the top, in intro-ducing notions like corporate management, corporate culture, and even that of management itself, it tends to obscure the fact that relations between senior officials and ministers are constitutional in nature. As we have seen, when Canadian officials answer questions from members of par-liament, they do so in the name of their minister. Faced with the complex-ities of day-to-day administration and the conflicting values that the system has thrust upon them, they need some fundamental reference point to which they may turn in case of doubt. As John Rohr has put it, "the con-stitution must serve as a source of a list of regime values for administra-tors."[47] At lower levels of administration, the law is a guarantor of democratic government: "Government by law is the most bureaucratic of all institutions because to a greater extent than other institutions it feels bound by its own rules."[48] In this respect a public manager must differ from a pri-vate one, since, while the latter may regard the law as a constraint, some-thing he must obey, the public manager must also uphold it. As Moe and Gilmour put it:

> Law-based principles of public administration are not quaint proverbs; nor are they impediments to sound government management prac-tices. They provide the necessary foundation for a growing and evolv-ing administrative system.[49]

Much of the public management movement evolved as a response to the rigidities and entitlements that came from the excesses of bureaucracy that were introduced in Canada during the period of growth of government ser-vices from 1945 to 1975. In trying to assess its likely consequences, we are not proposing, like King Canute, to resist the incoming tide of change. Nor do we think it profitable, in the words of Arnold Heeney, to fight to the end "in defence of ancient victories," as he found the attitude of some at the Civil Service Commission to be.[50] Nor yet do we think that we are belabouring the obvious. To be sure, Public Management proponents usu-ally say that they are aware that the state is not a business, but we saw above that the classic values of accountability and respect for the law tend to be eclipsed by it. In practice, very few public servants actually believe that government should be thought of as a corporation.[51]

To us, the greatest charge against managerialism is its reductionism and its lack of imagination. It tries to reduce a complex phenomenon to a single model drawn from business. We argued above that the appropriate image for the public administrator is the steward, not the entrepreneur. What remains to be pointed out is another curious paradox of management. Astley and Van de Ven have observed that there are two versions of organization theory, one which is basically deterministic and the other which is proactive in its outlook.[52] The deterministic school sees management as fine tuning, adapting organizations to changes occurring in the environment. The proactive outlook takes a strategic view of that environment, claiming that it is there to be acted upon.

The paradox of the New Public Management is that while its language is full of references to a proactive stance — where strategic planning, innovation, change, and growth are promoted — in its basic thrust it is profoundly deterministic. Its message is that there really are no choices, that deficits, structural economic change, and world trade competition are forcing governments of all developed countries to adopt the same policies. This obscures the fact that these same governments do things very differently. European countries accept a more corporatist form of national bargaining with business and labour, while Britain, the United States, and Canada have more liberal societies, where individual competition has supremacy.[53] It also masks the fact that there are other models of the new state than the market model. Both Guy Peters and Henry Mintzberg have proposed more complex typologies of organization.[54]

In sum, if the teleological model of administrative analysis is carried to the extreme, technique drives out the desirable. What is feasible informs what is desirable, but if feasibility is the only criterion for the desirable, we have allowed ourselves to become too limited. We cannot remain in thrall to the old bureaucratic paradigm; imaginative ways of doing public business are required. However, entrepreneurship does not seem to us to be the appropriate image for this new type of responsible public administrator.

4 · Lessons Drawn From This Study

If we return to the questions raised at the beginning of this study, we believe it is clear that there is a Canadian administrative culture, even if it is deeply divided by subcultures based on department or agency, rank, professional training, gender, and language. It is probable that region and age also have their impact, but we have not explored these variables.

The two subcultures that we put first are created by the rules of the administrative system. Administrative reorganizations, like Kali, the Hindu goddess of destruction and rebirth, break down old loyalties and create new ones. Rules governing classification, seniority and promotion also contribute to the creation of subcultures.

A good deal of the preceding pages deals with attempts to create a change of culture from the top down. Each administrative reform is designed to change behaviour, which in turn requires changes in perceptions and values. While most administrative reforms only achieve partial success, they have an educational function; that is, they change perceptions, if not values.

These attempts to change culture from the top down pass necessarily through deputy ministers and their assistant deputies. We recall that Linda de Leon postulated that the perception of an organization held by its members establishes their moral horizon regarding their work.[55] It seems clear that twenty years of management-type reform have discredited the hierarchical model with its reduced sense of personal responsibility. The contest seen today at the highest level of the Canadian administration would seem to be between the pluralist competition and the collegial models. The rules and practices introduced by Paul Tellier, former Clerk of the Privy Council, have partly succeeded in creating the collegial corporate management that he wanted. However, we saw that repeated budgetary cuts, restructuring, and downsizing have caused a revival of a more competitive, pluralistic culture.[56]

At lower levels, the various subcultures remain. They too can be affected by decisions taken from the top. Policies covering bilingualism and equal opportunity have created new groups of stakeholders, with their own values and perceptions. The introduction of collective bargaining also did this, by recognizing officially that there were lower-level participants in the administration who had the right to defend their own interests in the face of their administrative and political masters.

The shift that recent changes have tried to introduce in the culture of the Canadian administration has been away from the traditional values of the Westminster system (fidelity, discretion, permanence, objectivity, and neutrality) to new values proposed by the New Public Management movement (flexibility, business orientation, results-orientation, customer service, innovation, and personal accountability).

The frameworks of values we presented in Chapter 1 have been overtaken by these changes. The values identified by Dunsire (discipline, stewardship, fairness, and public service as vocation) have, with the possible exception of fairness, been eclipsed by more dynamic values. While government and administrative leaders act and talk as though we can respect all of these values simultaneously, the message of the last few years is that results count more than the means used to obtain them.[57]

This is the main cultural legacy of the New Public Management movement. As many authors have noted, one of the profound debates of our time is that between public and private values.[58] Part of the promise of NPM has been to propose ways to get around traditional constraints, for example, by considerable decentralization, as in Special Operating Agencies, and by contracting out. Some adherents, like Osborne and Gaebler and Borins, maintain that the NPM is necessary precisely to preserve the public sector, not to undermine it.[59]

However, a great debate is required about the place the citizens of our societies wish to reserve to public values, which cannot always be reduced to commercial transactions. At the same time, it must be noted that high taxes and complicated bureaucratic systems have created sympathy within the wider political culture for NPM-type changes.

Our task is not to resolve such a debate, although we place more worth on a number of the values of the Westminster model than the NPM does. Moreover, politics, being rooted in interests as well as in values, will always give rise to conflict and debate. The apparently insulated administrative world of the classic Westminster model was surrounded by strife and clamour. This agitation has appeared within the public sector as conflict over sex, age, language, cultural origins, pay, and benefits. Today's administration is more politicized than yesterday's. This does not seem likely to change.

Public administration is about the daily life of the state and of those whose task it is to prepare and implement state policies. In finding its place in the new public space, the Canadian federal administration will have to find a culture based on cooperation and inclusion. As the Task Force on Public Service Values and Ethics reported, it is not a question of choosing between the "old" and the "new" values of the public service, but of finding a "new synthesis between the public management approach, with its emphasis on users, customers and clients, and the more holistic direction represented by the public administration perspective."[60]

5 · Conclusion

The two approaches utilized in the study of administrative culture of the Canadian federal administration should not be seen as contradictory: each is incomplete without the other. No amount of factual analysis can allow one to escape certain moral judgements, fundamental choices about both the public service and public life in this country. On the other hand, the kind of all-embracing anthropological approach we advocate for the study of culture aims at informing moral judgements with the best possible understanding of the causes and the consequences of certain patterns of behaviour. This is what we have attempted in this volume.

The Public Service of Canada has served Canada well. It has given dependability and reliability to the institution of governance, and it has answered the challenge by shifting its orientation from a homogeneous administrative system to a multifaceted administrative culture. Its performance is superior when compared to many nations, and it is accommodating demands for change, as signalled by *Public Service 2000* and the *Programme Review*. The accommodation for change may be more readily acceptable at the senior management level than at lower levels. However, for the majority of public servants, these reforms and the New Public Management movement are a direct threat to their job security; thus they engender survival strategies that may not be conducive to a productive and responsible administration. The administrative culture of Canada is exhibiting a different and sometimes contradictory administrative ethos: different because it is no longer wedded only to the traditional (inherited) bureaucratic values, but must accommodate the new management (business-based) values, and contradictory in the sense that the two groups — senior management and other employees — envision their role and status differently. But one thing is clear: for the orderly functioning of the Canadian democratic society, the Canadian administrative culture will have to act as the custodian of traditional public administration values and ideals while accommodating a number of the New Public Management values. That accommodation is needed if we do not wish to keep on considering Canadian bureaucracy as a barrier to sustainable development in Canada.

This study began with our general concern for the values and ideals of the Canadian administrative system and our interest in understanding the linkages between the realm of public servants and factors influencing their culture. We were also interested in knowing what happened to some of the inherited civil service ideals — such as government service as a vocation, exemplary conduct, and life dedicated for the cause of the nation — in light of the New Public Management movement. Our study should be regarded only as a mapping expedition of a flowing stream, not a static pond, because we have attempted to highlight only the main patterns of development and to show the directions in which the administrative culture of Canada is moving. We hope that this overview will enable readers to appreciate the complex world of our administrators.

Notes

1 P.J. Chartrand and K.L. Pond, "Chemine-
ment des carrières de direction dans la
fonction publique du Canada," *Relations
industrielles*, 24:2 (1969): 318-29.

2 C. Pollitt, *Managerialism and the Public
Service* (Oxford: Basil Blackwell, 1990)
19-22; and C. Hood, "A Public Management for All Seasons?," *Public Administration* 69 (1991): 11-15.

3 Peter Aucoin, "Administrative Reform in
Public Management: Paradigms, Prin-
ciples, Paradoxes and Pendulums,"
Governance 3:2 (1990): 115-37.

4 Donald Savoie, *Thatcher, Reagan, Mulroney: In Search of a New Bureaucracy*
(Toronto: University of Toronto Press,
1994), 279-80.

5 J. Simpson, *Spoils of Power*, (Don Mills:
Collins, 1988); Sharon Sutherland, "The
Canadian Federal Government: Patronage,
Unity, Security and Purity," *Corruption,
Character and Conduct*, ed. J.W. Langford
and A. Tupper (Toronto: Oxford
University Press, 1993) 113-50; and Stevie
Cameron, *On the Take* (Toronto:
Macfarlane Walter and Ross, 1994).

6 O.P. Dwivedi has advocated this aspect
in the following terms: "All governmental acts, if they are to serve the present
and future generations well, must be
measured against some higher law. That
law cannot be a secular law because it is
limited in vision as it is framed by imper-
fect people in their limited capacities.
That law has to be, perforce, based on the
principles of higher spiritual and philosophical foundations. Administrative
theology is one such foundation which
can provide an important base to a moral
and responsible statecraft." See his article, "Moral Dimensions of Statecraft: A
Plea for an Administrative Theology,"
Canadian Journal of Political Science 20:4
(December 1987): 705. The authors of this
volume appreciate the difficulty in the

use of the term "administrative theology,"
because for some it may be equated with
religious fervour or even a kind of
bureaucratic theocracy. Certainly, this is
not the purpose because the concept, as
suggested here, involves a notion of duty
and service to members of the public, as
well as the responsibility for their welfare;
further, the concept is reconciled with
the higher values of democratic secularism and morality.

7 *Public Service 2000* 14.

8 Frederick C. Mosher, *Democracy and the
Public Service* (New York: Oxford
University Press, 1968) 109.

9 See Chester I. Barnard, *The Functions of
the Executive* (Cambridge, Mass.:
Harvard University Press, 1948) ch. xvii.

10 Norman Lewis and Diane Longley,
"Ethics and the Public Service," *Public
Law* (1994): 598.

11 Lewis and Longley.

12 P. Hennessy, "Genetic Code of Conduct
Inherited by Mandarins," *The Independent* (UK), 5 June 1989.

13 On the "new" institutionalism, see James
G. March and Johan P. Olsen, *Redis-
covering Institutions: The Organizational
Basis of Politics* (New York: Free Press,
1989); Lynn G. Zucker, "Institutional
Theories of Organization," *Annual
Review of Sociology* 13 (1987): 443-64; and
R. Kent Weaver and Bert A. Rockman,
eds., *Do Institutions Matter?* (Washing-
ton DC: Brookings Institution, 1993).

14 Christopher Hood and Michael Jackson,
"Keys For Locks in Administrative
Argument," *Administration and Society*,
25:4 (1994): 467-88.

15 H. Brinton and W.L. Boyd, "Contracting for the Hollow State," a paper presented to the annual meeting of the American Political Science Association, Washington DC, August 1993.

16 Andrew Dunsire, "Administrative Doctrine and Administrative Change," *Public Administration Bulletin* 13 (1973): 39, cited by Hood and Jackson 468.

17 David Wolfe, "Les dimensions politiques des deficits," in G. Bruce Doern (ed.) *Les dimensions politiques de la politique economique*, vol. 40 (Ottawa: Approvisionnements et services, 1985).

18 Task Force on Program Review, *An Introduction to the process of Program Review* (Ottawa: Supply and Services, 1986) 20-22; and Gazette News Services, "Ottawa is Throwing Away Billions a Year, Nielsen Task Force Reports," *The Gazette* (Montreal) 12 March 1986: A1.

19 Stéphane Dion, "Les avantages du Québec fédéré; l'évolution du fédéralisme canadien" *Choix: Série Québec-Canada* (Montréal: Institut de recherches en politiques publiques, 1993) 7-9; and Eugene Swimmer, "Six and Five," in Alan Maslove (ed.) *How Ottawa Spends, 1984: the New Agenda* (Toronto: Methuen, 1984) 240-281.

20 Mohamed Charih, *La guerre des experts* (Montréal: Agence d'Arc, 1990).

21 Douglas Hartle, "The Report of the Royal Commission on Financial Management and Accountability (the Lambert Report): A Review," *Canadian Public Policy* v:3 (1979): 366-81.

22 Savoie, *The Politics of Public Spending* 338.

23 Martin Tomkin, *Processus décisionnel gouvernemental: analyse du système d'acquisition du défense au Canada*, diss., Université de Montréal, 1995.

24 Gilles Bouchard, "Les relations fonctionnaires-citoyens: un cadre d'analyse," *Canadian Public Administration* 34:4 (1991): 604-21; and J.I. Gow, "Frauds and Victims: Some Difficulties in Applying the Notion of Service to the Clientele in the Public Sector," *Canadian Public Administration* 38:4 (1995): 557-77.

25 Gow, "Frauds and Victims."

26 Barbara Wake Carroll and David Siegel, *Service in the Field: Field-Level Public Servants in the Policy Process* (Montreal and Kingston: McGill-Queen's University Press and IPAC, 1999) 200.

27 E.S. Savas, *Privatization: the Key to Better Government* (Chatham NJ: Chatham House, 1987) 172: and Lionel Ouellet, "La privatisation: un instrument de management public?," *Canadian Public Administration* 30:4 (1987): 570-71.

28 J.I. Gow, "Managing All Those Contracts: Beyond Current Capacity?," *Public Administration Present and Future*, ed. Mohamed Charih and Arthur Daniels (Toronto: IPAC and Ecole nationale d'administration publique, 1997) 235-61.

29 Milward and Boyd, "Contracting For the Hollow State" and "The Hollow Corporation," *Business Week* 3 March 1987: 57-81.

30 J. Stewart, ""Contracting for Program Evaluation Resources," *Canadian Journal of Programme Evaluation* 2:2 (1987): 73-75: and Pierre J. Hamel and Nancy Guénette, "La nécessaire concurrence," *Le Devoir* 17 and 18 March 1994.

31 Peter Larson, "Canada Must Pay Its Top Civil Servants What CEO's Earn," *The Gazette* (Montreal) 26 September 1994: F16.

32 Patricia Ingraham, "Of Pigs and Pokes and Policy Diffusion: Another Look at Pay-for-Performance," *Public Administration Review* 53:4 (1993): 348-56; Ingraham, "Pay For Performance in the States," *American Review of Public Administration* 23:3 (1993): 190-200; and James L. Perry. "Merit Pay in the Public Sector: the Case for the Failure of Theory," *Public Personnel Administration* 7 (1986): 57-69.

33 Hood and Jackson 478.

34 Ronald C. Moe, "The 'Reinventing Government' Exercise: Misinterpreting the Problem, Misjudging the Consequences," *Public Administration Review* 54:2 (1994): 111-22.

35 Bruce William Milne, "Democratic Administration: Beyond Current Reforms," annual conference of the Canadian Political Science Association, Ottawa, 6-8 June 1993.

36 Henry Mintzberg, *The Nature of Managerial Work* (New York: Harper and Row, 1973).

37 Douglas Hartle made this point when reviewing the Lambert Commission's report (see note 20). Also, Stephen J Elkin, "Toward a Contextual Theory of Innovation," *Policy Sciences* 16 (1983): 367-87.

38 Sutherland, "The Al-Mashat Affair."

39 This was a major finding of Campbell and Szablowski. Another way of looking at this is to note the list of exceptions to the Access to Information Act, Statutes of Canada 1980-1981-1982-1983, c.III. This may be taken as a fair representation of the values that the Liberal government at the time considered too political or too sensitive for disclosure to the public.

40 Hood and Jackson 478.

41 J.E. Hodgetts, *Public Management: Emblem of Reform for the Canadian Public Service* (Ottawa: Canadian Centre for Management Development, 1991) 13. This was a prophetic conclusion to the John L. Manion Lecture, given on 27 March 1991, for the Al-Mashat affair became just such a controversy within two months of its delivery.

42 Nicole Morgan, "Conservative View of the Civil Service," *The Globe and Mail* 9 July 1994.

43 Sharon Sutherland, "Responsible Government and Ministerial Responsibility: Every Reform Is Its Own Problem," *Canadian Journal of Political Science* 24:1 (1991):96-100.

44 Adrien Payette, "Eléments pour une conception du management public," *Management Public*, ed. R. Parenteau (Sillery: Les Presses de l'Université du Québec, 1992) 15.

45 See Chapter 1, p. 27.

46 David Rosenbloom, "Have an Administrative Rx? Don't Forget the Politics!," *Public Administration Review* 53:6 (1993) 503-507, and Martin Minogue, "Theory and Practice of Public Policy and Administration," *Policy and Politics* 11:1 (1983): 63-85.

47 John Rohr, *Ethics for Bureaucrats* (New York: Marcel Dekker, 1978) 67, as cited by Kathryn G. Denhardt, *The Ethics of Public Service* (Westport: Greenwood Press, 1988) 20.

48 Marshall E. Dimock, "Bureaucracy Self-Examined," Merton *et al.* 399.

49 Ronald C. Moe and Robert S. Gilmour, "Rediscovering Principles of Public Administration: the Neglected Foundation of Public Law," *Public Administration Review* 55:2 (1995): 143.

50 A.D.P. Heeney, *The Things That Are Caesar's* (Toronto: University of Toronto Press, 1972) 147.

51 Gow, *Learning From Others* 56, found that only 2 per cent of the respondents to his survey of IPAC members favoured the corporation as the most appropriate metaphor for public administration. In what is to us quite a realistic fashion, they overwhelmingly chose either a complex system (43 per cent) or a living organism (28 per cent).

52 W. Graham Astley and Andrew Van de Ven, "Central Perspectives and Debates in Organization Theory," *Administrative Science Quarterly* 28 (1983): 245-73.

53 Gérard Boismenu, "Systèmes de représentation des intérêts et configurations politiques: les sociétés occidentales en perspective comparée," *Canadian Journal of Political Science* 27:2 (1994): 309-44.

54 Guy B. Peters has developed four models of governance in *The Public Service, The Changing State and Governance* (Ottawa: Canadian Centre for Management Development, 1993). His models are based on the market, the participatory state, flexible government, and deregulating government. Henry Mintzberg, in "Managing Government, Governing Management," *Harvard Business Review* (May-June 1996): 75-83, argues that there are privately owned organizations, publicly owned ones, cooperative organizations, and organizations without owners (like universities, hospitals, and charities). To these models, we might add that of the professional organization, where the customer is not always right, even if the professionals are in private business. See John Langford and Kenneth Kernaghan, *The Responsible Public Servant* (Halifax: the Institute for Public Policy, 1989) 113.

55 Chapter 1 (note 71).

56 Eleanor Glor, "Culture and Value Changes in the Federal Public Service: the Implications," *Optimum* 25:3 (1994/95): 15. "The recent changes (in the Public Service) are definitely not about cooperation: they are solutions developed by small elites and centrally driven."

57 Carolyn Ban, *How Do Public Managers Manage? Bureaucratic Constraints, Organizational and Potential for Reform* (San Francisco: Jossey-Bass, 1995) 277.

58 Jane Jacobs, *Systems of Survival: A Dialogue of the Moral Foundations of Politics* (New York: Vintage Books, 1992); Amitai Etzioni, ed., *Rights and The Common Good: The Communitarian Perspective* (New York: St. Martin's Press, 1995): Paul Thomas, "Beyond the Buzz Words: Coping With Change in the Public Sector," *International Review of Administrative Science* 62:1 (1996): 5-29: Donald Savoie, "What's Wrong With the New Public Management," *Canadian Public Administration* 38:1 (1995): 112-21; Benjamin Barber, *From Jihad to McWorld* (New York: Ballantine Books, 1995); Rosenbloom; Moe; Hood; Glor.

59 Osborne and Gaebler xviii-xix; Sandford Borins, "The New Public Management Is Here To Stay," *Canadian Public Administration* 38:1 (1995): 122-32.

60 Government of Canada, *A Strong Foundation: Report of the Task Force on Public Service Values and Ethics: A Summary* (Ottawa: Privy Council Office, February 1997) 10-11.

Index

FROM BUREAUCRACY TO PUBLIC MANAGEMENT

Stillman, Richard J. 24
Substantive Values 27
Supreme Court of Canada 73, 99
Szablowski, George 105, 106, 113
Task Force, Public Service Values and
 Ethics (Tait Task Force) 75, 76,
 148, 149, 151, 180
Taylor, Charles 31
Taylor, Frederick W. 69, 125
Teleological Approach 28, 29-30, 34,
 168, 170-178
Tellier, Paul 81, 105, 126, 135, 136, 147,
 179
Therrien, Eugene 108
Thompson, V.A. 126
Traditional Values 44, 78, 141, 144, 179
Treasury Board 21, 65, 69, 76, 77, 78,
 80-83, 94, 95, 103, 106, 111, 112,
 129, 132, 133, 136, 137, 138, 139,
 149, 164, 166, 174
Trudeau, Pierre E. 48, 49, 51, 95, 103,
 105, 113
Typologies of Values 26-28

United Empire Loyalists 44, 49
United Kingdom 56, 67, 161
United States 20, 24, 43, 45, 46, 52, 53,
 55, 56, 67, 69, 71, 98, 125, 128, 129,
 138, 178

Values 17-22, 22-24, 26-32, 32-34, 41,
 43, 44, 46, 47, 49, 54, 63, 66, 67,
 71, 75, 76, 78, 80-82, 89, 110, 113,
 126, 127, 140, 141, 144, 148, 149,
 151, 152, 161, 162, 164-166, 169, 171,
 175, 177, 179, 180, 181
 Elite 110-113
 Fundamental 28
 Instrumental 27
 New Public Management 142-143
 Political 34, 175
 Public Administration 24-28
 Regime 47, 63, 66-80, 177
 Study of 23, 26
 Substantive 27
 Traditional 44, 78, 141, 144, 179
 Typologies 26-28
Van de Ven, Andrew 178

Verba, Sydney 21
Vietnam War 29

Waldo, Dwight 25, 28
War Veterans 70
Weber, Max 24, 27, 93, 162
Western Canada 49
Western World 25
Westminster Model 34, 83, 89, 92,
 94, 104, 115, 162, 167, 180
Whitaker, Reg 51, 52
Whitehall Model, Canadian Version
 163
Whitley Councils 79, 114
Wildavsky, Aaron 25, 30
Wilson, V. Seymour 128
Wolfe, David 172
Woodrow Wilson 24, 55, 125, 165
World War II 17, 45, 52, 70, 103, 114,
 116, 172

Zero-Base Budgeting System 55
Zussman, David 112, 148, 164